1986

The Ada Companion Series

There are currently no better candidates for a co-ordinated low-risk and synergetic approach to software development than the Ada programming language. Integrated into a support environment, Ada promises to give a solid standards-orientated foundation for higher professionalism in software engineering.

This definitive series aims to be the guide to the Ada software industry for managers, implementors, software producers and users. It deals with all aspects of the emerging industry: adopting an Ada strategy, conversion issues, style and portability issues, and management. To assist the organised development of an Ada-orientated software components industry, equal emphasis is placed on all phases of life cycle support.

Some current titles:

Life cycle support in the Ada environment
Ed. J. McDermid and K. Ripken

Portability and style in Ada
Ed. J. C. D. Nissen and P. J. L. Wallis

Ada: Language, compilers and bibliography
Ed. M. W. Rogers

Ada for multi-microprocessors
Ed. M. Tedd, S. Crespi-Reghizzi and A. Natali

Proceedings of the Third Joint Ada Europe/Ada TEC Conference
Ed. J. Teller

Ada for specification: possibilities and limitations
Ed. S. J. Goldsack

Ada in use
Ed. J. G. P. Barnes and G. A. Fisher

Concurrent programming in Ada
A. Burns

Concurrent programming in Ada®

Concurrent programming in Ada

ALAN BURNS

Lecturer in Computer Science
University of Bradford

The right of the
University of Cambridge
to print and sell
all manner of books
was granted by
Henry VIII in 1534.
The University has printed
and published continuously
since 1584.

CAMBRIDGE UNIVERSITY PRESS

Cambridge

London   New York   New Rochelle

Melbourne   Sydney

Published by the Press Syndicate of the University of Cambridge
The Pitt Building, Trumpington Street, Cambridge CB1 2RP
32 East 57th Street, New York, NY 10022, USA
10 Stamford Road, Oakleigh, Melbourne 3166, Australia

First published 1985

Printed in Great Britain at the University Press, Cambridge

Library of Congress cataloguing data available

British Library Cataloguing in Publication Data
Burns, Alan, 1953–
    Concurrent programming in Ada.–(Ada companion series)
    1. Ada (Computer program language)
    I. Title   II. Series
    001.64′24   QA76.73.A15

ISBN 0 521 30033 9

This book is dedicated in dearest memory to my father for
concurrently programming two sons who raised many exceptions
which he always managed to handle.

CONTENTS

FOREWORD

The Ada tasking model is one of the most interesting aspects of the language. Indeed, Ada is the first standard language for embedded systems to include tasking intrinsically within the language at all; earlier languages of the JOVIAL, CORAL66 and RTL/2 generation have relied upon the facilities of some independent underlying operating system. Furthermore, the Ada tasking model is of a rather high level nature being based upon the quite recent concepts in the CSP language of Tony Hoare.

Ada has thus taken a bold double step by not only including tasking but also using a high level model. Although some aspects of Ada tasking are as yet unproven in live applications, it seems unlikely that serious practical difficulties will be revealed; as with any new tool there will no doubt be minor problems which will be overcome by pragmatic means.

The use of tasking is unfamiliar to most programmers; for the small but important practical community who do know the problems of programming parallel activities, some Ada concepts will probably seem rather remote from the techniques with which they are familiar such as semaphores.

This book is thus very welcome; Alan Burns has written a most readable and very complete account of Ada tasking. It will be of great value to the programmer about to use Ada for embedded systems by giving much practical guidance. It will also make available an account of tasking to those quite unfamiliar with the topic and thereby dispel a certain amount of the mysticism which surrounds it. For those interested in the development of programming languages it probes in depth many interesting areas and includes much material that is otherwise not readily available; it concludes with a very thought provoking list of suggestions regarding how the Ada tasking model might be improved in the future.

The addition of this book to the Ada Companion Series increases the importance of the series as a vital component of every Ada programmer's library.

July 1985   J.G.P.Barnes
Reading

PREFACE

The development of the Ada programming language forms a unique and, at times, bizarre contribution to the history of computer languages. As all users of Ada must know by now the language design was a result of competition between a number of organisations each of which attempted to give a complete language definition in response to a series of requirements documents. The "IRONMAN" document formed the basis for the early designs and its successor "STEELMAN" provided the final specification. An important aspect of the resulting language, Ada, is the model it presents for providing **concurrent** or parallel programming. This model is both complex and new, but is not the inevitable consequence of the specification requirements; indeed, the three other competing language designs for the "Ada" prize proposed quite different (and conservative) designs.

This book gives a detailed description and an assessment of that part of the Ada language that is concerned with concurrent programming. No prior knowledge of concurrent programming (in general) or Ada tasking (in particular) is assumed in this book. However, readers should have a good understanding of at least one high-level sequential programming language. The Ada language is defined by the **Ada Language Reference Manual** (ARM, 1983) which was given an ANSI standard in 1983 and is a draft ISO standard.

This book is aimed both at professional software engineers and students of computer science (and other related disciplines). Already, many million lines of Ada code have been produced world wide, and over the next decade a wide range of applications will be designed with Ada in mind as the target language. It is important that Ada programmers do not restrict themselves to a subset of the language on the dubious assumption that tasking is not appropriate to their work or for fear that the tasking model is too complex. Tasking is an integral part of the language and programmers must be familiar with, if not experienced in, its use. Due to space considerations, books that describe the entire language may not deal adequately with the tasking model; this book therefore concentrates, exclusively, on this model.

Students studying real-time programming, software engineering, concurrent programming or language design should find this book useful in that it gives a comprehensive description of the features that one language provides. Ada is not merely a product of academic research (as are many concurrent programming languages) but is a language for actual use in the information technology industry. Its model of tasking has therefore had to deal with the orthogonality of the entire language design and the interaction between tasking and non-tasking features. Consequently, the study of Ada's model of concurrency should be included in those advanced courses mentioned above. However, this does not imply that the tasking model is free from controversy, has a proven semantic basis or is amenable to efficient implementation. The nature of these areas of 'discussion' are dealt with, as they arise, in this book.

The first chapter gives a brief overview of the important non-concurrent features of the language. No attempt is made to be exhaustive, and readers completely unfamiliar with Ada are recommended to supplement this book with some appropriate text (there are many to choose from, for example Barnes, 1984).

Chapters 2 and 3 look, in detail, at the uses of concurrent programming and the inherent difficulties of providing inter-process communication. There is, as yet, no agreement on which primitives a concurrent programming language should support and, as a consequence, many different styles and forms exist. In order to fully understand the Ada tasking model it is necessary to appreciate these different approaches and the problems faced by the user of a language that supports multi-processing.

The Ada task is introduced in chapter 4 and the rendezvous and the important select statement are considered in the following two chapters. Task termination and the relationship between tasks and exceptions are dealt with in chapter 7. Within the Ada language, the task and the package form the two main building blocks of programs. Chapter 8 compares these two constructs (together with generics) and indicates where one can use a package and where one must employ a task. Consideration is also given to the specification of packages that contain synchronisation tasks in their bodies.

Another important feature of the tasking model is the ability, within a program, to create tasks dynamically by the use of an allocator. This allows for useful agent tasks such as messengers and mailboxes to be used when required. Unfortunately, deallocation problems can cause difficulties here; these agents and the difficulties are explained in chapter 9.

Within most concurrent programs the need to provide safe but efficient access to non-shareable resources that can, by definition, only be used by one process at a time forms one of the major design difficulties. In chapter 10, resource management is examined and a general purpose resource control generic package is given. This generic is structured so that it employs a set of reusable agents, thereby making the algorithm reliable in the face of clients being aborted.

Whenever you introduce more than one process into a system there is a need to schedule the executions of these processes and, where desirable, allow for priority levels to be used to indicate the relative importance of each process. Chapter 11 describes the scheduling of Ada tasks and describes the entry family facility that can be used to circumvent the 'first in first out' structure of the rendezvous queue.

Chapter 12 switches to the important low-level facilities that Ada supports; these are necessary to create device driver tasks for embedded systems. Here, Ada is still largely untried and I have no direct experience of producing such code in Ada. A number of possible difficulties are discussed.

The use of agents, while perhaps representing good programming style, introduces a proliferation of tasks. Unfortunately, the design of the rendezvous does not lend itself easily to the production of efficient code. Multitasking programs may therefore not perform adequately in time-critical applications. The possibility of providing optimisations that will improve performance is discussed in chapter 13 as is the use of distributed and multiprocessor systems.

The issue of portability is, of course, a significant one in software production and the designers of Ada have paid particular attention to this requirement. Unfortunately the characteristics of particular implementations inevitably impinge on the semantics of tasking structures. This is discussed in chapter 14.

In chapter 15 all the factors that effect programming style are brought together in order to provide a comprehensive overview of the features (and restrictions) available for those who are developing concurrent programs in Ada.

The focus of attention in chapter 16 is the formal specification of the tasking model and the verification of programs that contain tasks. This is a complex and controversial issue and only a brief discussion is given.

The material presented in this book reflects the authors experience in both using and teaching Ada tasking. Teaching experience has been obtained by writing and presenting courses at the University of Bradford (UK) and by developing educational material for The Instruction Set (a company specialising in software training and consultancy).

The programs presented in this book have been developed using the University of York (UK) compiler and tested on the validated Rolm system.

Braille Copies.

Braille copies of this book, on paper or versabraille cassette, can be made available. Enquires should be address to Dr Alan Burns, Postgraduate School of Computing, University of Bradford, BRADFORD, West Yorkshire, UK.

Acknowledgements.

It would be impossible to thank all those who have, directly or indirectly, helped me to formulate my ideas and put them in the form of a book. I must however explicitly mention John Barnes, Carol Burns, Paul Luker, John Nissen, John Robinson, Mike Rogers, Chris Jones, the staff at The Instruction Set and the University of York (UK) Ada compiler development team. The manuscript preparation and presentation was managed by Ian W. Morrison who painstakingly developed a collection of incomprehensible macros for controlling the layout of the text. His work is gratefully acknowledged. Finally I would like to give a special thanks to Andy Wellings for many thought provoking and enjoyable discussions. The material in this book reflects, significantly, the substance of these discussions.

July 1985   Alan Burns
Bradford

1 THE ADA LANGUAGE

Ada was primarily (although in the end not exclusively) designed for the programming of embedded systems; that is where the computer hardware and software form a crucial part of some larger engineering system. The computer will at least monitor, and probably control, the operations of the larger system. To do this it will need to exchange data and control information with a variety of devices both analogue and digital. And yet many of the problems with which the design project for Ada was concerned are not the detailed ones of some one-off control system but the complexity problems associated with giving life-cycle support to the software production process. These difficulties relate to problem and program size as well as to the management of software production. McDermid and Ripken (1984) give a set of characteristics for a demanding, but by no means untypical, embedded project:

```
size of source code              50,000 lines
life expectancy of system        30 years
reliability requirements         very high
configuration of target hardware highly distributed
size of development team         100
```

The management of this type of project is therefore both complex and critically important. Two complementary methods or approaches are used to overcome some of the difficulties associated with the complexity arising out of program size; decomposition and abstraction. Decomposition, as the name suggests, involves the systematic break down of the complex system into smaller and simpler parts. At each step in the decomposition there is an appropriate level of description and a method of documenting or expressing this description. Abstraction allows for the consideration of detail, particularly that appertaining to implementation, to be postponed, and thereby simplifies both the system itself and the objects contained within the system. The use of decomposition and abstraction pervades the entire engineering process and has influenced the design of the Ada language and associated programming methods. This is discussed in more detail by Downes and Goldsack (1982).

1.1 Overall Style

As the IRONMAN requirements document was largely written in a Pascal-like terminology it is not surprising that, at a lexical level, Ada bears a close resemblance to Pascal. Ada's data structures are conventional and only lack the set construct from those of Pascal. Control structures are also similar, with Ada possessing a more flexible loop construct that allows exit from the loop at any point within it. The first major distinction between the two languages comes from Ada's block structure. A block consists of, (i) the declaration of any objects that are local to the block (if there are no such objects then this declaration part may be omitted), (ii) a sequence of statements, and (iii) a collection of exception handlers (these handlers may be omitted and are considered later in this chapter):

```
declare
  <declarative part>
begin
  <sequence of statements>
exception
  <exception handlers>
end;
```

A block itself may be declared in any place in the program where a statement may be written. Blocks, which may be named, can contain other blocks and they therefore form a useful method of giving decomposition within a program unit. When a block is executed, the declarative part is said to be elaborated and the sequence of statements executed; in both operations it may be necessary to evaluate expressions.

The scope rules for blocks in Ada are somewhat different from other languages. Informally they can be described as follows:

(i) The scope of an identifier is the block in which it is declared and all blocks enclosed within.

(ii) An identifier is in scope immediately following its declaration.

(iii) The visibility of an identifier matches its scope unless an identical identifier is declared in an inner block, in which case the original identifier is not directly visible.

A simple example will indicate the nature of Ada's block structure:

```
TOP : declare       -- a named block
                    -- TOP is not a label
                    -- for a goto statement
      A : INTEGER := 42;    -- initial values can be
                            -- given to most objects.
      B : INTEGER := A + 3;  -- A is visible.
   begin
      A := A + B;               -- A equals 87
      declare
         A : INTEGER := 10;
         C : INTEGER;
      begin
         C := B;       -- C equals 45.
         C := A;       -- C equals 10.
         C := TOP.A;   -- C now equal to 87.
      end;
      B := A;  -- B equals 87 and C
               -- is now out of scope.
   end TOP;
```

The predefined scalar types in Ada are INTEGER, CHARACTER, BOOLEAN, FLOAT and DURATION (for use with real-time see section 4.4); from these it is possible to derive new types. In addition there are anonymous types such as 'universal_integer' and there may be implementation dependent types such as LONG_INTEGER. A type may also be constructed by defining all allowable values which objects of that type may take, (these are called enumeration types). With all types it is possible to define a subtype that restricts the range of values of the parent type. It is not possible however to use a subtype to restrict the operators that are associated with that type.

```
declare
   type NEW_INT is new INTEGER;
   type SMALL_INT is new INTEGER range -32..+31;
   type DAY is (MONDAY, TUESDAY, WEDNESDAY, THURSDAY,
                FRIDAY,SATURDAY, SUNDAY);
   subtype POS_INT is NEW_INT range 1..NEW_INT'LAST;
   subtype WEEKDAY is DAY range MONDAY..FRIDAY;
   START : DAY := MONDAY;
   A : NEW_INT;
   B : POS_INT;
   C : INTEGER;
begin
   A := B; -- legal.
   B := A; -- legal, but the value may be out of range
           -- and cause an exception to be raised
           -- during execution.
   A := C; -- illegal, this is a type clash as A is
           -- NEW_INT and C is INTEGER.
end;
```

Ada is a strongly typed language; a compiler is therefore of use not only as a translator but also as a tool for testing the logical consistency of incomplete programs, for example ones in which abstract types have not yet been constructed.

In the above example an attribute is employed ('LAST) to indicate the largest integer supported. Attributes are used throughout the language to give information about types and objects. They are particularly useful for manipulating arrays.

Procedures and functions are known collectively as subprograms. They are specified by giving a name, a complete description of the parameters and, if the subprogram is a function, the type of the return object:

```
procedure QUADRATIC(A,B,C  :  in FLOAT;
                    R1, R2 :  out FLOAT;
                    OK     :  out BOOLEAN);

function  MINIMUM(X,Y,Z : in INTEGER) return INTEGER;
```

The parameters must have their type and their mode specified. Three such modes are allowed :

in   Within the subprogram the parameter acts as a local constant – a value is assigned to the formal parameter on entry to the procedure or function. This is the only mode allowed for functions. It is the default mode.

out   Within the subprogram the parameter acts as a write–only variable – a value is assigned to the calling parameter upon termination of the subprogram.

in out Within the subprogram the parameter acts as a variable – upon entry to the subprogram a value is assigned to the formal parameter, upon termination the value attained is passed back to the calling parameter.

Interestingly, these parameter modes do not dictate the method of implementation which could be either by copy or by reference (for scalar types copy must be used). Indeed the Language Reference Manual makes it quite clear that:

> "The execution of a program is erroneous if its effect depends on which mechanism is selected by the implementation." (ARM 6.2.7).

A subprogram body consists of a repeat of the specification plus whatever declarations and statements are needed to 'implement' the specification:

```
function MINIMUM(X,Y,Z : in INTEGER) return INTEGER is
begin
  if X <= Y then
    if X < Z then return X;
    else return Z;
    end if;
  elsif Y <= Z then return Y;
    else return Z;
  end if;
end MINIMUM;

procedure QUADRATIC(A,B,C  : in FLOAT;
                    R1, R2 : out FLOAT;
                    OK     : out BOOLEAN) is
  Z : constant FLOAT := B**2 - 4.0*A*C;
begin
  if Z < 0.0 or A = 0.0 then
    OK := FALSE;
    R1 := 0.0; -- arbitrary value.
    R2 := 0.0;
    return;    -- return from procedure before
               -- reaching physical end.
  end if;
  OK := TRUE;
  R1 := (-B + SQRT(Z))/(2.0*A);
  R2 := (-B - SQRT(Z))/(2.0*A);
end QUADRATIC;
```

Parameters of mode 'in' can have default expressions, the value of which is used if a call of the subprogram does not contain an actual matching parameter. Calls, in general, can make use of the usual positional notation or employ name notation to remove positional errors and increase readability:

```
function WAGE(GRADE    : UNIVERSITY_POST;
             HOURS    : FLOAT := 40.0;
             OVERTIME : FLOAT := 0.0) return FLOAT;
```

Calls to this function could take the form:

```
PAY := WAGE(SECRETARY, 40.0, 0.0);
PAY := WAGE(SECRETARY);                 -- uses default values.
PAY := WAGE(GRADE => SECRETARY); -- uses name notation.
PAY := WAGE(PROFESSOR, HOURS => 30.0);
PAY := WAGE(GRADE => LECTURER, OVERTIME => 25.0);
```

All subprograms can be called recursively and are reentrant.

1.2 Packages

The package is the single most important construct in Ada. It serves as the logical building block of large complex programs and is the most natural unit of separate compilation. In addition the package provides for data hiding and the definition of abstract data types. A package definition has two parts, the specification (which itself may consist of a private as well as a

visible part) and the body. The body contains the code necessary to implement
the specification. Its inner details are hidden from the rest of the program and
in terms of program development the body of a package will usually be
constructed later and take the form of a separately compiled unit. The general
form of a package is:

```
package <name> is
  -- visible declarations of constants, types,
  -- variables and subprograms.
private
  -- hidden type and constant declaration, if any.
end <name>;

package body <name> is
  -- internal declarations.
begin
  -- sequence of statements for
  -- initialising the package.
end <name>;
```

If the sequence of statements in the package body consists only of the null
statement then the package body need only contain the bodies of units
specified in the package specification. An example of the use of a package to
define an abstract data type would be one that provided complex arithmetic
for the rest of the program (Barnes, 1984). This package will need to specify
the type COMPLEX, the usual arithmetic operations and a set of functions for
converting from type FLOAT to COMPLEX and vice versa:

```
package COMPLEX_ARITHMETIC is
  type COMPLEX is private;
  function "+"(X,Y : COMPLEX) return COMPLEX;
  function "-"(X,Y : COMPLEX) return COMPLEX;
  function "*"(X,Y : COMPLEX) return COMPLEX;
  function "/"(X,Y : COMPLEX) return COMPLEX;
  function COMP(A,B : FLOAT)   return COMPLEX;
  function REAL_PART(X : COMPLEX) return FLOAT;
  function IMAG_PART(X : COMPLEX) return FLOAT;
private
  type COMPLEX is
  record
    REAL : FLOAT;
    IMAG : FLOAT;
  end record;
end COMPLEX_ARITHMETIC;
```

This package defines operators, "+", "-", "*" and "/" for objects of type
COMPLEX. These operators are said to *overload* the usual operators.
Overloading is allowed for all subprograms in Ada as long as the meaning is
unambiguous.

By defining COMPLEX to be private no assumption can be made (outside this package) about the structure of the type; in this example it is implemented as a record, however it could just as easily have been constructed as a two component array. If a type has been tagged as being private then the following operations are allowed in the rest of the program where the package is in scope:

(i)   Objects of that type can be declared.

(ii)   Subprograms supplied with the type can be called.

(iii)   Two objects of that type can be compared for equality.

(iv)   Values of that type can be assigned to objects.

If it is desirable to remove the possibility of assignment and equality tests then the type can be declared as being 'limited private'.

The body of the above package would have the structure:

```
package body COMPLEX_ARITHMETIC is

    function "+"(X,Y : COMPLEX) return COMPLEX is
    begin
      return (X.REAL + Y.REAL, X.IMAG + Y.IMAG);
    end "+";

    function "-"(X,Y : COMPLEX) return COMPLEX is
    begin
      return (X.REAL - Y.REAL, X.IMAG - Y.IMAG);
    end "-";

    -- similarly for "*" and "/".

    function COMP(A,B : FLOAT) return COMPLEX is
    begin
      return (A,B);
    end COMP;
    function REAL_PART(X : COMPLEX) return FLOAT is
    begin
      return X.REAL;
    end REAL_PART;

    -- similarly for IMAG_PART.

end COMPLEX_ARITHMETIC;
```

The clear distinction between specification and body should imply that the private part of a package specification is contained in the body where it would be appropriately hidden. This would however make implementation very difficult due to the rules of separate compilation in Ada (Young, 1982).

If COMPLEX_ARITHMETIC were a precompiled library unit then an example of the use of the package would take the form:

```
with COMPLEX_ARITHMETIC; use COMPLEX_ARITHMETIC;
procedure MAIN is
   A,B,C  : COMPLEX;
   SIGNAL : array (1..10) of COMPLEX;
begin
   A := COMP(0.0,1.0);
   B := A + COMP(1.0,1.0);
   C := (A + B)/A;
   -- note, A.REAL := 1.0 would be illegal.
end MAIN;
```

The 'with' clause names the precompiled library unit (or units) upon which MAIN is dependent. Only those units upon which there is a direct dependence should be specified. Library units can themselves have 'with' clauses, thereby supporting a hierarchy of dependencies. Clearly the recompilation of any unit necessitates the recompilation of all units that depend upon it. The 'use' clause provides direct visibility of declarations that appear in the visible part of the named package. If 'use COMPLEX_ARITHMETIC;' was omitted from the above example then the names of all objects from the package would need to be prefixed by the package name, for example:

```
A,B,C : COMPLEX_ARITHMETIC.COMPLEX;
```

Separate compilation can also be achieved by the use of subunits which are either package, subprogram (or task) bodies. A subunit is removed from its immediate surrounding unit and compiled later:

```
package body COMPLEX_ARITHMETIC is
   function "+"(X,Y : COMPLEX) return COMPLEX
                        is separate; -- a program stub
   ...
```

The separate compilation of this subunit (which must name its parent unit) would take the form:

```
separate (COMPLEX_ARITHMETIC)
function "+"(X,Y : COMPLEX) return COMPLEX is
begin
   return (X.REAL + Y.REAL, X.IMAG + Y.IMAG);
end "+";
```

Subunits provide for the top down construction of programs; they also have the facility for giving access to additional library units:

```
with LIB_UNIT;
separate(PARENT)
procedure INNER(...) is
   .
   .
   .
end INNER;
```

Unless explicitly stated no other part of PARENT will have access to LIB_UNIT;

The package construct provides both for decomposition and abstraction and it therefore has an important role in any design method. Module specification will invariably lead to package specification and the 'implementation' of package bodies gives a natural partition to project work. The link between package specification and implementation is however merely a syntactical one, there is no formal means by which the semantics of the implementation can be specified using standard Ada. This shortcoming has led to the development of a number of methods for specifying the semantics of package and subprogram bodies. Two general approaches have been suggested: one involves the use of formal comments, the other uses additional subprograms to 'test' the behaviour of implementation code. Formal comments are, in effect, extensions to the language definition and may use Ada-like syntax (Snyder & Gorden, 1983) or algebraic axioms (Krieg-Bruckner & Luckham, 1980; Hill, 1983 and 1984). Subprogram additions (Pyle, 1983) are usually applied to test pre-condition, post-condition and invariant properties of the implementation. They have the advantage that readily available Ada-specific tools such as a compiler, can be used to good effect at the design stage.

No book on concurrent programming would be complete without the bounded buffer example and this book will be no exception. This example not only illustrates the use of packages and generics but it is also relevant as the use of buffers is an important feature in concurrent programming. A bounded buffer is constructed as an array with two pointers; one pointer indicates the next free slot on the array, the other indicates the slot containing the next object to be removed. As the array is of a fixed finite size the pointers must wrap around the array. For this reason the structure is often called a **circular buffer.** Consider, first, a package that defines appropriate operations for a single buffer (let REC be some type that is in scope):

```
package STORE is
  procedure GIVE(R : REC);
  procedure TAKE(R : out REC);
end STORE;

package body STORE is

  SIZE   : constant := 128;   -- size of buffer.
  subtype VECTOR_RANGE is INTEGER range 0..SIZE-1;
  VECTOR : array (VECTOR_RANGE) of REC;
  TOP    : VECTOR_RANGE := 1; -- next free slot.
  BASE   : VECTOR_RANGE := 1; -- slot containing next
                              -- REC to be removed.
```

```
     procedure GIVE(R : REC) is
     begin
       VECTOR(TOP) := R;
       TOP := (TOP + 1) mod SIZE;
     end GIVE;

     procedure TAKE(R : out REC ) is
     begin
       R := VECTOR (BASE);
       BASE := (BASE + 1) mod SIZE;
     end TAKE;

   end STORE;
```

This example clearly shows the data hiding properties of packages; neither VECTOR, TOP nor BASE are accessible from outside the package. Only procedures GIVE and TAKE are defined to be visible and therefore callable. As it stands the above code is unreliable, as attempts to take from an empty buffer or place into a full one are not trapped. However, before considering exception handling, the package specification will be expanded so that it allows more than one buffer to be declared:

```
     package STORE is
       type BUFFER is limited private;
       procedure GIVE(R : REC; B : in out BUFFER);
       procedure TAKE(R : out REC; B : in out BUFFER);
     private
       SIZE : constant := 128;
       subtype VECTOR_RANGE is INTEGER range 0..SIZE-1;
       type VEC is array (VECTOR_RANGE) of REC;
       type BUFFER is
       record
         VECTOR : VEC;
         TOP    : VECTOR_RANGE := 1;
         BASE   : VECTOR_RANGE := 1;
       end record;
     end STORE;

     package body STORE is
       procedure GIVE(R : REC; B : in out BUFFER) is
       begin
         B.VECTOR(B.TOP) := R;
         B.TOP := (B.TOP + 1) mod SIZE;
       end GIVE;

       procedure TAKE(R : out REC; B : in out BUFFER) is
       begin
         R := B.VECTOR(B.BASE);
         B.BASE := (B.BASE + 1) mod SIZE;
       end TAKE;
     end STORE;
```

Buffers can then be declared and used as follows:

```
with DATA_DECS;   use DATA_DECS;
with STORE;   use STORE;
procedure MAIN is
   BUFF1, BUFF2 : BUFFER;
   BUFFERS : array(1..64) of BUFFER;
   CLIENT : REC;
begin
   -- produce value for CLIENT
   GIVE(CLIENT,BUFF2);
   -- etc
end MAIN;
```

As the above example shows the package is a means of encapsulating related objects in a program. It is nevertheless a static and passive construct; it is strictly a compile-time facility that should exhibit no run-time overheads. These characteristics will be compared with those of the task in later chapters. The idea of a package is not new in programming languages. In fact the class construct in SIMULA (Dahl *et al*, 1968) is probably the first example of an abstraction mechanism. Following SIMULA a number of Pascal derivatives have introduced some form of class structure; for example, concurrent Pascal (Brinch Hansen, 1975) and Pascal Plus (Welsh & Bustard, 1979). The concurrent programming language Modula (Wirth, 1977a,b,c) uses the idea of a module to give a structure similar to that of a package although the specification of the visible part is much more rudimentary. The main criticism that can be levelled at the Ada package is its use of open scope rules whereby all objects visible at the point of package declaration are automatically accessible inside the package (Young, 1982). This is to be compared with Modula where, in a module specification, all external objects that are used in the module have to be explicitly named in a 'use clause'.

1.3 Exception Handling

During the execution of a program, events or conditions may occur which might be considered 'exceptional'. With commercial or numerical computing such conditions can be catered for by an appropriate run-time error message followed by program termination. This is not acceptable with embedded systems, where the software must be tolerant of both hardware and software faults. Two broad classifications of exception can be isolated:

> **Error Conditions.** Arithmetic overflow, storage exhaustion, array-bounds violation, subrange violations, peripheral timeouts, etc.

Abnormal Program Condition. Type clash in user input, need for special algorithm to deal with singularities etc.

In order to deal with error conditions, the run-time system must bring such errors to the program's attention – predefined exceptions are said to be raised. With abnormal program conditions it is usual to raise exceptions explicitly within the software :

```
if <condition> then raise <exception>; end if;
```

For both of these situations it is necessary for control to pass to a specified sequence of statements which is called the exception handler. These exception handlers are separated, textually, from the place at which the error is raised so that the normal behaviour of the program is easier to see. The raised exception is therefore, in many ways, an up-market goto statement and its widespread use can lead to the kind of unmaintainable spaghetti code that high level languages are designed to avoid. Because of this, Ada contains a limited form of exception handling (c.f. PL/1) that should really be used only for error conditions. For example the Ada model of exceptions does not allow for an automatic return to the point of the error from within the exception handler.

Any program block (or subprogram) in Ada may contain handlers that can catch exceptions raised during the execution of that block, for example:

```
declare
  BAD_DATA : exception;   -- user defined exception.
begin
  -- sequence of statements containing:
  if <condition> then raise BAD_DATA; end if;
exception
  when BAD_DATA =>
    -- sequence of statements to be
    -- executed if this exception is raised.
  when CONSTRAINT_ERROR =>
    -- handler for predefined exception.
  when others => handler for all other exceptions.
end;
```

the optional handler 'others' is guaranteed to catch all exceptions raised in the block (excluding those already mentioned and therefore explicitly handled) although within the handler for others it is not possible to find out which exception has actually been raised.

When an exception is raised, the appropriate exception handler is executed and the block terminates. If no handler is to be found in the local block then the exception is propagated to containing blocks until it is handled or, if there is no such handler in the main program block, the program itself terminates. Where an exception is raised and not handled in a subprogram the subprogram is terminated and the named exception is raised again at the point of call of that subprogram. In this way, the exception is propagated down the dynamic chain of subprogram calls. If a user defined exception goes out of scope due to its propagation then the exception becomes anonymous and can only be caught with 'when others'.

For real-time languages, a major requirement of the exception handling mechanism is that it should incur no run-time overheads in situations of normal execution. This is feasible for Ada but is not an implementation requirement.

The bounded buffer example can now be expanded so that buffer overflow and underflow are managed by the use of exceptions. The package specification now becomes:

```
package STORE is
   type BUFFER is limited private;
   procedure GIVE(R : REC; B : in out BUFFER);
   procedure TAKE(R : out REC; B : in out BUFFER);
   OVERFLOW, UNDERFLOW : exception;

   private
     SIZE: constant := 128;
     subtype VECTOR_RANGE is INTEGER range 0..SIZE-1;
     type VEC is array (VECTOR_RANGE) of REC;
     type BUFFER is
       record
         VECTOR     : VEC;
         TOP, BASE  : VECTOR_RANGE := 1;
         CONTENTS   : INTEGER range 0..SIZE := 0;
       end record;
   end STORE;
```

Within the body of STORE the procedures GIVE and TAKE would now have the form:

```
procedure GIVE(R : REC; B : in out BUFFER) is
begin
   if B.CONTENTS = SIZE then raise OVERFLOW; end if;
   B.VECTOR(B.TOP) := R;
   B.TOP := (B.TOP + 1) mod SIZE;
   B.CONTENTS := B.CONTENTS + 1;
end GIVE;
procedure TAKE(R : out REC; B : in out BUFFER) is
begin
   if B.CONTENTS = 0 then raise UNDERFLOW; end if;
   R := B.VECTOR(B.BASE);
   B.BASE := (B.BASE + 1) mod SIZE;
   B.CONTENTS := B.CONTENTS - 1;
end TAKE;
```

It is thus the responsibility of the user of this package to trap overflow and underflow exceptions:

```
declare
    -- the following is an example
    -- of a protected call on GIVE
    TEMP_REC : REC; -- if the buffer is full an element
                    -- will be taken off and
                    -- 'thrown away'
begin
    STORE.GIVE(A_REC,A_BUFFER);
exception
    when STORE.OVERFLOW =>
        STORE.TAKE(TEMP_REC,A_BUFFER);
        STORE.GIVE(A_REC,A_BUFFER);
end;
```

If the exceptions are not trapped the program will terminate.

The package STORE illustrates an interesting 'feature' of the interaction between exceptions and packages. In the specification of STORE there are two subprograms and two exceptions and yet without some formal comment it is not possible to know which exceptions can be raised by which subprograms unless one looks into the body of the package. This is clearly against the philosophy of packages and is a genuine problem with large library units. For example TEXT_IO (the specified library package for straightforward input and output) has some 84 subprograms and 8 exceptions. Obviously not all exceptions can be raised by each subprogram but unless 'others' is used to catch all exceptions (in which case it is not possible to find out which of the eight exceptions was raised), an over-elaborate handler must be associated with all subprogram calls.

1.4 Generics

An essential feature of library units should be a generality which will allow them to be used over a wide range of applications. This generality can be achieved in a limited sense by the appropriate choice of subprogram parameters (with default values). However the strong typing model of Ada prevents flexibility. Generics make possible the production of reusable software components and they represent an important and central feature of the Ada language. A generic is a template (with parameters) from which actual subprograms and packages can be constructed. This construction, or **instantiation** as it is usually called, involves the association of formal and calling parameters at compile time; the parameters themselves being either data values, types or subprograms.

Generic instantiation is more powerful than mere macro expansion. A detailed analysis of the Ada model is, however, of only tangential significance to this book and therefore will not be undertaken. To complete this introductory chapter the bounded buffer example will be expanded so that the record type REC becomes a generic parameter. Within the package STORE, the only property of REC that is used is assignment and therefore within the package REC acts as a private type; the specification of the generic package is thus:

```
generic
  type REC is private;
package STORE is
  type BUFFER is limited private;
  procedure GIVE(R : REC; B : in out BUFFER);
  procedure TAKE(R : out REC; B : in out BUFFER);
  OVERFLOW, UNDERFLOW : exception;
private
  -- as before
end STORE;
package body STORE is separate; -- as before
```

From this generic a package may be instantiated for any type other than one that is limited private:

```
declare
  type DATE is
    record
      DAY    : INTEGER range 1..31;
      MONTH  : INTEGER range 1..12;
      YEAR   : INTEGER range 1066..2066;
    end record;
  package DATE_STORE is new STORE (REC => DATE);
  package INT_STORE is new STORE (REC => INTEGER);
  BUFF1, BUFF2 : INT_STORE.BUFFER; -- two buffers.
  IN_TRAY : DATE_STORE.BUFFER;        -- a date buffer.
begin
  null;
end;
```

Buffer structures are important in concurrent programs and this generic package is a usable and useful program component. However in the above form it is unreliable for all but sequential programs.

2 THE NATURE AND USES OF CONCURRENT PROGRAMMING

Any language, whether computer or natural, has the dual property of allowing expression whilst limiting the conceptual framework over which that expressive power may be applied. Pascal, FORTRAN and COBOL share the common property of being sequential languages. Programs written in these languages have a single thread of control. They start executing in some state and then proceed, by executing one statement at a time, until the program terminates. The path through the program may differ due to variations in input data but for any particular execution of the program there is only one path. A modern computer system will, by comparison, consist of one or more central processors and many I/O devices, all of which are operating in parallel. Moreover, an operating system that provides for interactive use will always support many executing programs (called processes), in the sense that they are being time-sliced onto the available processors. The effect of fast process switching is to give behaviour almost indistinguishable from true parallelism. In the programming of embedded systems one must deal with the inherent parallelism of the larger system. A real-time language must therefore provide some facility for multi-programming. This can be achieved by specifying a standard interface to a multi-processing operating system or by allowing multiple process systems to be expressed in the language itself.

Ada provides for the direct programming of parallel activities. Within an Ada program there may be a number of tasks each of which has its own thread of control. It is thus possible to match the parallel nature of the application area with syntactical forms that reflect these structures. This has proved to be an invaluable aid in the production of clear and correct software. Languages whose conceptual framework includes parallelism are known as concurrent programming languages. Ada is such a language but it is by no means the first (or last!), for example Modula, CHILL, Mesa, CSP, Pascal Plus and occam all deal with this concept although in radically different ways. In addition to these procedural language there are also functional languages such as Arctic (Dannenberg, 1984) and OWL (Donner, 1983), and data-flow languages (Dennis & Weng, 1979; Dennis, 1980; McGraw, 1982) available for the specification and implementation of real-time systems.

In general each individual thread of control within a concurrent program is known as a process, although Ada uses the term 'task'. No distinction is made, in this book, between tasks and processes. The execution of a process can be by any of three methods:

(i)   All processes may share a single processor.

(ii) Each process may have its own processor and the processors share common memory.

(iii) Each process may have its own processor and the processors are distributed (i.e. they are connected by a communications network).

Hybrids of these three methods are also possible. Ada is designed for all the above situations (the full implications of this will be considered later). Because of the different implementation methods the term concurrent, rather then parallel, is of more use in this area. Two processes are said to be executing in **parallel** if at any instant they are both executing. Therefore in the above classifications only cases (ii) and (iii) are truly parallel.

By comparison two processes are said to be **concurrent** if they have the potential for executing in parallel. A concurrent program is thus one that has more than one thread of control. Execution of this program will, if there are processors available, run each of these threads of control in parallel. Otherwise each of the threads will be interleaved. The important concept is therefore concurrency (as it encompasses all three of the above cases) rather than whether, or not, the implementation of concurrency involves parallelism or pseudo-parallelism.

> *"Concurrent programming is the name given to programming notation and techniques for expressing potential parallelism and for solving the resulting synchronisation and communication problems. Implementation of parallelism is a topic in computer systems (hardware and software) that is essentially independent of concurrent programming. Concurrent programming is important because it provides an abstract setting in which to study parallelism without getting bogged down in the implementation details." (Ben-Ari, 1982).*

The problems of synchronisation and communication are considered in the next chapter.

2.1 Uses of Concurrent Programming

Concurrent programming is primarily of use in the programming of embedded real-time systems. A system is 'real-time' if its specification has time dependent features. Virtually all embedded systems are inherently parallel, the software must therefore control the simultaneous operations of the coexisting hardware components. Typically this is achieved by associating with each external device a process that controls the input and output operations of that device. These processes, together with the necessary management processes, comprise the software model. Embedded systems themselves are to be found in a wide variety of applications, for example:

```
process control
air traffic control
industrial robots
domestic appliances
environmental monitors
operating system kernels
```

The implementation of these multi-task systems can be achieved by integrating sequential programs, but this necessitates the support of an underlying operating system that will map the programs onto the processes and allow data communication. This is done by the use of common memory areas and the provision of safe operating system procedures.

The use of a concurrent programming language may preclude operating system support, in which case the run-time system of the language implementation must control scheduling; and data communication (plus synchronisation) is programmed directly in the language. This leads to the second use of tasks; they may serve as control agents (for example, providing buffers) that will be of use to the active processes of the embedded system.

Concurrency is also of value in efficiently mapping software onto multiprocessor hardware to exploit the properties of concurrent algorithms. For instance the need to sort 10,000 objects (a standard sequential problem) may be more effectively undertaken as ten parallel processes each sorting 1,000 objects, followed by a merge operation. Here the distinction between true and pseudo-parallelism is important: as the above algorithm will almost certainly be less efficient than a standard approach if the processes are time-sliced onto a single processor. The hardware architecture can therefore have a serious effect upon certain aspects of the portability of concurrent programs.

Finally, software engineering principles indicate that the implementation languages should, wherever possible, mimic the structure of the application domain. If the application contains inherent parallelism then the design and construction of the software product will be less error-prone, easier to prove correct and easier to adapt if concurrency is available in the design and implementation languages. Two examples of this type of use of Ada are in the development of information processing system prototypes (Kirkham et al, 1984; Burns and Kirkham, 1985) and dialogue control systems (Burns & Robinson, 1984a,b). In the first of these a data-flow description of an information processing system consists of, primarily, tasks (where information is processed) and data-flows which link these tasks. The transformation of this description into a series of sequential programs is time consuming and error-prone. With a concurrent language such as Ada the implementation is straightforward and can be undertaken almost automatically.

A dialogue control system, DCS, enables the application software (which may be multi-tasking) and the user interface implementation to be designed separately and programmed as concurrent objects. The DCS provides a flexible multi-levelled interface, (Robinson & Burns, 1985), which can be used by the application software to interact with the human users of the system. This is achieved by allowing the tasks in the application software to communicate, in a controlled way, with the tasks in the DCS. This logic naturally extends to viewing the software, the interface and the user as concurrent elements of the same system.

These two quite different examples indicate that concurrent programming is not just concerned with coding embedded systems but is a quite fundamental language structure. The wide availability and use of Ada will allow programmers from many differing application domains to have available, if necessary, concurrent programming facilities. It is therefore important that all users of Ada understand the tasking model.

2.2 Process Representation

There are several notations used to specify the concurrent components of a program and different methods are also employed to indicate when a process should start executing and when it should terminate. Coroutines were one of the first methods of expressing concurrency although the coroutines themselves could not actually execute in parallel. A coroutine is structured like a procedure; at any one time a single coroutine would be executing, with control being passed to another coroutine by means of the **resume** statement. The scheduling of the coroutines is therefore explicitly expressed in the program. A resumed coroutine will continue executing, from its last executing state, until it again encounters a resume statement. The resume statement, itself, names the coroutine to be resumed.

Coroutines have been used, primarily, in discrete event simulation languages and were provided in SIMULA (Nygaard & Dahl, 1978) although they have reappeared recently in Modula 2 (Wirth, 1982). Because coroutines are not adequate for true parallel processing they are not available in Ada. Instead Ada, like many other concurrent programming languages, uses a direct representation of processes which, as has been noted, are called tasks. Moreover the execution of a task is started by, in effect, the scope rules of the language. This is in contrast to languages such a Algol68 (van Wijngaarden *et al*, 1975) and CSP (Hoare, 1978) where execution is started by a cobegin .. coend structure:

```
cobegin
  P1; P2; P3;
coend;
```

this will cause the concurrent execution of processes P1, P2 and P3.

In chapter 4 a detailed examination of task declaration is given. However, a more informal description will be of use at this stage. Consider the following program skeleton:

```
procedure MAIN is
  task A;
  task B;  -- two tasks have been declared
           -- and named.
         .
         .
         .
  task body A is separate;  -- implementation
                            -- of task A.
  task body B is separate;
begin
  -- A and B are now both executing concurrently.
         .
         .
         .
end MAIN;
```

The task has a similar syntactical structure to that of the package. In the sequence of statements of procedure MAIN three concurrent objects are executing, the two tasks (A and B), and the statements of the procedure. The procedure will itself only terminate when all these statements have been executed and the two tasks have terminated. Execution of tasks A and B is deemed to commence immediately after 'begin', that is before any of the statements of MAIN.

2.3 A Simple Embedded System

In order to illustrate some of the advantages and disadvantages of concurrent programming a simple embedded system will now be considered. Figure 2.1 outlines this simple system; a process T takes readings from a set of thermo-couples (via an analogue to digital converter, ADC) and makes appropriate changes to a heater (via a digital to analogue converter, DAC). Process P has a similar function but for pressure. Both T and P must communicate data to process S which presents measurements to an operator via a screen. The overall objective of this embedded system is to keep the temperature and pressure of some chemical process within defined limits. A real system of this type would clearly be more complex allowing, for example, the operator to change the limits. However, even for this simple system, implementation could take one of three forms:

(i)   T, P and S are written as separate programs and use operating system primitives for program/process interaction.

(ii)   A single program is used which ignores the logical concurrency of T, P and S. No operating system support is required.

(iii) A single concurrent program is used which retains the logical structure of T, P and S. No operating system support is required.

With embedded system it is rare for the processor to have any resident operating system, therefore (i) is usually inappropriate. Rather, the code will be targeted onto a 'bare' processor from a host computer that supports an Ada programming environment. In order to simplify the structure of the central software the following packages will be assumed to have been implemented:

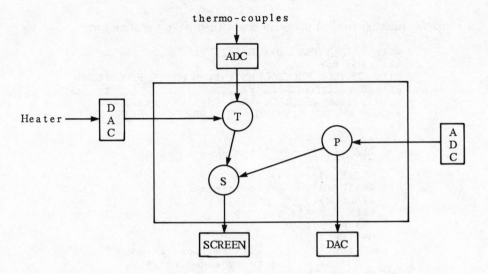

Figure 2.1

```
package DATA_TYPES is
   type TEMP_READING is new INTEGER range 10..500;
   type PRESSURE_READING is new INTEGER range 0..750;
   type HEATER_SETTING is (ON,OFF);
   type PRESSURE_SETTING is new INTEGER range 0..9;
end DATA_TYPES;
with DATA_TYPES; use DATA_TYPES;
package IO is
   -- procedures for data exchange with the environment.
   procedure READ  (TR : out TEMP_READING); -- from ADC.
   procedure READ  (PR : out PRESSURE_READING);
   -- this is an example of overloading; two reads
   -- are defined but they have a different type
   procedure WRITE (HS : HEATER_SETTING);    -- to DAC.
   procedure WRITE (PS : PRESSURE_SETTING);
   procedure WRITE (TR : TEMP_READING);      -- to screen.
   procedure WRITE (PR : PRESSURE_READING);
end IO;

with DATA_TYPES; use DATA_TYPES;
package CONTROL_PROCEDURES is
   -- procedures for converting a reading into
   -- an appropriate setting for output.
   procedure TEMP (TR : TEMP_READING;
                   HS : out HEATER_SETTING);
   procedure PRES (PR : PRESSURE_READING;
                   PS : out PRESSURE_SETTING);
end CONTROL_PROCEDURES;
```

A simple sequential control program could then have the structure:

```
with DATA_TYPES; use DATA_TYPES;
with IO; use IO;
with CONTROL_PROCEDURES; use CONTROL_PROCEDURES;
procedure CONTROLLER is
  TR : TEMP_READING; PR : PRESSURE_READING;
  HS : HEATER_SETTING; PS : PRESSURE_SETTING;
begin
  loop
    READ(TR);      -- from ADC.
    TEMP(TR,HS);
    WRITE(HS);     -- to DAC.
    WRITE(TR);     -- to screen.
    READ(PR);
    PRES(PR,PS);
    WRITE(PS);
    WRITE(PR);
  end loop;        -- infinite loop, common
                   -- in embedded software.
end CONTROLLER;
```

This code has the immediate handicap that temperature and pressure readings must be taken at the same rate which may not be in accordance with requirements. The use of counters and appropriate if statements will improve the situation, however there remains a serious drawback, that while waiting to read a temperature no attention can be given to pressure (and vice versa). Moreover, if there is a system failure that results in, say, control never returning from the temperature READ, then in addition to this problem no further pressure READs would be taken.

An improvement to this sequential program can be made by including in the package IO two boolean functions, READY_TEMP and READY_PRES, to indicate the availability of an item to read. The control program then becomes:

```
with DATA_TYPES; use DATA_TYPES;
with IO; use IO;
with CONTROL_PROCEDURES; use CONTROL_PROCEDURES;
procedure CONTROLLER is
  TR : TEMP_READING; PR : PRESSURE_READING;
  HS : HEATER_SETTING; PS : PRESSURE_SETTING;
begin
  loop
    if READY_TEMP then
      READ(TR);
      TEMP(TR,HS);
      WRITE(HS);   -- assuming write to be reliable.
      WRITE(TR);
    end if;
```

```
        if READY_PRES then
          READ(PR);
          PRES(PR,PS);
          WRITE(PS);
          WRITE(PR);
        end if;
      end loop;
    end CONTROLLER;
```

This solution is more reliable; unfortunately the program now spends a high proportion of its time in a 'busy loop' polling the input devices to see if they are ready. Busy-waits are, in general, unacceptably inefficient. They tie up the processor and make it very difficult to impose a queue discipline on waiting requests. Moreover programs that rely on busy-waiting are difficult to design, understand or prove correct (Andrews & Schneider, 1983).

The major criticism that can be levelled at the sequential program is that no recognition is effectively given to the fact that the pressure and temperature cycles are entirely independent subsystems. In Ada this can be rectified by coding each system as a task:

```
    procedure CONTROLLER is    -- same package
                               -- dependencies as before.
      task T;
      task P;
      task body T is
        TR : TEMP_READING; HS : HEATER_SETTING;
      begin
        loop
          READ(TR);
          TEMP(TR,HS);
          WRITE(HS);
          WRITE(TR);
        end loop;
      end T;
      task body P is
        PR : PRESSURE_READING; PS : PRESSURE_SETTING;
      begin
        loop
          READ(PR);
          PRES(PR,PS);
          WRITE(PS);
          WRITE(PR);
        end loop;
      end P;
    begin
      null;
    end CONTROLLER;
```

Tasks T and P execute concurrently and each contains an indefinite loop within which the control cycle is defined. While one task is suspended waiting for a read the other may be executing; if they are both suspended a busy loop is not executed. The logic of the application is reflected in the code; the inherent parallelism of the domain is represented by concurrently executing tasks in the program.

One major problem however remains with this two task solution. Both T and P send data to the screen, but the screen is a resource that can only sensibly be accessed by one process at a time. In Figure 2.1 control over the screen was given to a third process, S; the controller program should therefore possess three tasks. This has transposed the problem from that of concurrent access to a non-concurrent resource to one of inter-task communication. It is necessary for tasks T and P to pass data to task S. Moreover S must ensure that it deals with only one request at a time. These requirements and difficulties are of primary importance in the design of concurrent programming languages. Therefore before considering in detail how Ada faces these problems the next chapter will concentrate on inter-process communication and what structures other concurrent languages have employed.

3 INTER-PROCESS COMMUNICATION

The major difficulties associated with concurrent programming arise from process interaction. Rarely are processes as independent of one another as they were in the simple example of the previous chapter. One of the main objectives of embedded systems design is to specify those activities that should be represented as processes, and to indicate the nature of the interfaces between these concurrent objects. Before considering language structure, however, it is necessary to discuss the inherent properties of inter-process communication. This will be attempted by consideration of the following topics:

Data Communication.
Synchronisation.
Deadlocks and Indefinite Postponements.
System and Performance Reliability.

It is these themes that have influenced the design of the Ada tasking model.

3.1 Data Communication

The partitioning of a system into tasks invariably leads to the requirement that these tasks exchange data in order for the system to perform sensibly. For example, a device driver (a process with sole control over an external device) will need to receive requests and return data (if it were an input request) from other processes.

Data communication is, in general, based upon either shared variables or message passing. Shared variables are objects that more than one processes have access to; communication can therefore proceed by each process referencing these variables when appropriate. Message passing involves the explicit exchange of data between two processes by means of a message that passes from one process to the other via some agency. For distributed systems where processors do not have common memory, shared variables are clearly difficult to map onto the hardware architecture. With non-distributed systems, shared variables and message passing are appropriate although messages tend to require greater run-time support. Ada provides for shared variables and a type of message passing structure.

Although shared variables are a straightforward means of passing information between processes their unrestricted use is unreliable and unsafe. Consider the following assignment:

X := X + 1;

This will most probably be implemented in three stages:
(i)   Copy value of X into some register.
(ii)   Add 1 to register.
(iii)   Store value of register in address for X.

If two or more processes are assigning values to X (called multiple- update) it is possible from the nature of the concurrency for unexpected values to be given to the shared variable. For example let processes P1 and P2 concurrently execute the above assignment; a possible sequence of actions is (let X be initially zero):
(a) P1 copies value of X into its register (X(P1) = 0).
(b) P1 adds 1 to its register (X(P1) = 1).
(c) P2 copies value of X into its register (X(P2) = 0).
(d) P2 adds 1 to its register (X(P2) = 1).
(e) P2 stores its value of X (X = 1).
(f) P1 stores its value of X (X = 1).

This interleaving of the executions of P1 and P2 results in X having the final value of 1 rather than the expected value 2. Only if the assignment to X was an indivisible operation (this is achieved, for example, with the fetch-and-add instruction on the Ultracomputer see Schonberg & Schonberg, 1985) would the integrity of the variable be assured. Because of this multiple update problem shared variables are usually only employed in concert with operators that give indivisible operations (see section 3.7).

3.2 Synchronisation

Although processes execute essentially independently there are situations where it is necessary for two or more processes to coordinate their executions. For example, in order for a process to receive a message it is necessary for another process to have first sent this message. Synchronisation is simply defined as one process possessing knowledge about the state of another process. In most instances data communication will necessitate synchronisation. Indeed, with the Ada tasking model communication and synchronisation are closely related in the same basic mechanism.

With languages that allow communication through shared objects there are two particularly important classes of synchronisation: **mutual exclusion** and **condition synchronisation.** The execution of a program implies the use of **resources** (files, devices, memory) many of which can only be safely used by one process at a time. A shared variable is itself an example of such a resource. Mutual exclusion is a synchronisation that ensures that while one process is accessing a shared variable (or other non-concurrent resource) no other process can possibly gain access. The sequence of statements that manipulates the shared resource is called a critical section. It may be a single assignment (such as the X := X + 1; described above) or may be more complex (for example, a file update). One means of defining mutual exclusion is to treat a critical section as an indivisible operation. The complete actions on the resource must therefore have been performed before any other process could execute a possibly corrupting action.

Condition synchronisation is necessary when a process wishes to perform an operation that can only sensibly or safely be performed if another task has itself taken some action or is in some defined state. If two processes are communicating via a shared variable then the receiver of the data must be able to know that the sender has made the appropriate assignment to this variable. In this case the sender does not need to synchronise with the receiver; in other cases the data communication may be in both directions or the sender may wish to know that the receiver has taken the data. Here both processes must perform condition synchronisation.

Another example of condition synchronisation comes with the use of buffers as described in chapter 1. Two processes that pass data between them may perform better if the communication is not direct but via a buffer. This has the advantage of de-coupling the processes and allows for small fluctuations in the speeds at which the two processes are working. The use of this structure (two processes communicating via a buffer) is commonplace in concurrent programs and is known as the producer-consumer system. Two condition synchronisations are necessary if a finite buffer is used. Firstly the producer process must not attempt to deposit data onto the buffer if the buffer is full. Secondly the consumer process cannot be allowed to extract objects from the buffer if the buffer is empty. In Ada the buffer itself can simply be constructed as a task and hence the required synchronisations are between tasks.

3.3 Deadlocks and Indefinite Postponements

The above synchronisations, although necessary, lead to difficulties that must be considered in the design of concurrent programs (rather than in the design of concurrent languages in which it is impracticable to remove the possibility of these difficulties arising). Deadlocks are the most serious condition and entail a set of processes being in a state from which it is impossible for any of the processes to proceed. Consider two processes P1 and P2 and two non-concurrent resources R1 and R2. Access to the resources must be via critical sections that preclude further access. Let P1 have access to R1 and P2 access to R2; the program structure may then allow the following interleaving:

```
P1 retains access to R1 but also requires R2

P2 retains access to R2 but also requires R1
```

Mutual exclusion will ensure that concurrent access does not take place, but unfortunately as a consequence both P1 and P2 are deadlocked, neither can proceed.

The testing of software rarely removes other than the most obvious deadlocks; they can occur infrequently but with devastating results. Two distinct approaches to the deadlock problem can be taken. One can attempt to prove that deadlocks are not possible in the particular program under investigation. Although difficult this is clearly the correct approach to take and is helped by programming in an appropriate style (see chapter 15). Alternatively one can attempt to avoid deadlocks whilst having contingency plans available if they do occur. These actions can be grouped together under three headings:

(i)   Deadlock Avoidance
(ii) Deadlock Detection.
(iii) Recovery from Deadlock.

Avoidance algorithms attempt to look ahead and stop the system moving into a state that will inevitably lead to a deadlock. Recovery is never painless and must involve, for real-time systems, the aborting (or backing off) of at least one process with the pre-emptive removal of resources from that process. Deadlocks are a particular problem with operating systems and considerable work has been done on deadlocks within this context (see, for example, Peterson and Silberschatz, 1983).

Indefinite postponement (sometimes called lockout or starvation) is a less severe condition whereby a process that wishes to gain access to a resource, via a critical section, is never allowed to because there are always other processes gaining access before it. If entry to a critical section is in the order of the requests that have being made then indefinite postponement is not possible. However, if processes have priorities, and the order of entry is dependent on these priorities, then a low priority process may be postponed indefinitely by the existence of higher priority requests. Even if the postponement is not indefinite, but indeterminate, making assertions about the program's behaviour may be impossible.

A different way of looking at indefinite postponements is to consider the opposite criteria, namely that of **fairness** (Lehmann et al, 1981), which may be defined as an equal chance for equal priority processes, or **liveness** (Ben-Ari, 1982). These properties imply that if a process wishes to perform some action then it will, eventually, be allowed to do so. In particular if a process requests access to a critical section then it will gain access in some finite time . If requests are being actively processed and there is a defined upper limit on how long a process will be delayed then the synchronisation mechanism is said to be **bounded fair.**

3.4 System Performance and Reliability

Both mutual exclusion and condition synchronisation give rise to situations in which a process must be delayed; it cannot be allowed to continue its execution until some future event has occurred. Message based systems similarly require processes to be suspended. A receiver process must wait until a message arrives and, in other circumstances, a sender process may wish to have it confirmed that the message has reached its destination before proceeding.

One method of 'holding back' a process would be to have it execute a busy wait loop testing a continuation flag. This approach was criticised in the previous chapter as being grossly inefficient. What is more, fairness is impossible to prove on a system using busy waits. Rather, what is required is a mechanism by which a process is 'put to sleep', only to be awakened when circumstances are right for it to proceed. As this future event may be waited upon by a number of processes (although only one may proceed when it occurs, i.e. access to a critical section) it is necessary to queue processes and to have an appropriate run-time support system for managing this queue. The combination of fairness and process queues gives the foundation for an acceptable system performance. Particular communication methods, and implementation, will nevertheless have varying effects upon this performance.

Reliability is of paramount importance with embedded systems where software failure may be costly or dangerous. With inter-process communication the model to be applied in a language should be both reliable in itself and lead to the production of reliable programs. The possibility of misinterpreting parts of the model should be eliminated, and implementation factors should not infringe upon the semantics of the language. These points will be considered later with respect to Ada.

One aspect of reliability is of general significance; the effect of a single process failure upon the rest of the process system. Failure may be due to internal errors or to external circumstances (i.e. being aborted); in both cases the impact on all other processes should be minimal. A reliable model will allow a process to terminate without any effect upon existing processes. However, attempts to communicate or synchronise with a terminated process must be catered for. A process failing whilst executing a critical section presents particular difficulties. A graceful termination may still lead to deadlock if it does not release its mutual exclusive hold over the critical section.

With pure message-based languages, reliability implies that systems should be resilient to not only process failure but also message loss. This can be difficult. If process P1 sends a message to process P2, and expects a reply, what action should it take if the reply has not materialised? Does it assume that the original message was lost, or the reply is lost, or that P2 has failed? An easy approach for the language is to assume that the run-time system implements a completely reliable communication system. This may take the form of an atomic transaction (Lomet, 1977). An atomic transaction is either fully executed or is not executed at all. Therefore if the reply message is received P2 has acted, once, upon the request; if a reply is not received then P2 has taken no action - it is as if P2 never received the original request. Implementation of atomic actions is, however, expensive (Liskov, 1981).

3.5 Dining Philosophers Problem

The dining philosophers problem is a system, which does not contain computers, that illustrates well the points made in the above sections. Although it is described in many books on concurrent programming no apologies are given for including a brief description here. Five Chinese philosophers are seated, permanently, around a circular table, between each philosopher there is a single chopstick (i.e. there are only five chopsticks). Each philosopher can be considered as a concurrent process whose existence is entirely made up of either eating or thinking (I think therefore I am; I am therefore I eat!).

Even though each philosopher is well versed in Chinese culture they find it impossible to eat with only one chopstick. Therefore at most only two philosophers can be eating at any one time. The chopsticks are a scarce non-concurrent resource (i.e. they cannot be broken in two!). It is assumed that philosophers are too polite to lean across the table to obtain a chopstick (and too engrossed in thought to leave and find more) and thus they only make use of the chopsticks at either side of them. This philosopher system illustrates many of the important aspects of inter-process communication:

(i)   Data Communication - chopsticks may be passed directly from one philosopher to another or be held in a pool of available resources.

(ii)   Mutual Exclusion - access to each chopstick must be via a critical section as two philosophers cannot have concurrent access to the same chopstick.

(iii)   Condition Synchronisation - a philosopher cannot pick up a chopstick until it is free (on the table).

(iv)   Deadlocks - a solution of the form:

```
loop
   pickup left chopstick
   pickup right chopstick
   eat;
   put down left chopstick
   put down right chopstick
   think;
end loop;
```

will lead to a deadlock if all philosophers pick up their left chopstick.

(v)   Indefinite Postponement - it is possible for two philosophers to starve (literally) the philosopher sitting between them. If they eat alternatively the middle philosopher will never have both chopsticks.

(vi)   Efficient Waiting - should a philosopher who wishes to eat constantly check on the amount of food remaining on their neighbour's plate, or should the philosopher sleep and rely on a neighbouring philosopher to wake them up when at least one chopstick is free?

(vii) System Reliability - will the death of a philosopher unduly alarm the others? (Yes if it is while eating and the chopsticks depart with the dying philosopher.)

An Ada solution to the dining philosophers problem is given later.

3.6 Shared Variables

From the above analysis it is clear that the Ada tasking model should be reliable, have an efficient wait mechanism, provide for synchronisation, data communication and in particular mutual exclusion, and should enable software to be designed that is free from deadlocks and indefinite postponements. The simplest way that two Ada tasks can interact is via variables that are in scope for both tasks; however, the safe use of these shared variables is not straightforward, as was illustrated by the multiple update problem described above. It is possible to give mutual exclusion by using only shared variables but a reliable solution that is free from deadlocks and indefinite postponements is not trivial. The following code implements Dekker's algorithm (Francez & Pnueli, 1978) for mutual exclusion:

```
procedure DEKKER is
  task T1;
  task T2;
  type FLAG is (UP, DOWN);
  FLAG_1, FLAG_2 : FLAG := DOWN;
    -- flag up implies intention to enter
    -- critical section.
  TURN : INTEGER range 1..2 := 1;
    -- used to arbitrate between tasks if they
    -- both wish to enter critical section concurrently.
  task body T1 is
  begin
    loop
      FLAG_1 := UP;
      while FLAG_2 = UP loop
        if TURN = 2 then
          FLAG_1 := DOWN;
          while TURN = 2 loop
            null; -- busy wait.
          end loop;
          FLAG_1 := UP;
        end if;
      end loop;
      -- critical section.
      TURN := 2;
      FLAG_1 := DOWN;
      -- rest of task.
    end loop;
  end T1;
```

```
task body T2 is
begin
  loop
    FLAG_2 := UP;
    while FLAG_1 = UP loop
      if TURN = 1 then
        FLAG_2 := DOWN;
        while TURN = 1 loop
          null;  -- busy wait.
        end loop;
        FLAG_2 := UP;
      end if;
    end loop;
    -- critical section.
    TURN := 1;
    FLAG_2 := DOWN;
    -- rest of task.
  end loop;
end T2;

begin
  null;
end DEKKER;
```

In order to protect the critical section three extra shared variables are necessary. When T1 wishes to enter its critical section it first announces this to T2 by raising its flag (FLAG_1); if T2 is executing the 'rest of process' then FLAG_2 will be down and T1 can proceed safely into its critical section. However if an interleaving of T1 and T2 leads to both flags being raised concurrently then the shared variable TURN will arbitrate; if TURN=2 then T1 will relinquish its request to enter its critical section by lowering its flag. Only when TURN takes the value 1 (i.e. when T2 has left its critical section) will T2 reset its flag. The switching of the value of TURN eliminates indefinite postponement.

This solution can be extended to more then two tasks but the protocols get even more complex. Hopefully the above program illustrates the difficulties of using shared variables as the basis for inter-process communication. The criticism can be summarised as follows:

(a) An unreliable (rogue) task that misuses shared variables will corrupt the entire system, hence unreliable.

(b) Only busy wait possible.

(c) Programming synchronisations and communications is non-trivial and error prone.

(d) Testing programs may not examine rare interleavings that break mutual exclusion or lead to deadlocks.

(e) With large programs, readability, and hence understanding, is poor.

(f) Analysis of code, i.e. proving the non-existence of deadlocks, is almost impossible with large programs.

(g) No concurrent programming language relies entirely upon shared variables.

(h) There may be no shared physical memory!

As shared variables are clearly inappropriate, other methods have been derived (a comprehensive survey of these methods is to be found in Andrews & Schneider, 1983). Three such methods will be described briefly here: semaphores, monitors and rendezvous. These represent the major structures used in language design; moreover Ada incorporates an adaptation of the rendezvous, which can itself be used to program semaphores and monitors.

3.7 Semaphores

Semaphores were originally designed by Dijkstra (1968a,b) to give simple primitives for the programming of mutual exclusion and condition synchronisation. A semaphore is a non-negative integer variable that apart from initialisation can only be acted upon by two procedures WAIT and SEND (called P and V by Dijkstra and WAIT and SIGNAL in other descriptions). An Ada package could define semaphores, e.g.:

```
package SEMAPHORE_PACKAGE is
   type SEMAPHORE is limited private;
   procedure WAIT (S : in out SEMAPHORE);
   procedure SEND (S : in out SEMAPHORE);

private
   type SEMAPHORE is
     record
       SEM : NATURAL := 1;
     end record;
end SEMAPHORE_PACKAGE;
```

The actions of WAIT and SEND can be described as follows:

```
SEND(S) executes      S.SEM := S.SEM + 1;

WAIT(S) executes      if S.SEM = 0 then
                        delay until S.SEM > 0;
                      end if;
                      S.SEM := S.SEM - 1;
```

The delay implies, on implementation, a queue mechanism; a process executing a WAIT on a zero semaphore will be suspended until the semaphore becomes non-zero. This will occur only when some other process executes a SEND on that semaphore. The additional important property of SEND and WAIT is that they are **indivisible operators.** Because of this property the mutual update of a semaphore (by the concurrent executions of WAITs and SENDs) is guaranteed to be reliable. Mutual exclusion can now be coded quite easily:

```
with SEMAPHORE_PACKAGE; use SEMAPHORE_PACKAGE;
procedure MUTUAL_EXCLUSION is
  MUT : SEMAPHORE;
  task T1;
  task T2;
  task body T1 is
  begin
    loop
      WAIT(MUT);
      -- critical section.
      SEND(MUT);
      -- rest of task.
    end loop;
  end T1;

  task body T2 is
  begin
    loop
      WAIT(MUT);
      -- critical section.
      SEND(MUT);
      -- rest of task.
    end loop;
  end T2;

begin
  null;
end MUTUAL_EXCLUSION;
```

The semaphore is initially set to the value one, so the first process (task T1 say) to execute WAIT will not be delayed but will change the value of the semaphore to zero. If the other task now executes WAIT it will be suspended; only when T1 executes SEND (i.e. when it has left the critical section) will T2 be allowed to continue. The generalisation of this program to any number of tasks presents no further difficulties. If there are n tasks suspended on a zero semaphore then a SEND will unblock exactly one of them. SEND will increment the semaphore, one blocked task will proceed and in doing so it will decrement the semaphore back to zero (on implementation these pointless assignment to the semaphore can be eliminated in cases when a SEND unblocks a waiting process).

The initial value of the semaphore sets the maximum concurrency through the critical section. If the value is one then mutual exclusion is assured; alternatively if it has a value of, say, six then up to six processes may have concurrent access. For condition synchronisation a value of zero is often employed; the condition that some process is waiting for can be announced by executing a SEND. By executing a WAIT on a semaphore initialised to zero the waiting process will be suspended until the condition has occurred.

Although semaphores give appropriate synchronisations that will allow, for example, safe data communication using shared variables, they can be criticised as being too low-level and not sufficiently structured for reliable use (Barnes, 1982). Just as with shared variables, a simple misuse of a semaphore, although less likely, will still corrupt the whole program. What is more it cannot be assumed that all processes will make reference to the appropriate semaphore before entering their critical sections. If mutual exclusion is used to protect a non-concurrent resource, then reliability requires all calling processes to use the appropriate protocols. A different approach would have the resource itself protecting usage – this is essentially the solution adopted with monitors. Finally, a semaphore solution is only partially reliable when faced with process failure. If a process terminates, or is aborted, while executing a critical section then it will never SEND, no other process will gain access and deadlock is almost certain to ensue.

3.8 Monitors

A monitor is an encapsulation of a resource definition and all operators that manipulate the resource. In Ada terms a monitor can be viewed as a package in which only procedures are defined in the specification; the resource is hidden in the monitor body and can only be accessed via these procedures. However, unlike a package, a monitor exercises control over calls to its external subprograms. Specifically, execution of monitor procedures is guaranteed, by definition, to be mutually exclusive. This ensures that variables declared in a monitor body can never be subject to concurrent access (this is not the case with ordinary packages). Monitors are a form of Critical Control Regions (Hoare, 1972 and Brinch Hansen, 1972, 1973a, 1981) and have been refined by the work of Dijkstra (1968b), Brinch Hansen (1973b) and Hoare (1974). They are to be found in numerous programming languages such as Mesa (Mitchell et al, 1979), Pascal Plus (Welsh & Bustard, 1979) and Modula (Wirth, 1977a,b,c,d), but not Ada.

If one considers a syntax for a monitor similar to that of an Ada package then a simple resource control monitor would have the form:

```
monitor SIMPLE_RESOURCE is
  -- this monitor controls access to 8 identical
  -- resources by providing acquire
  -- and release operators.
  procedure ACQUIRE;
  procedure RELEASE;
end SIMPLE_RESOURCE;

monitor body SIMPLE_RESOURCE is
  RESOURCE_MAX : constant := 8;
  R : INTEGER range 0..RESOURCE_MAX := RESOURCE_MAX;
  -- R is the number of free resources.
  procedure ACQUIRE is
  begin
    if R = 0 then BLOCK; end if;
    R := R - 1;
  end ACQUIRE;

  procedure RELEASE is
  begin
    R := R + 1;
  end RELEASE;
end SIMPLE_RESOURCE;
```

Tasks that wish to make use of this resource need use no mutual exclusion protocols for the calling of either ACQUIRE or RELEASE. Mutual exclusion is catered for by there being only one execution of ACQUIRE or RELEASE allowed at any one time.

The above code recognises, but does not deal with, the call of an ACQUIRE procedure when there are no resources available. This is an example of a condition synchronisation, for the ACQUIRE cannot be successful until a call of RELEASE is made. Although it would be possible to give this synchronisation using a semaphore defined within the monitor Hoare (1974) proposed a simpler primitive. This primitive is called a **condition variable** or **signal** and is again acted upon by two procedures, which by analogy will also be known here as WAIT and SEND. Unlike a semaphore which has an integer value a condition variable has no associated variable. However, a simple way of understanding the properties of a condition variable is to think of it as a semaphore which always has the value zero. The actions of WAIT and SEND are therefore as follows:

WAIT (cond_var) always blocks calling process.

SEND (cond_var) will unblock a waiting process if there is one, otherwise it has no lasting effect.

With condition variables the simple monitor defined above can now be fully coded as:

```
monitor body SIMPLE_RESOURCE is
  RESOURCE_MAX : constant := 8;
  R   : INTEGER range 0..RESOURCE_MAX := RESOURCE_MAX;
  CR  : CONDITION_VARIABLE;

  procedure ACQUIRE is
  begin
    if R = 0 then WAIT(CR); end if;
    R := R - 1;
  end ACQUIRE;

  procedure RELEASE is
  begin
    R := R + 1;
    SEND(CR);
  end RELEASE;
end SIMPLE_RESOURCE;
```

If a process executes ACQUIRE when R=0 then it will become blocked and in doing so it releases its mutual exclusive hold on the monitor so that other processes may call RELEASE or ACQUIRE. When RELEASE is called the execution of SEND will unblock the waiting process which can then proceed. This action could lead to a difficulty as now there are two processes active in the monitor; the unblocked process and the process that freed it. Different methods are used to ensure the reliability of the monitor in these circumstances, the simplest being that the execution of SEND must be the last action in the procedure. In effect, therefore, the process exits the monitor and passes mutual exclusive control to the unblocked process. If no process is blocked on the condition variable then one process delayed upon entry to the monitor is freed.

The monitor is a flexible programming aid that provides the means to tackle, reliably, most of the problems encountered with inter-process communication. Their use provides a clear distinction between synchronisation and data communication, the latter being provided by shared objects. However the monitor, like a package, is a passive construction. There is no mechanism within the monitor for the dynamic control of the order of executions of incoming procedure calls. Rather they must be handled in a predefined order and then blocked if their complete execution is not, at that time, possible. A further criticism of monitor-based languages is that condition synchronisation outside the monitor must be provided by a further mechanism. In Modula this is achieved by allowing signals to be a general language feature. However, signals (condition variables) suffer from the same criticism as semaphores, they are too low-level for reliable use.

This subsection is completed by a further example. The simple. resource control monitor described above is expanded so that requests state the number of resources required. Only when all these resources are available will control pass back to the calling process. Release of resources will cause all blocked processes to check, in turn, to see if enough resources are now available for them. If they are, they proceed; if not, they cycle back and become reblocked on the same condition variable. The reason for giving this example here is that the problem is surprisingly difficult to code reliably in Ada (see chapter 10):

```
monitor RESOURCE_CONTROL is
  procedure ACQUIRE (AMOUNT : NATURAL);
  procedure RELEASE (AMOUNT : NATURAL);
end MONITOR;

monitor body RESOURCE_CONTROL is
  RESOURCE_MAX : constant := 8;
  R : INTEGER range 0..RESOURCE_MAX := RESOURCE_MAX;
  CR : CONDITION_VARIABLE;
  BLOCKED : NATURAL := 0; -- number of blocked processes
  QUEUED  : NATURAL;      -- number of blocked processes
                          -- at time of resource release
  procedure ACQUIRE (AMOUNT : NATURAL) is
  begin
    if R < AMOUNT then
      loop
        BLOCKED := BLOCKED + 1;
        WAIT(CR);
        BLOCKED := BLOCKED - 1;
        QUEUED := QUEUED - 1;
        if R >= AMOUNT then
          R := R - AMOUNT;
          if QUEUED > 0 then SEND(CR); end if;
          return;
        end if;
      end loop;
    else
      R := R - AMOUNT;
    end if;
  end ACQUIRE;

  procedure RELEASE (AMOUNT : NATURAL) is
  begin
    R := R + AMOUNT;
    QUEUED := BLOCKED;
    SEND(CR);
  end RELEASE;
end monitor;
```

This algorithm assumes a FIFO queue on the condition variable and has introduced unreliable elements in order to simplify the code (e.g. it assumes that processes will only release resources they have previously received). The actual nature of the resource and how it is passed to the calling process for use is similarly omitted for clarity.

3.9 Rendezvous

Semaphores were introduced for synchronisation to protect shared variables, however, a possible extension to the semaphore idea would be for it itself to carry the data to be communicated between the synchronised processes. This is the basis for the design of message passing primitives. One process will SEND a message, another process will WAIT for it to arrive. If the process executing the SEND is delayed until the corresponding WAIT is executed then the message passing is said to be **synchronous.** Alternatively, if the SEND process continues executing arbitrarily then one has **asynchronous** message passing. The drawback with the asynchronous structure is that the receiving process cannot know the present state of the calling process; it only has information on some previous state. It is even possible that the process initiating the transfer no longer exists by the time the message is processed.

One of the main issues to be addressed in the design of a message based concurrent programming language is how destinations, and sources, are designated. The simplest form is for the unique process name to be used; this is called direct naming:

```
send <message> to <process-name>
```

A symmetrical form for the receiving process would be:

```
wait <message> from <process-name>
```

Alternatively an asymmetric form may be used if the receiver is only interested in the existence of a message rather than from where it came:

```
wait <message>
```

The asymmetric form is particularly useful when the nature of the inter-process communication fits the **client/server** relationship. The server process renders some utility to any number of client processes (usually one client at a time!). Therefore the client must name the server in sending it a message. By comparison the server will cycle round, receiving requests and performing the service. This may necessitate the return of a reply message, but the address for this will be contained in the original message rather than in the syntax of the way it was received.

Where direct naming is inappropriate, **mailboxes** or **channels** may be used as intermediaries between the sending and receiving processes.

```
send <message> to <mailbox>

wait <message> from <mailbox>
```

In the special case where only one process may wait on a mailbox (although many processes may send) then the shared entity is called a **port** (Balzer, 1971).

With all of these message structures the receiving process, by executing a wait, commits itself to the synchronisation and will be suspended until an actual message arrives. This is, in general, too restrictive; the receiving process may have a number of ports to choose from or it may be in a state that would make it inappropriate to process particular messages. For example, a buffer control process would not wish to wait on an 'extract' message if the buffer is empty. Dijkstra (1975) proposed that commands should be guarded and selective in order to achieve a flexible program structure. A guarded command has the following form:

```
guard => statement
```

where guard is a boolean expression; if the guard is true then the statement may be executed. Selection is achieved through the use of an alternative statement which in Ada is constructed as follows:

```
select
   G1 => S1;
or
   G2 => S2;
or

       .
       .
       .

or
   Gn => Sn;
end select;
```

For example:

```
select
   BUFFER_NOT_FULL => WAIT <place_message>
or
   BUFFER_NOT_EMPTY => WAIT <extract_message>
end select;
```

If more than one guard is true a non-deterministic choice is made from the open alternatives. An important aspect of the guard statement is whether or not the boolean expression can take into account information contained in the message. The language SR (Andrews, 1981, 1982) does allow a process to 'peek' at its incoming messages; Ada, as will be shown later, does not.

The combination of direct naming and synchronous communication together with the use of guarded and selective statements provides a communication structure known as a **rendezvous.** This has been used in the languages CSP (Communicating Sequential Process; Hoare, 1978) and occam (Hoare, 1983). The motivations for basing inter-process communication on the rendezvous are three fold:

(i)   The use of shared variables is so clearly unreliable it should not be allowed by the language.

(ii)   Data communication and process synchronisation should be considered as inseparable activities.

(iii)   The communication model should be simple and amenable to analysis.

In CSP both communicating partners are considered and treated equally. Assume a variable (of type VEC) is to be passed between process A and process B; let AR and BR be of type VEC then the transmission has the form:

```
In process A
   B!AR

In process B
   A?BR
```

Both processes name their partner; when A and B are ready to communicate (i.e. when they execute the above statements) then a rendezvous is said to take place with data passing from the object AR in A to BR in B. The process that executes its command first will be delayed until the other process is ready to rendezvous. Once the communication is complete the rendezvous is broken and both processes continue their executions independently and concurrently. In the CSP model a rendezvous is restricted to unidirectional data communication.

Occam supports a similar communication structure; the main distinction being the use of a unidirectional channel (rather than direct naming) for inter-process communication. The design of occam has been closely coupled with the development of the transputer (a VLSI processor with on-chip RAM and four communication links; May and Taylor, 1984), as a result its execution is likely to be efficient and the distribution of programs on a network of transputers can be directly represented. A channel is thus implemented as a word in memory (if the two processes concerned are on the same transputer) or as a standard link between transputers (if the processes themselves are on separate processors). The scheduling of processes is also supported at a fundamental level within the hardware.

Occam is the lowest level at which the transputer will be programmed. It is however an abstract programming language which, although it is much simpler than Ada, is clearly a powerful method of representing and implementing parallel algorithms, at least on a transputer type network architecture.

Finally in this section a brief description must be given of another high level message-passing construct, namely, **remote procedure calls.** Many applications necessitate the coupling of messages in the form of a request followed by a reply. Process A sends a message to process B; B processes the message and sends a reply message to A. Because this type of communication is common it is desirable to represent it directly in concurrent programming languages.

Procedures, in general, provide this form of processing; **in** parameters are processed to produce **out** parameters. Therefore a simple construct is to allow a process to call a procedure defined in another process. Hence the term remote procedure call:

```
remote procedure SERVICE (A : in SOME_TYPE;
                          B : out SOME_OTHER_TYPE) is
begin
  -- use value of A.
  -- produce value for B.
end SERVICE;
```

Unfortunately this simple structure is not sufficient. If the procedure updates any of the variables of its process, then reentrant access will be unsafe. There is a need to allow the owner process to exercise some control over the use of its procedures. This can be achieved by replacing the procedure by an **accept** statement in the body of the process code:

```
if SOME_CONDITION then
  accept SERVICE (A : in SOME_TYPE;
                  B : out SOME_OTHER_TYPE) do
    .
    .
    .
  end accept;
end if;
```

for the calling process however the communication still has the style of a procedure call. The language DP (Distributed Processes; Brinch Hansen, 1978) was the first to make use of remote procedure calls. It enables an active process to 'export' a collection of procedures in a manner that recreates the rules governing the access of monitor procedures.

3.10 The Ada Tasking Model and its Assessment

Inter-task communication in Ada can be by either of two methods:
- (i)   shared variables.
- (ii) an adapted rendezvous structure.

Although shared variables are allowed, no protection primitives such as semaphores or monitors are supplied. Moreover, all necessary communications can be achieved solely by use of the rendezvous mechanism. Indeed the direct, unprotected, sharing of variables between tasks should if possible be avoided (Nissen & Wallis, 1984). However the rendezvous can be used to construct protection primitives such as monitors that allow objects to be safely shared.

The rendezvous itself is a combination of the mechanisms employed in CSP and DP:

> *"With respect to concurrent programming Ada's main innovation is the rendezvous form of the remote procedure call." (Andrews & Schneider, 1983)*

It differs from the rendezvous of CSP in that:
- (i)   the naming is asymmetric – the calling task names (directly) the called task, but not vice versa.
- (ii) during the rendezvous data may pass in both directions.

Nevertheless Ada and CSP have the following features in common:
- (i)   Tasks wishing to rendezvous are blocked until their partner also indicates a wish to rendezvous.
- (ii) Guarded and selective commands allow flexible program structures.

The rendezvous in Ada, unlike CSP, is not just a simple data transfer but may consist of quite complex processing in order to construct the reply parameters. It takes the form of an **accept** statement as outlined in the previous section on remote procedure calls and is known as an **extended rendezvous.**

The following chapters deal with the syntax and semantics of the Ada tasking model. Criticisms of the model exist, for example, Hoare (1981a) and Wellings (1984a, 1985a), but it is difficult to define appropriate criteria for assessing languages in terms of their treatment of concurrency. Bloom (1979) however suggests a method for evaluating communication and synchronisation mechanisms. He defines three basic requirements of any such mechanism:

(i) Modularity – the resources of the system should be defined abstractly and these definitions should be distinct from those of resource usage. Resources and the operators defined for them should be encapsulated together. Synchronisation requirements should be catered for at the time of operator design not operator usage.

(ii) Expressive power – the ability to program directly the required synchronisations; in particular to be able to express the constraints on condition synchronisation.

(iii) Ease of use – the ease with which the expressive power of the language may be used to implement complex resource allocation requirements.

The application of this method to Ada will be considered later after the concurrent elements of the language have been fully described.

4 ADA TASK TYPES AND OBJECTS

In chapter 2 tasks were introduced, informally, in order to illustrate some of the properties of concurrent programs. The Ada Language Reference Manual (ARM 1983) defines the full syntax as follows:

```
<task_declaration> ::= <task_specification>;

<task_specification> ::=
   task [<type>] <identifier> [is
      {<entry_declaration>}
      {<representation_clause>}
   end [<task_simple_name>]] ;

<task_body> ::=
   task body <task_simple_name> is
      [<declarative_part>]
   begin
      <sequence_of_statements>
   [exception
      <exception_handler>
      {<exception_handler>}]
   end [<task_simple_name>] ;
```

The full declaration of a task type consists of its specification and body; the specification can contain only entries and representation clauses - the latter being used solely for interrupt handling, (see section 12.4). Example specifications are:

```
task type CONTROLLER;  -- this task has no entries.

task type BUFFER is
   entry PUT (C : CHARACTER);
   entry GET (C : out CHARACTER);
end BUFFER;

task type TIMER is
   entry NEXT_START;
end TIMER;
```

```
task type RESOURCE is
  entry SEIZE;
  entry RELEASE;
end RESOURCE;
```

Entries define those parts of the task that can be accessed from other external tasks. They represent the remote procedures that are available externally; associated with each entry will be at least one accept statement.

The value of an object of a task type is a task having the entries specified (if any) and an execution defined by the task body. This body may consist of some hidden data declarations and a sequence of statements. A task type can be regarded as a template from which actual tasks are created. Consider the following simple task type:

```
task type CHARACTER_COUNT;

task body CHARACTER_COUNT is
  use TEXT_IO;
  DIGIT_COUNT, CHAR_COUNT, REST : NATURAL := 0;
  CH : CHARACTER;
begin
  loop
    GET(CH);  -- GET is defined in TEXT_IO.
    case CH is
      when '0'..'9' =>
        DIGIT_COUNT := DIGIT_COUNT + 1;
      when 'a'..'z' | 'A'..'Z' =>
        CHAR_COUNT := CHAR_COUNT + 1;
      when others =>
        REST := REST + 1;
    end case;
    exit when CH = '?';
  end loop;
  PUT(DIGIT_COUNT);  -- PUT is defined in TEXT_IO.
  PUT(CHAR_COUNT);
  PUT(REST);
end CHARACTER_COUNT;
```

All objects of type CHARACTER_COUNT will execute this sequence of statements.

A task type is limited private, therefore no operations, comparisons or assignments are allowed on task objects (it is possible to abort a task, this is considered later). The only action admissible is for an object to be declared as a task:

```
MAIN_CONTROLLER : CONTROLLER;
BUFF : BUFFER;
INPUT_ANALYSER : CHARACTER_COUNT;
POOL : array (1..10) of BUFFER;
```

```
type CHARACTER_BUFFER is
record
  CONTENTS : NATURAL := 0;
  BUFF : BUFFER;
end record;
```

A task object behaves as a constant in that it always designates the same task. However, the reserved word *constant* is not allowed as no explicit initialisation is possible with a task. Although subtype declarations are allowed there are no constraints applicable to task types. One *cannot*, for example, declare a subtype that has fewer entries than the task type which is its base.

Task objects and types can be declared in any declarative part including task bodies themselves. For any task type the specification and body must be declared together in the same unit with the body usually being placed at the end of the declarative part. The entries are in scope immediately after the task specification that defines them. As indicated in chapter 2 tasks can and should be used in any of three distinct circumstances (Pyle, 1981):

(i)   To model co-existing objects – active tasks.

(ii)   To provide synchronisation agents – passive tasks.

(iii) To define concurrent algorithms.

Care should be taken not to mix these roles; particularly the functions of active and synchronisation tasks. As a general guideline the following points should be taken into account when designing concurrent programs:

(a) Active tasks should communicate with each other via synchronisation tasks – these will often take the form of buffers.

(b) Access to resources should be controlled by synchronisation tasks.

(c) Synchronisation tasks should be defined within packages.

(d) Active tasks should contain no entries but call (directly or indirectly) the entries of synchronisation tasks.

(e) A synchronisation task should contain entries and restrict itself to whatever processing is necessary to satisfy each entry call.

(f) Tasks used to define concurrent algorithms should be contained within procedures or functions. They should terminate naturally.

The use of active and synchronisation tasks necessitates the use of a rendezvous, the discussion of which is deferred till the next chapter. Some algorithmic tasks however require no rendezvous; the following is a short example from Young (1983). A procedure is required that will calculate both the sum and differences of two large integer arrays:

```
type VECTOR is array (1..10_000) of INTEGER;

procedure SUMDIF (A, B  : VECTOR;
                  SUM   : out VECTOR;
                  DIFF  : out VECTOR);
```

Although a sequential solution is quite straightforward it is possible to define a concurrent structure that may, with hardware support, be more efficient. Consider the following two concurrent structures for SUMDIF:

```
procedure SUMDIF (A, B  : VECTOR;
                  SUM   : out VECTOR;
                  DIFF  : out VECTOR) is
  task type MINUS;
  M : MINUS;

  task body MINUS is
  begin
    for I in VECTOR'RANGE loop
      DIFF(I) := A(I) - B(I);
    end loop;
  end MINUS;
begin
  for I in VECTOR'RANGE loop
    SUM(I) := A(I) + B(I);
  end loop;
end SUMDIF; -- method one

procedure SUMDIF (A, B  : VECTOR;
                  SUM   : out VECTOR;
                  DIFF  : out VECTOR) is
  task type MINUS;
  task type ADD;
  M : MINUS;
  AD : ADD;

  task body MINUS is
  begin
    for I in VECTOR'RANGE loop
      DIFF(I) := A(I) - B(I);
    end loop;
  end MINUS;
  task body ADD is
  begin
    for I in VECTOR'RANGE loop
      SUM(I) := A(I) + B(I);
    end loop;
  end ADD;
begin
  null;
end SUMDIF; -- method two.
```

In the first method there are two concurrent processes, the task and the main sequence of SUMDIF; whereas in the second example three processes exist, the two tasks (M and AD) and the main sequence. In method two, however, the procedure itself consists of only the null statement. Both of these structures are acceptable, the first involves fewer tasks; the second has a more symmetric form. In each case the tasks terminate naturally and the procedure itself terminates and returns appropriate values after the contained tasks have finished. (A detailed discussion on task termination is given in chapter 7.) Finally, this simple example illustrates that the concurrency deployed is only at an implementation level. The rest of the program, that makes use of SUMDIF, is unaware that tasks have been employed. The body of the procedure may indeed have been coded in this manner only after the program was moved onto a hardware system that could exploit true parallelism. This usage of tasks is in stark contrast to the employment of active and synchronisation agents where the recognition of co-existing objects will take place at the topmost level of design.

4.1 Anonymous Task Types

In the example used above a task type was declared followed by a single object of that type. This may appear long winded and indeed Ada allows a short hand form to be used that hides the explicit declaration of the type. There can, therefore, be anonymous task types in an identical way to there being anonymous array types. For the direct declaration of a task the reserved word 'type' is omitted from the specification:

```
task MINUS;
task body MINUS is separate;
```

MINUS now refers to the task object not its type. The declaration of an anonymous task type is interpreted as being equivalent to the declaration of its type followed, immediately, by the declaration of the object:

```
task type MINUS_TYPE;
MINUS  : MINUS_TYPE;
task body MINUS_TYPE is separate;
```

As no construct in Ada allows direct reference to the task's body this form is unambiguous.

4.2 Task Activation and Execution

In a number of languages, for example CSP, a command is used explicitly to start the execution of a process. The most common such command is the **cobegin .. coend** structure. Ada has no such facility: rather task execution is started implicitly. Execution of a task object starts immediately after the elaboration of the declarative part in which the task object was declared:

```
declare
  task type Z;
  task A;
  B, C : Z;
  I, J : INTEGER;
  task body Z is ...
  task body A is ...
begin
  -- the tasks A, B and C start their
  -- executions concurrently.
  I := 4;
  J := 2;
    .
    .
    .
end;
```

Thus between 'begin' and the first statement of the parent block all tasks start their executions. If a task object is declared in a package specification then it commences its execution after the elaboration of the declarative part of the package body:

```
package BUFFERING is
  task BUFFER is
    entry PUT (C : CHARACTER);
    entry GET (C : out CHARACTER);
  end BUFFER;
end BUFFERING;

package body BUFFERING is
  task body BUFFER is separate;
begin
  -- BUFFER starts executing here.
  null;
end BUFFERING;
```

A task is said to be **created** by its elaboration.

The initial phase of a task's activity is called the **activation** of the task. It consists of the elaboration of the declarative part, if any, of the task body. The following points appertain:

(i)   All task activations proceed concurrently (for tasks declared in the same unit).

(ii)   Following activation, the execution of the task object is defined by the appropriate task body.

(iii)   A task need not wait for the activation of other concurrently created tasks.

(iv)   A task may attempt to communicate with another task which although created has not yet been activated. The calling task will be delayed.

(v)   The first statement of the parent block can only be executed after the activation of all created tasks.

Program errors can lead to exceptions being raised during these initial phases of a task's existence. If an exception is raised in the elaboration of the parent then a created task becomes terminated and is never activated. Alternatively if an exception is raised during a task's activation then the task becomes completed (a completed task becomes terminated when, and only when, any dependent tasks have terminated; if their are no dependent tasks a completed task immediately becomes terminated) and the predefined exception TASKING_ERROR is raised prior to the first executable statement of the parent. This exception is raised after all created tasks have been activated (whether successfully or not) and is raised at most once. As the associated exception handler must be at the outermost level of the parent, little direct error recovery is possible. The attribute CALLABLE can however be used to at least identify the rogue task:

```
declare
  task A;
  task B;
  task body A is ...
  task body B is ...
begin
  null;
exception
  when TASKING_ERROR =>
    if not A'CALLABLE then
      PUT("TASK A FAILED DURING ACTIVATION");
    end if;
    if not B'CALLABLE then
      PUT("TASK B FAILED DURING ACTIVATION");
    end if;
    if A'CALLABLE and B'CALLABLE then
      PUT("SOMETHING STRANGE IS HAPPENING");
    end if;
end;
```

The boolean attribute CALLABLE is defined to yield the value TRUE if the designated task is neither COMPLETED, TERMINATED nor ABNORMAL. (An abnormal task is one that has been aborted; the conditions necessary for an abnormal task to become terminated are discussed in chapter 7). In the above example if task B fails in its elaboration than the parent will cause the appropriate error message to be displayed. Task A will however be unaffected by this and will proceed in its execution. The parent block will only terminate if, and when, A subsequently terminates.

Figure 4.1 summarises the points that have been made in this section. It shows the early states of a task and the actions necessary for a task to move from one state to another. This diagram will be expanded later.

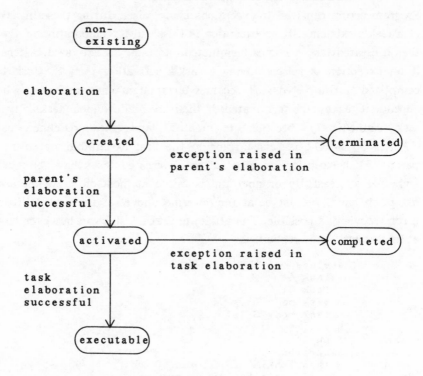

Figure 4.1

4.3 Task Dependency

In the previous section reference was made to the parent of a task; this is a common concept in multi-process systems. Each task in Ada must depend upon a parent (**master** is the term used in the ARM). A master can be a block, a subprogram, a task or a library package. As the package is a passive compile-time construct it cannot, in general, act as a master:

```
procedure FRED is
  package JILL is
    task T;
  end JILL;
  package body JILL is separate;
```

```
begin
  null;
end FRED;
```

In this contrived example the master of T is FRED not JILL. Unfortunately this rule cannot be applied to library packages as they are at the outermost level of the program. Therefore any task declared in a library package must have that package as a master.

With nested tasks and subprograms masters will themselves depend upon other masters. This chain of dependency is particularly important when considering the termination of subprograms and tasks.

The master of a task is that construct whose execution created the task object:

```
package BUFFER_LIBRARY is
  task type Z;
  task A;
end BUFFER_LIBRARY;   -- a library package.

with BUFFER_LIBRARY; use BUFFER_LIBRARY;
-- A is active.
procedure MAIN is
  B : Z;
begin
  -- A and B active. A's master is BUFFER_LIBRARY,
  -- B's master is MAIN.
  null;
end MAIN;
```

4.4 Real Time

Access to a real-time clock is provided by the predefined library package CALENDAR:

```
package CALENDAR is
  type TIME is private;

  subtype YEAR_NUMBER   is INTEGER  range 1901..2099;
  subtype MONTH_NUMBER  is INTEGER  range 1..12;
  subtype DAY_NUMBER    is INTEGER  range 1..31;
  subtype DAY_DURATION  is DURATION range 0.0..86_400.0;

  function CLOCK return TIME;

  function YEAR    (DATE : TIME) return YEAR_NUMBER;
  function MONTH   (DATE : TIME) return MONTH_NUMBER;
  function DAY     (DATE : TIME) return DAY_NUMBER;
  function SECONDS (DATE : TIME) return DAY_DURATION;

  procedure SPLIT  (DATE    : in  TIME;
                    YEAR    : out YEAR_NUMBER;
                    MONTH   : out MONTH_NUMBER;
```

```
                         DAY        : out DAY_NUMBER;
                         SECONDS    : out DAY_DURATION);

        function TIME_OF (YEAR       : YEAR_NUMBER;
                         MONTH      : MONTH_NUMBER;
                         DAY        : DAY_NUMBER;
                         SECONDS    : DAY_DURATION := 0.0)
                                    return TIME;

        function "+"  (LEFT : TIME;        RIGHT : DURATION)
                             return TIME;
        function "+"  (LEFT : DURATION; RIGHT : TIME)
                             return TIME;
        function "-"  (LEFT : TIME;        RIGHT : DURATION)
                             return TIME;
        function "-"  (LEFT : TIME;        RIGHT : TIME)
                             return DURATION;

        function "<"  (LEFT, RIGHT : TIME) return BOOLEAN;
        function "<=" (LEFT, RIGHT : TIME) return BOOLEAN;
        function ">"  (LEFT, RIGHT : TIME) return BOOLEAN;
        function ">=" (LEFT, RIGHT : TIME) return BOOLEAN;

        TIME_ERROR : exception;
        -- This exception can be raised by TIME_OF,
        -- "+", and "-".
   private
        -- implementation dependent.
   end;
```

A value of the private type TIME is a combination of the date and the time of day, where the time of day is given in seconds from midnight. Seconds are described in terms of a subtype DAY_DURATION which is, in turn, defined by means of DURATION. This fixed point type DURATION is one of the predefined **scalar** types and has a range which, although implementation dependent, must be at least $-86\_400.0 .. +86\_400.0$. The value 86_400 is the number of seconds in a day. The accuracy of DURATION is also implementation dependent.

The current time is returned by the function CLOCK. Conversion between TIME and program accessible types such as YEAR_NUMBER is provided by subprograms SPLIT and TIME_OF. In addition some arithmetic and boolean operations are specified. CALENDAR therefore defines an appropriate structure for an abstract data type for time. The following code tests to see if some time-critical sequence of statements executes in 1.7 seconds:

```
declare
  START, FINISH : TIME;
  INTERVAL : DURATION := 1.7;
begin
  START := CLOCK;
  -- sequence of statements.
  FINISH := CLOCK;
  if FINISH - START > INTERVAL then
    raise TIME_ERROR;  -- a user defined exception.
  end if;
end;
```

As well as having access to a real-time clock, tasks must also be able to delay themselves for a period of time. This enables a task to be queued on some future event rather than busy wait on calls to the CLOCK function:

```
START := CLOCK;    -- to delay 10 seconds.
loop
  exit when CLOCK - START > 10.0;
end loop;
```

Ada provides an explicit delay statement:

```
delay 10.0;
```

The expression following 'delay' must yield a value of the pre-defined type DURATION. It is important to appreciate that 'delay' is an approximate time construct, the inclusion of which in a task indicates that the task will be delayed by at least the amount specified. There is no upper bound given on the actual delay. Where tasks share a processor the delay may indeed be considerably longer than that indicated. The significant point is that the delay cannot be less than that given in the delay statement. Consider task T:

```
task body T is
begin
  loop
    ACTION;
    delay 5.0;
  end loop;
end T;
```

Here ACTION cannot be called twice in any five second interval. Two subsequent calls may, however, be separated by any time interval greater than this value. If a five second interval is desired, the time over-run is called **local drift** - it cannot be eliminated using normal Ada constructs. The time taken to execute the above loop in task T consists of, at least, five seconds plus the execution time of ACTION plus a small overhead for the loop (a jump instruction). If ACTION should be called at regular five second intervals then on each iteration of the loop there will be an addition to a **cumulative drift.** This can be eliminated by delaying less than five seconds (Barnes, 1984):

```
task body T is
  INTERVAL : constant DURATION := 5.0;
  NEXT_TIME : TIME;
begin
  NEXT_TIME := CLOCK + INTERVAL;
  loop
    ACTION;
    delay NEXT_TIME - CLOCK;
    NEXT_TIME := NEXT_TIME + INTERVAL;
  end loop;
end T;
```

This removes cumulative drift but not local drift.

5 ADA INTER-TASK COMMUNICATION

In chapter 3 a brief description of a simple rendezvous mechanism, as it is applied in CSP, was given. The designers of Ada have adapted this mechanism to produce a structure that is, in some senses, a hybrid of the CSP method and a remote procedure call. Within a task the 'procedures' that are callable externally are defined as entries and are declared in the task specification. A calling task issues an 'entry call' on the called task which either 'accepts' this request or not. If the call is accepted a rendezvous takes place. Consider the following simple code:

```
task A;                              task B is
                                        entry CALL;
                                     end B;


task body A is                       task body B is
begin                                begin
  loop                                 loop
     .                                    .
   B.CALL;   <---- rendezvous ---->    accept CALL;
     .                                    .
   end loop;                           end loop;
end A;                               end B;
```

In this example no data passes between the tasks; nevertheless A and B are synchronised at the point of the rendezvous. Note that the naming protocol is asymmetric. The destination of the rendezvous call is named directly by incorporating the task identifier in the entry call (i.e. B.CALL). By contrast the source of the call is not designated by the accept statement. Task B will accept a call on its entry from *any* other task.

Data is communicated between tasks via the parameters defined in the entry specification:

```
task BUFFER is
  entry PLACE (C : CHARACTER);
  entry TAKE  (C : out CHARACTER);
end BUFFER;
```

```
task body BUFFER is
  CHAR : CHARACTER;
begin
  loop
    accept PLACE (C : CHARACTER) do
      CHAR := C;
    end PLACE;
    accept TAKE (C : out CHARACTER) do
      C := CHAR;
    end TAKE;
  end loop;
end BUFFER;
```

The above task implements a single character buffer; the buffer itself is represented by the variable CHAR. The statements in the task body indicate that the execution of this task will involve accepting a call to PLACE, then a call to TAKE, then another call to PLACE, then TAKE etc. A call to PLACE, when accepted, will involve the transfer of a character from the calling task to CHAR. Similarly a call to TAKE, once the rendezvous commences, will mean that the current value of CHAR will be copied to the entry parameter. The structure of the task body ensures that a character cannot be removed from the buffer until a value has been given to it.

The active tasks that wish to use this buffer will make calls of the form:

```
GET(CH);   -- TEXT_IO for character CH.
BUFFER.PLACE(CH);
```

and

```
BUFFER.TAKE(CH);
PUT(CH);
```

This use of a task for implementing a buffer should be compared with a solution based on a package:

```
package BUFFER is
  procedure PLACE (C : CHARACTER);
  procedure TAKE  (C : out CHARACTER);
end BUFFER;
package body BUFFER is
  CHAR : CHARACTER;
  procedure PLACE (C : CHARACTER) is
  begin
    CHAR := C;
  end PLACE;
  procedure TAKE (C : out CHARACTER) is
  begin
    C := CHAR;
  end TAKE;
end BUFFER;
```

Although calls to these procedures would have an identical form (e.g. BUFFER.PLACE(CH)) the actions taken by the package and the task are quite distinct; in particular the package cannot control:

(a) The order in which calls to PLACE and TAKE are accepted.

(b) The simultaneous execution of PLACE and TAKE.

(c) The simultaneous execution of PLACE (or TAKE) by more than one external task.

The package implementation is clearly unsafe; however the task (by its ability to control access to itself) can be used to give reliable code.

What the package and task approaches have in common is their ability to hide the buffer variable CHAR. The task, like the package, is a module structure that has a distinct specification and body.

In addition, this straightforward buffer example illustrates another important distinction between the use of packages and tasks. This distinction is concerned, however, with implementation. If a task T executes one of the package subprograms, then this procedure will be executed on the stack for task T. Having executed the procedure, T will continue; there will have been no context switch. By comparison a task object of task type BUFFER will have its own stack. The accept statement will therefore be executed on the stack for BUFFER not T. At least two context switches are necessary in order to execute the rendezvous. More will be said on this later.

5.1 The Entry Statement

As has been indicated, entries are similar to procedures; their parameter modes are the same (*in, out* and *in out* - with *in* being the default). The rules for parameter association are also identical.

```
<entry_declaration> ::=
  entry <identifier>
        [(<discrete_range>)] [<formal_part>] ;

<formal_part> ::=
  (<parameter_specification>{;<parameter_specification>})

<parameter_specification> ::=
   <identifier_list> : <mode><type_mark>[:=<expression>]

mode ::= [in] | out | in out
```

For example:

```
entry READ (I : out ITEM);
entry HALT;
entry MIXTURE (A : ITEM; B : out ITEM; C : in out ITEM);
```

```
entry NEXT (X : out ITEM: I : INTEGER := 1);
```

The optional 'discrete_range' in the entry declaration is used to declare a family of distinct entries all of which will have the same formal-part, (see 5.4).

A single entry (i.e. not a family) will overload a subprogram (TASK.ENTRY may be identical to PACKAGE.SUBPROGRAM), an enumeration literal or another entry if they have the same identifier. For example, a task implementing a buffer for characters may define GET entries for single characters and strings:

```
subtype STR is STRING (1..8);
task CHAR_BUFF is
  entry PUT (C  : CHARACTER);
  entry GET (C  : out CHARACTER);
  entry GET (ST : out STR);
end CHAR_BUFF;
```

The body for this task will be defined so that a call to GET (ST : out STR) will only be accepted if the buffer contains more than seven characters.

Unlike a package a 'use' clause cannot be employed with a task to shorten the length of the calling identifiers, however a procedure can rename an entry:

```
procedure PUT (C : CHARACTER) renames BUFFER.PLACE;
```

5.2 The Accept Statement

For each and every entry defined in a task specification there must be at least one accept statement in the corresponding task body. Interestingly, the ARM is not specific on this point and it is therefore possible that a compiler may not flag as an error the lack of an appropriate accept statement. Nevertheless if there is no accept statement for some entry E then a call to E will never be handled and the associated task may be blocked indefinitely.

An accept statement specifies the actions to be performed when an entry is called and the formal part of the accept statement must conform exactly to the formal part of the corresponding entry.

```
<accept_statement> ::=
  accept <entry_simple_name> [(<entry_index>)]
                                   [<formal_part>] [do
    <sequence_of_statements>
  end [<entry_simple_name>]] ;
```

The sequence of statements may contain subprogram calls, entry calls, accept statements and inner blocks. There are, however, good reasons for making the accept statement as simple as possible. The code it contains should be only that which is necessary for the rendezvous. If it contains extra statements then the calling task will be held up unnecessarily. Where the sequence of statements is precisely *null* then there is nothing to *do* and the accept statement can be terminated by a semicolon following the formal part. A task body may contain more than one accept statement for the same entry. Example accept statements are:

```
accept READ (I : out ITEM) do
  I := SOME_VALUE;
end READ;

accept HALT;

accept NEXT (X : out ITEM; I : INTEGER := 1) do
  J := J + I;
  X := SOME_ARRAY(J);
end NEXT;
```

Let REC be defined by:

```
type REC is
record
  I : INTEGER;
  F : FLOAT;
  S : STRING (1..21);
end record;
```

Then a task that controls access to a single keyboard and VDU may have the structure:

```
task IO_CONTROL is
  entry GET (R : out REC);
  entry PUT (R : REC);
    .
    .
    .
end IO_CONTROL;
```

For PUT the accept statement might have the form:

```
accept PUT(R : REC) do
  PUT(R.I);   -- This procedure is constructed
              -- from TEXT_IO.
  PUT(R.F);
  PUT(R.S);
end PUT;
```

However this ties up the rendezvous for the time it takes to output the three items; a better structure would be:

```
declare
  TEMP_REC : REC;
begin
  accept PUT(R : REC) do
    TEMP_REC := R;
  end PUT;
  PUT(TEMP_REC.I);
  PUT(TEMP_REC.F);
  PUT(TEMP_REC.S);
```

With the GET entry some user prompts are necessary; these must be undertaken during the rendezvous:

```
accept GET(R : out REC) do
  PUT("VALUE FOR I?"); GET(R.I);
  PUT("VALUE for F?"); GET(R.F);
  PUT("VALUE for S?"); GET(R.S);
end GET;
```

User errors on I/O are unavoidable and exceptions are bound to occur from time to time. A reliable accept statement for GET would therefore be:

```
accept GET(R : out REC) do
  loop
    begin
      PUT("VALUE FOR I?"); GET(R.I);
      PUT("VALUE FOR F?"); GET(R.F);
      PUT("VALUE FOR S?"); GET(R.S);
      return;
    exception
      when others => PUT("INVALID ENTRY: START AGAIN");
    end;
  end loop;
end GET;
```

This represents a sizeable accept statement that will hold the rendezvous for a comparatively large amount of time. An alternative structure would be for the calling task to first make a request (via another entry) for the record and later make a separate entry call to GET the record. The calling task would therefore make two entry calls:

```
IO_CONTROL.REQUEST;
IO_CONTROL.GET(SOME_REC);
```

The task IO_CONTROL would then have the following code in its sequence of statements:

```
accept REQUEST;
loop
  begin
    -- This is as before but with record
    -- variable TEMP_REC.
  end;
end loop;
accept GET(R : out REC) do
  R := TEMP_REC;
end GET;
```

This has simplified the accept statements but at the cost of a further rendezvous. The use of a two rendezvous structure is necessary for a number of particular communication problems. It is not without its own difficulties as will be indicated in chapter 10.

5.3 Synchronisation and Communication

A rendezvous takes place when:

(a) a task makes an entry call, and

(b) the called task is in a position to accept that entry call.

Whichever task gets into one of the above conditions first will wait until the other task is ready to rendezvous. This 'wait' is achieved by suspending the execution of the first task. Associated with each entry is a queue. A task that is suspended on an entry call is placed on the queue associated with that entry. Each task can therefore only be present on one queue at a time. The manipulation of the queue is the responsibility of the run-time system. To provide for the safe use of these structures an implementation must ensure that the necessary pointer updates are undertaken as an indivisible operation. This is needed to provide mutual exclusion over the shared objects that represent the queue.

When the buffer task executes an accept statement either the queue is empty or it is not.

(i) If the queue is empty the task is suspended.

(ii) If the queue is not empty a rendezvous takes place with the task at the head of the queue.

The queue structure is defined by the ARM to be FIFO, i.e. the calls are processed in the order in which they arrive.

Execution of the rendezvous is considered to be undertaken by the task that 'owns' the accept statement, the calling task is suspended (if it were not already) for the duration of the rendezvous. The rendezvous terminates when the accept statement terminates (i.e. when the last statement of the 'sequence of statements' is executed – N.B. a *return* statement is allowed in an accept statement). Both tasks then continue their executions independently and concurrently.

After activation, a task begins its execution and passes through a number of internal states. Figure 5.1 gives a representation of the important states that have so far been considered. This description takes no account of whether the executable task is actually running on a processor at that time. This is an implementation matter which should not impinge on the description of the model.

As indicated earlier communication is via the parameters of the entry call:

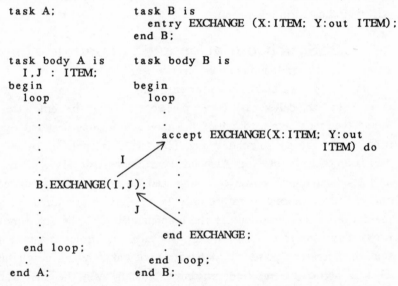

```
task A;              task B is
                       entry EXCHANGE (X: ITEM; Y: out  ITEM);
                     end B;

task body A is      task body B is
  I,J : ITEM;
begin                begin
  loop                 loop
    .                    .
    .                    .
    .                       accept EXCHANGE(X: ITEM; Y: out
    .                I                        ITEM) do
    .                    .
    B.EXCHANGE(I,J);     .
    .                J   .
    .                    .
    .                    > 
    .                    end EXCHANGE;
  end loop;              .
    .                  end loop;
end A;               end B;
```

At the beginning of the rendezvous the scalar parameters of *in* mode (and *in out*) are copied from the calling task to the formal parameters of the associated entry. When the rendezvous terminates, the parameters of *out* mode (and *in out*) are transcribed onto the calling parameters. Both of these actions are deemed to be synchronisation points and any variables shared by the two tasks are brought up to date (see section 5.6). For non-scalar parameters the effect, if not the mechanism, is the same.

The accept statements can only be placed within the body of a task; a call to an entry is usually also made from within a task body. In this latter case however it is allowed for an entry call to be generated from outside a task. This is usually employed to initialise a task.

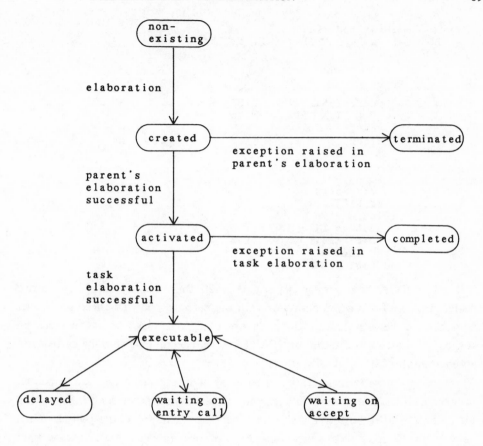

Figure 5.1

The following example is from Nissen and Wallis (1984) and uses the
initialisation section of a package to pass an index number to each task defined
within the package body. In this example the tasks model a set of lifts:

```
package body LIFT_SYSTEM is
  task type LIFT is
    entry START (N : LIFT_INDEX);
  end LIFT;

  LIFT_SET : array (LIFT_INDEX) of LIFT;
```

```
task body LIFT is
  LIFT_NUMBER : LIFT_INDEX;
        .
        .
        .
begin
  accept START(N : LIFT_INDEX) do
    LIFT_NUMBER := N;
  end START;
  loop
        .
        .
        .
  end loop;
end LIFT;
begin
  for L in LIFT_INDEX loop
    LIFT_SET(L).START(L);
  end loop;
end LIFT_SYSTEM;
```

If LIFT_INDEX has a range of, say, 1 .. 20 then twenty task objects are declared in the form of an array. Within the package body all these tasks will be activated before the 'for loop' is executed. All tasks will therefore be suspended waiting for a call to START; each in term will then be called and given a unique LIFT_NUMBER.

There is no method, in Ada, by which parameters can be passed to tasks at initiation time. It is necessary to serially transfer such information via an entry call (the active task must therefore define an entry point). With very large distributed systems (an array of ten thousand tasks rather then twenty!) this may cause serious congestion. Yemini (1982) has shown that there is no easy way around this serial bottleneck and suggests that this may make Ada unsuitable for certain classes of parallel algorithms. This task initialisation problem is discussed again in chapter 13.

5.4 Entry Families

Calls upon a single entry are processed strictly in the order in which they arrive. If a programmer wishes to handle such calls in some other predefined way then different entries must be used. This flexibility is usually sought to implement a priority structure that is different from 'first in first out'. Consider a server task that has the single entry REQUEST(...), and let the set of possible client tasks be partitioned into three priority levels - high, medium and low. The server task could then have the specification:

```
task SERVER is
  entry REQUEST_HIGH(...);
  entry REQUEST_MEDIUM(...);
  entry REQUEST_LOW(...);
end SERVER;
```

Within the body of this task calls to REQUEST_HIGH would be processed first, then calls to REQUEST_MEDIUM and then finally calls to REQUEST_LOW. The entries are distinct and therefore separate queues are supplied and supported for each. A more appropriate solution to this problem is possible however using a family of entries:

```
type PRIORITY is (HIGH,MEDIUM,LOW);

task SERVER is
  entry REQUEST (PRIORITY) (...);
end SERVER;
```

An entry call would then specify the priority of the request:

```
SERVER.REQUEST (MEDIUM) (...);
```

Within the body of the SERVER task accept statements for all possible priorities must exist, such as:

```
accept REQUEST (MEDIUM) (...) do
        .
        .
end REQUEST;
```

A family of entries is defined by adding a discrete range to the entry specification, for example:

```
entry READ (1..7) (I : out INTEGER);

entry WORK (DAY range MON .. FRI) (A : ACTION);

entry GET  (1 .. 5000) (R : out REC);
```

This last example illustrates that the family can be arbitrarily large. This would, of course, be difficult to achieve if each element had to be a distinct entry. (The size of families may be limited on some implementations).

The structure of the task SERVER is such that only one call to REQUEST should be processed at a time. If concurrent execution of REQUEST(HIGH), REQUEST(MEDIUM) and REQUEST(LOW) was allowed by the requirements of the system then an array of SERVER tasks would be a more appropriate structure:

```
type PRIORITY is (HIGH, MEDIUM, LOW);
task type SERVER is
  entry REQUEST(...);
end SERVER;
SERVERS : array (PRIORITY) of SERVER;
```

A high priority task would then call:

```
SERVERS(HIGH).REQUEST(...);
```

5.5 Three Way Synchronisation

Although a rendezvous can only take place between two tasks, nested accept statements can be used to tie together more than just two tasks. Consider a program in which a task (DEVICE) simulates the actions of an external device and where CONTROLLER is a task acting as a device driver and USER is some task that wishes to use the (input) device:

```
procedure THREE_WAY is
  task USER;
  task DEVICE;
  task CONTROLLER is
    entry DOIO (I : out INTEGER);
    entry START;
    entry COMPLETED (K : INTEGER);
  end CONTROLLER;
  task body USER is separate; -- includes calls to
                              -- CONTROLLER.DOIO(...).
  task body DEVICE is
    J : INTEGER;
    procedure READ (I : out INTEGER) is separate;
  begin
    loop
      CONTROLLER.START;
      READ(J);
      CONTROLLER.COMPLETED(J);
    end loop;
  end DEVICE;

  task body CONTROLLER is
  begin
    loop
      accept DOIO (I : out INTEGER) do
        accept START;
        accept COMPLETED (K : INTEGER) do
          I := K;
        end COMPLETED;
      end DOIO;
    end loop;
  end CONTROLLER;
begin
  null;
end THREE_WAY;
```

At the assignment of K to I, USER is in rendezvous with CONTROLLER, and the rendezvous itself is in rendezvous with DEVICE: three tasks are therefore synchronised.

5.6 Shared Variables

In addition to the rendezvous mechanism, and in many ways unfortunately, shared variables are also available for inter-task communication. None of the synchronisation aids associated with the safe use of shared variables are supported in Ada, consequently such variables should only be used with considerable care. Alternatively tasks can be constructed to provide synchronisation primitives that safeguard communications based on shared objects. Indeed an early version of Ada (1980) provided a predefined task type for semaphores. But the rationale behind the rendezvous construct is that synchronisation and communication are inseparable concepts that should be catered for in a single mechanism. This dictates that the use of shared variables between tasks should be avoided if at all possible. Only when it can be shown that two tasks (or more) are not updating the shared variable or are acting as coroutines, i.e. there is only ever one task wishing to execute at a time, should shared access to data be used. Notwithstanding this point there will be applications in which speed requirements necessitate the uncontrolled use of shared variables. In these situations errors must be tolerated. For example a task may scan data values that are being updated by other tasks; shared variables could be used if partially updated values are acceptable.

In many ways the existence of shared objects in Ada is a result of applying consistent and orthogonal scope rules:

```
procedure MAIN is
   X : DATA;
   task type T;
   A, B : T;
      .
      .
      .
   end MAIN;
```

Here the object X is in scope for the declaration of the type T, tasks A and B, and the task body associated with A and B. As a result X is accessible in both A and B and could be used to communicate between the two tasks.

Tasks are implemented as, essentially, separate programs and do not therefore share identical address spaces (see chapter 13). Hence to enable an implementation to optimise how, for example, a task may employ fast registers, Ada allows 'local' copies of shared scalar and access types to be held in a task's own address space. Therefore if X is a scalar type both A's and B's stack could have a (different) location for X. This could clearly lead to difficulties and consequently the following rules must be applied to all programs (ARM 9.11):

(i)   If a task reads a shared variable no other task must update it.

(ii) If a task updates a shared variable no other task must read or update it.

If these rules are broken the execution of the program is erroneous. There are therefore programs which are syntactically correct but whose execution is deemed to be erroneous.

At the start and completion of a rendezvous (and also at the start and termination of a task) there are what are termed synchronisation points. At these synchronisation points all copies of a shared variable are brought up to date. As a consequence of the above rules only one task, at most, will have updated any such variable. The rules therefore apply only to the execution of tasks between points of synchronisation. Two tasks could thus pass permission to update a variable between themselves via a rendezvous call. Note that a third task, not involved with the rendezvous, will not have its copy of the shared scalar object updated.

It is possible to force the run-time system to continually update all copies of a variable by using the pragma SHARED. This acts by making every read or update of a variable a synchronisation point for all tasks with access to that variable. The pragma must appear immediately after the variable declaration (i.e. in the same declarative part).

```
pragma SHARED (variable_simple_name);
```

The pragma can only apply to objects whose type is either scalar or access.

With true parallel systems, difficulties would occur if two tasks were updating a variable controlled by this pragma. In what order should simultaneous updates be applied? The ARM instructs that the pragma must be further restricted to objects whose reading and updating can be achieved as an indivisible operation. But this still leaves the implementation ambiguous, particularly in a distributed system where there may be a significant time delay for the necessary low level communication between the processors. For safety it must be possible for all copies of a shared object to be locked by a single instruction. A task wishing to read or update a locked variable will thus be delayed until the run-time system unlocks it. The overheads necessary with this type of structure are excessive and makes the pragma to all intents and purposes useless.

Interestingly, the 1980 draft version of Ada dealt with this updating difficulty not by the use of a pragma but by providing a generic procedure:

```
generic
   type SHARED is limited private;
procedure SHARED_VARIABLE_UPDATE(X : in out SHARED);
```

A call to an instantiated procedure would cause the variable's value to be brought up-to-date.

This section together with the earlier discussion on the use of shared variables should have convinced the reader that such variables are not part of the Ada programmer's toolkit.

6 THE SELECT STATEMENT

The select statement can be considered the most important element of the tasking model. It converts what would otherwise be a very restricted language into one that is non-deterministic and flexible. In particular it allows a task to accept entry calls in the order dictated by actual operation, rather than by some predefined structure, and it enables a task making an entry call not to be inevitably committed to the ensuing rendezvous:

```
<select_statement> ::= <selective_wait>
  | <conditional_entry_call> | <timed_entry_call>

<selective_wait> ::=
  select
    <select_alternative>
{ or
    <select_alternative> }
[ else
    <sequence_of_statements> ]
  end select;

<select_alternative> ::=
[ when <condition> => ]
    <selective_wait_alternative>

<selective_wait_alternative> ::= <accept_alternative>
  | <delay_alternative> | <terminate_alternative>

<accept_alternative> ::= <accept_statement>
                         [ <sequence_of_statements> ]

<delay_alternative> ::= <delay_statement>
                        [ <sequence_of_statements> ]

<terminate_alternative> ::= terminate;
```

6.1 Selective_Wait

The primary use of a select statement is to construct a task so that it can accept any one of a number of possible entry calls. This is the 'selective_wait' form of the syntax.

The select statement itself may simply consist of a number of alternatives separated by 'or':

```
select
  ALTERNATIVE_1;
or
  ALTERNATIVE_2;
or

      .
      .
      .

or
  ALTERNATIVE_N;
end select;
```

Execution of this statement entails the complete execution of one, and only one, alternative. The alternatives are of three types:

    (i)   accept alternative – the usual form.

    (ii)   delay alternative – used for programming timeouts.

    (iii)   terminate alternative – controls the termination of the task.

If none of the alternatives are immediately executable (i.e. there are no entry calls on the accept alternatives) then the task executing the select statement will be delayed.

Alternatively an 'else' clause (only one) may be added to the statement:

```
select
  ALTERNATIVE_1;
or

      .
      .
      .

or
  ALTERNATIVE_N;
else
  DEFAULT_ALTERNATIVE;
end select;
```

In the case where no alternatives are executable the 'default_alternative' will be chosen, which can be any sequence of statements. It follows that a select statement with an else clause cannot result in the task being delayed.

One of the criticisms of the select statement is that its use has a number of restrictions which can lead to some confusion on the part of the programmer. It is necessary to gain a full appreciation of the reasons for these restrictions before the natural use of the select statement will emerge (Burns 1984). The relationships between the various select alternatives can be summarised as follows:

- A selective wait must contain at least one accept alternative.
- A selective wait may contain one terminate alternative, or
- it may contain one or more delay alternatives, or
- it may contain an else part.
- The last three possibilities are mutually exclusive.

The full use of selective_wait will be introduced, in stages, by looking at the code required to implement a reliable and efficient circular integer buffer. Without the select statement the following code might be used:

```
task BUFFER is
  entry PLACE (I : INTEGER);
  entry TAKE  (I : out INTEGER);
end BUFFER;

task body BUFFER is    -- an N integer buffer
  N  : constant POSITIVE := 24;
  subtype N_RANGE is INTEGER range 0..N-1;
  TOP, BOTTOM : N_RANGE := 0;
  BUFF : array (N_RANGE) of INTEGER;
begin
  loop
    accept PLACE (I : INTEGER) do
      BUFF (TOP) := I;
    end PLACE;
    TOP := (TOP + 1) mod N;
    accept TAKE (I : out INTEGER) do
      I := BUFF(BOTTOM);
    end TAKE;
    BOTTOM := (BOTTOM + 1) mod N;
  end loop;
end BUFFER;
```

Although the data structures necessary to produce an N integer buffer are defined the task will actually only store one item at a time. This is because the loop statement forces PLACE and TAKE to be accepted in a strict alternating sequence. What is required is a structure that will allow PLACE and TAKE to be accepted arbitrarily:

```
task body BUFFER is    -- an N integer buffer
  N : constant POSITIVE := 24;
  subtype N_RANGE is INTEGER range 0..N-1;
  TOP, BOTTOM : N_RANGE := 0;
  BUFF : array (N_RANGE) of INTEGER;
```

```
begin
  loop
    select
      accept PLACE (I : INTEGER) do
        BUFF(TOP) := I;
      end PLACE;
      TOP := (TOP + 1) mod N;
    or
      accept TAKE (I : out INTEGER) do
        I := BUFF(BOTTOM);
      end TAKE;
      BOTTOM := (BOTTOM + 1) mod N;
    end select;
  end loop;
end BUFFER;
```

Note that the assignments to the variables TOP and BOTTOM are kept outside the rendezvous as they do not effect the calling task. Calls to PLACE and TAKE will now be accepted as required; furthermore if both PLACE and TAKE have outstanding calls upon them then the order of execution is not defined.

The select statement has allowed the order in which PLACE and TAKE are accepted to be determined by the dynamics of the executing program rather than the syntax presented by the programmer. However, with this example flexibility has resulted in an unreliable solution. As it stands there is no condition synchronisation imposed upon the calling tasks; a task could TAKE from an empty buffer or PLACE onto a full one. The select statement needs to restrict, in certain circumstances, the access to the accept alternatives; this is achieved by using guards. A guard has the form

```
when <boolean expression> ->
```

The following code now reliably implements a circular buffer.

```
task body BUFFER is
  N : constant POSITIVE := 24;
  subtype N_RANGE is INTEGER range 0..N-1;
  TOP, BOTTOM : N_RANGE := 0;
  BUFF : array (N_RANGE) of INTEGER;
  ITEMS : INTEGER range 0..N := 0;
begin
  loop
    select
      when ITEMS /= N ->
      accept PLACE (I : INTEGER) do
        BUFF(TOP) := I;
      end PLACE;
      TOP := (TOP + 1) mod N;
      ITEMS := ITEMS + 1;
    or
```

```
      when ITEMS /= 0 =>
      accept TAKE (I : out INTEGER) do
        I := BUFF(BOTTOM);
      end TAKE;
      BOTTOM := (BOTTOM + 1) mod N;
      ITEMS := ITEMS - 1;
    end select;
  end loop;
end BUFFER;
```

It is precisely because the condition synchronisations cannot be provided for in a solution using subprograms (such as that given in chapter 1), that a buffer in a concurrent program must be structured as a task.

A select alternative is said to be 'open' if it does not contain a guard or if the boolean condition associated with the guard evaluates to TRUE. Otherwise the alternative is 'closed'. On execution of the select statement the first action to be taken is for all the guards to be evaluated; all open alternatives are thus determined. For this execution of the select statement closed alternatives are no longer considered. If one or more open accept alternatives has an outstanding entry call then one (an arbitrary choice) of these accept alternatives is chosen. The accept statement is executed, the rendezvous takes place, any statements following the accept (within that branch of the select statement) are executed and the execution of the select statement is then complete.

If, however, no open accept alternative has an outstanding entry call then, if there is an else part this will be executed, otherwise the task will be suspended on the select statement. The first entry call on an open accept alternative will re-activate the select statement and that alternative will be chosen.

The boolean expression associated with the guard has no particular properties; it is however strongly recommended that shared variables should not be used. This would be a particularly inappropriate form of synchronisation and is likely to lead to unforeseen actions by the program; these being due to the fact that the guard is only evaluated once and is not 're-tested' when an entry call is made. The following code controls calls to the entries CLOCK_IN and CLOCK_OUT. The specification of this task requires that CLOCK_IN is not allowed before 08.30 hours (constant START). Let WORKS_CLOCK be some function that provides the time in the right form:

```
loop
  select
    when WORKS_CLOCK > START =>
    accept CLOCK_IN (N : STAFF_NUMBER) do
                    .
                    .
                    .
    end CLOCK_IN;
  or
    accept CLOCK_OUT (N : STAFF_NUMBER) do
                    .
                    .
                    .
    end CLOCK_OUT;
  end select;
end loop;
```

This code, though superficially correct, is wrong. Consider the following interleaving:

(i)   Call to CLOCK_OUT at 8.20

(ii) select statement is then immediately re-executed; the guard is FALSE so CLOCK_IN deemed to be closed.

(iii) Call to CLOCK_IN at 8.45 – NOT ACCEPTED.

Indeed no calls to CLOCK_IN would be processed until a call to CLOCK_OUT had terminated that particular execution of the select. A correct but inappropriate solution to this requirement would be to use an else clause:

```
loop
  select
    when WORKS_CLOCK > START =>
    accept CLOCK_IN (N : STAFF_NUMBER) do
                    .
                    .
                    .
    end CLOCK_IN;
  or
    accept CLOCK_OUT (N : STAFF_NUMBER) do
                    .
                    .
                    .
    end CLOCK_OUT;
  else
    null;
  end select;
end loop;
```

Although this is now correct, in the sense that a call to CLOCK_IN would be accepted at 8.45, it is very inefficient. This solution is, in effect, employing a busy-wait which is not only wasteful of processor cycles but could lead to indefinite postponement of all other tasks on a single processor system. The correct solution to this problem must employ a reference to WORKS_CLOCK inside (or immediately after) the accept statement. Below are two possibilities:

```
(i)    accept CLOCK_IN (N : STAFF_NUMBER
                        OK : out BOOLEAN) do
       if WORKS_CLOCK <START then
          OK := FALSE;
          return;
       end if;
       OK := TRUE;
       START_TIME(N) := WORKS_CLOCK;
       end CLOCK_IN;

(ii)   accept CLOCK_IN (N : STAFF_NUMBER) do
          TEMP_N := N;
       end CLOCK_IN;
       if WORKS_CLOCK < START then
          START_TIME(TEMP_N) := START;
       else
          START_TIME(TEMP_N) := WORKS_CLOCK;
       end if;
```

As the above discussion indicates the else clause should only be used when absolutely necessary. Its existence in the language encourages the use of 'polling' (Gehani & Cargill, 1984). Polling is characterised by a task actively and repeatedly checking for the occurrence of some event. Unless a task can genuinely proceed with useful work in the situation where an entry call is not immediately outstanding, then the task should delay itself on a select statement without an else clause.

An example of the appropriate use of an else clause would be in the control of a process where there may, or may not, be new control data available:

```
loop
  select
    accept NEW_DATA (...) do
       ... -- update control parameters
    end NEW_DATA;
  else
    null;
  end select;
  GENERATE_CONTROL_SIGNALS(...);
  delay X;
end loop;
```

6.2 The Exception PROGRAM_ERROR

If all the accept alternatives have guards then there is the possibility in certain circumstances that all the guards will be closed.

Moreover, in this situation if the select statement does not contain an else clause then it becomes impossible for the statement to be executed. This invidious position could be catered for in two ways:

(a) The situation is deemed to be an error.

(b) The select statement becomes equivalent to 'null' and the task continues execution.

The designers of Ada decided upon the first solution and the exception PROGRAM_ERROR is raised at the point of the select statement if no alternatives are open. With the buffer example the two guards (ITEM /= N and ITEM /= 0) can only both be FALSE if N = 0; this value is not contained in the subtype POSITIVE therefore PROGRAM_ERROR cannot be raised in this select statement. In general there will normally exist a relationship between the guards that will allow an analysis of the code to prove that the exception cannot be raised. There will however be situations where this is not the case. Consider the following examples from Wellings (1984d):

```
1.    if A then                2.    select
         accept B;                       when A =>
      end if;                               accept B;
                                      end select;
3.    select
         when A =>
            accept B;
      else
         null;
      end select;
```

These three examples involve a single accept statement B and the condition A. If A is FALSE we do not wish to accept B, but if A is TRUE we may wish to

(a) accept an entry call before proceeding, or

(b) accept an entry call if and only if one is presently outstanding.

Example 1 caters for (a), example 3 caters for (b); example 2 is unnecessary and would cause an exception to be raised if A is FALSE.

With two accept statements and two conditions the situation is more complex:

```
4.    if A then                5.    select
         accept B;                       when A =>
      elsif C then                          accept B;
         accept D;                    or
      end if;                            when C =>
                                            accept D;
                                      end select;
```

```
6.  select
      when A = >
        accept B;
    or
      when C =>
        accept D;
    else
      null;
    end select;
```

The equivalent of case (b) is again easily catered for (example 6) in that an open accept alternative will be taken if a call is outstanding. Example 4 does not, however, deal appropriately with the first case, for if A and C are both TRUE then B will always be chosen in preference to D even when there is an outstanding call to D but not B. True indeterminacy can only be provided by the code in example 5; but this code will fail when A and C are both FALSE. If A and C are not related then it is clearly not possible to prove that A = C = FALSE cannot occur. In these circumstances the select statement itself must be 'guarded'; the correct solution to the above problem is therefore:

```
if A or C then
  select
    when A =>
      accept B;
  or
    when C =>
      accept D;
  end select;
end if;
```

6.3 The Delay Alternative

The mechanism of the rendezvous is such that, whichever of the two tasks is ready to rendezvous first must wait until the other task is ready. This delay could be indefinite, which is unacceptable in embedded systems where tasks will be involved in real-time interactions with the external system. Most languages involved in embedded work allow a timeout facility that will enable a task to take alternative action if some event has not occurred within a period of real-time. In Ada, timeouts are provided on entry calls and accept statements – although the latter is a more powerful facility as a task can then timeout on more than one possible alternative action.

The select statement is used to give a task the ability to choose between accepting an entry call or delaying for a defined time period. The delay statement is used to provide a timeout capability on the select statement. The following task monitors interrupts to check that they are occurring at a rate of at least one per minute:

```
task TIMEOUT is
  entry INTERRUPT;
end TIMEOUT;

task body TIMEOUT is
  TIME_INT : constant DURATION := 60.0;
begin
  loop
    select
      accept INTERRUPT;
    or
      delay TIME_INT;
        PUT("DEVICE OFF LINE");
    end select;
  end loop;
end TIMEOUT;
```

The delay alternative is selected if no other action is taken (i.e. no other
alternative is executable) during TIME_INT. Once the delay alternative is
selected the sequence of statements following the delay is executed. With the
example above, sixty seconds will elapse during which time, if an entry call to
INTERRUPT is made, then that accept alternative will be selected. After
approximately (i.e. not less than) one minute the delay alternative will be
chosen and the message DEVICE OFF LINE will be printed out. This action
terminates the select statement; in the above program, the loop will cause re-
execution and a further delay will be initiated. If the task responsible for
generating the entry call has failed, in some sense, then the warning message
will be displayed at approximately one minute intervals.

If one compares the actions of the else clause and the delay
alternative it is clear that to have both in the same select statement would be
meaningless. The else clause defines an action to be taken, immediately, if no
other alternative is executable. Whereas the delay suspends the owner task for
some period of real-time. For these reasons the language does not allow a
select statement to contain a delay alternative and an else part. Interestingly,
as type DURATION has a range including 0.0, it is possible to delay for zero
time. The following are therefore equivalent (for some sequence of statements
C):

```
select                                  select
  accept A;                               accept A;
or                                      or
  accept B;                               accept B;
else                                    or
  C;                                      delay 0.0;
end select;                                 C;
                                        end select;
```

It can therefore be argued that the else structure is redundant.

If the expression associated with the delay statement requires evaluation then this is done at the same time as the guards are being analysed, that is at the beginning of the execution of the select statement. More than one delay alternative is allowed, although for any particular execution of the select statement only the delay with the smallest time interval will act as the timeout. Delay alternatives like accepts can be guarded, in which case the delay will be ignored if the guard is FALSE.

Finally in this section two code fragments will be compared in order to illustrate the distinction between the delay alternative and the delay statement.

```
S1 : select                    S2 : select
       accept A;                      accept A;
     or                            else
       delay 10.0;                    delay 10.0;
     end select;                    end select;
```

If there is an outstanding entry call on A then these select statement will behave identically, i.e. the call to A will be accepted. The distinction arises when there is no waiting call. In S1 the delay alternative will allow a call to A to be accepted if one arrives in the next ten seconds. S2 gives no such provision; if there is no outstanding call the else part is executed, this happens to be an ordinary delay statement and so the task is delayed for ten seconds. If a call to A did arrive after, say, four seconds, S2 would not accept it. There is also a clear distinction between the behaviours of the following program fragments

```
select                         select
  accept A;                      accept A;
or                             or
  delay 10.0;                    delay 20.0;
  delay 10.0;
end select;                    end select;
```

The first will accept a call to A only during the first ten seconds (it will then delay for a further ten seconds), the second example will accept a call during the entire twenty second interval.

This apparent dual role for the delay statement does cause confusion to programmers learning the language (Burns, 1984); it is unfortunate that another identifier such as 'timeout' was not used. To improve the readability of programs with timeouts it is recommended that all statements in a delay alternative, following the delay statement, are further indented.

6.4 The Terminate Alternative

In chapter 2 it was argued that three distinct kinds of tasks can be identified; one of these classes - the synchronisation agent (or passive task) - is usually structured so that it indefinitely loops round performing some function for other processes in the system. The task does not therefore terminate naturally and some action must be taken if it is desired to complete the executions of all such tasks dependent on a master. This termination can be programmed directly using a special entry (which must be called by the master):

```
task body FRED is
  .
  .
  .
begin
  .
  .
  .
  loop
    select
      accept GOODNIGHT;
      exit;
    or
      .
      .
      .
    end select;
  end loop;
end FRED;
```

However, as this situation is common a special select alternative is provided:

```
select
  terminate;
or
  .
  .
  .
end select;
```

The terminate alternative consists of only the single statement 'terminate' which can be guarded. It is not possible to include a sequence of statements that will allow the task to control its own demise. If the master of the task wishes to terminate and all other tasks dependent on that master are either already terminated or are similarly delayed on a select statement with an open terminate alternative then all tasks plus the master will terminate together. Because all remaining tasks must be suspended on select statements there can be no outstanding entry calls (no task could have made such a call). The terminate alternative cannot thus be selected if there is a queued entry call for any entry of the task. It is not therefore necessary, in normal circumstances, to guard the terminate alternative. As the inclusion of a terminate alternative indicates that on the execution of this select statement the task may have no further work to do, it would be illogical to also include a delay alternative or an else clause in the same select statement. These possible combinations are therefore prohibited. Only in device driver tasks where an entry call may originate from outside the program (see chapter 12) is there a need for a more flexible programming structure.

6.5 Conditional and Timed Entry Calls

A calling task can avoid committing itself to a rendezvous by executing a conditional or timed entry call. This allows for the programming of a timeout on an entry call. Consider a call on the entry TAKE of a task T:

```
select
  T.TAKE(K);
  NEW_K_AVAILABLE := TRUE;
else
  NEW_K_AVAILABLE := FALSE;
end select;
if NEW_K_AVAILABLE then
     .
     .
     .
```

This is a conditional entry call, the syntax of which is defined by:

```
<conditional_entry_call> ::=
  select
    <entry_call_statement>
    [ <sequence_of_statements> ]
  else
    <sequence_of_statements>
  end select;
```

A conditional entry call issues an ordinary entry call that is cancelled if a rendezvous is not immediately possible.

> "The entry call is cancelled if the execution of the called task has not reached a point where it is ready to accept the call (that is, either an accept statement for the corresponding entry, or a select statement with an open accept alternative for the entry), or if there are prior queued entry calls for this entry. If the called task has reached a select statement, the entry call is cancelled if an accept alternative for this entry is not selected." (ARM 9.7.2)

The term 'immediate' does not strictly mean 'straight away', therefore, but allows for whatever time is necessary to investigate the state of the called task.

A conditional entry call should only be used when the task can genuinely do other productive work, if the call is not accepted. Care should be taken not to program polling, or busy-wait, solutions.

For timeout purposes the timed entry call can allow a period of time to elapse before cancelling the call:

```
select
  T.TAKE(K);
or
  delay X;
  raise TIMEOUT_ERROR;
end select.
```

Again the delay alternative should be used only where necessary, with the action taken (if the delay alternative is chosen) usually being seen as an error condition (hence the use of a user defined exception). The syntax of the timed entry call is defined as:

```
<timed_entry_call> ::=
  select
    <entry_call_statement>
    [ <sequence_of_statements> ]
  or
    <delay_statement>
    [ <sequence of statements> ]
  end select;
```

Note, the conditional entry call uses an 'else', the timed entry call an 'or'. Moreover they cannot be mixed, nor can two entry call statements be included. Indeterminate entry calls are not therefore, strictly, possible.

A timed entry call issues an entry call that is cancelled if a rendezvous is not started within a given delay. This has considerable implications for an implementation; not only must a task be able to place itself at the back of an entry queue, but the run-time system must provide for a task being removed from any position in a queue. The time requirement specified by the delay alternative includes whatever time is necessary to pass the entry call to the called task. With distributed systems this message passing overhead may be significant. If X is the time it takes to communicate with the called task then a timed entry call with a delay of Y ($Y <= X$) will always fail even if the task is able to rendezvous. A conditional entry call in this situation would succeed. What is more, if the timed entry call is made with a time value of zero (or negative) then it is deemed to act like a conditional call (ARM 9.7.3.4). This leads to the situation that a timed entry call with delay zero would succeed whereas a call with delay Y (0 < Y <= X) would fail.

It is also important to realise that the timed entry call only times out on the start of the rendezvous. What may actually be needed is a timeout on the completion of the rendezvous. Once the rendezvous has started then, however long it takes, the called task cannot timeout. An error could even make it impossible for the associated accept statement to terminate and there is nothing the called task can do about it. Implementation of a timeout on completion would, of course, be very difficult as a rendezvous would need to be cancelled half way through. This could leave the called task in some undetermined state. One approach here would be to define the accept statement as an **atomic action** - if the rendezvous is terminated before completion, the task would be returned to the state it was in prior to executing the accept. Unfortunately this presents further difficulties if the rendezvous has made entry calls on other tasks!

The timed entry call that Ada provides can be used sensibly in two ways. Firstly, if the accept statement is simple and short then the timed entry call is a reasonable approximation to a true timeout. Secondly, if the accept statement is complex or long then the single request should be split into two timed entry calls (let INTERVAL be the overall time limit):

```
START_TIME := CLOCK;
select
  T.CALL_IN(X); -- Pass data to called task.
or
  delay INTERVAL;
  raise TIME_OUT_ERROR;
end select;
INTERVAL := INTERVAL - CLOCK + START_TIME;
select
  T.CALL_OUT(Y);  -- Receive results from called task.
or
  delay INTERVAL;
  raise TIMEOUT_ERROR;
end select;
```

Within task T both CALL_IN and CALL_OUT would be very simple data transfer accept statements:

```
accept CALL_IN (X : ITEMS) do
  TEMPX := X;
end CALL_IN;
      -- sequence of statements transforming
      -- TEMPX to TEMPY.
```

```
accept CALL_OUT (Y : out SOME_OTHER_ITEMS) do
   Y := TEMPY;
end CALL_OUT;
```

The disadvantage of this approach is that it introduces a second rendezvous.

6.6 Mutual Exclusion and Deadlocks

The select statement introduces a further set of states into which an executing task can be placed. Figure 6.1 illustrates these new states and those already given in Figure 5.1. This completes the diagram for the active task; all the possible situations in which a task can find itself are included. With a single (or limited) processor system it should be remembered that the state 'executable' merely indicates an ability to execute. It may be that the run-time system has not actually scheduled that task to execute. Nevertheless, when it next has access to a processor it will continue to execute. A state change cannot occur while a task is swapped out (i.e. not actually executing), unless it is aborted, see section 7.1.

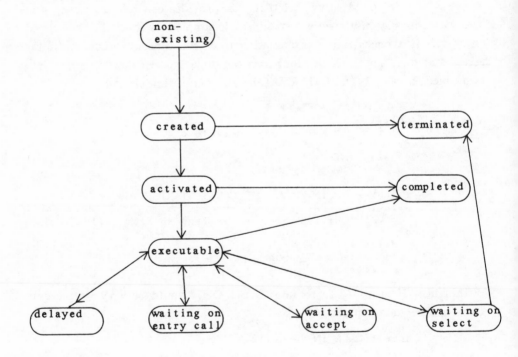

Figure 6.1

In chapter 3 a number of the inherent difficulties associated with concurrent programming were considered. Of paramount importance is insuring the integrity of resources that should not be accessed by more than one task at a time (non–concurrent resources). This integrity is usually assured by defining a critical section of code that must be protected by mutual exclusion. That is, while task A is in its critical section all other tasks must be inhibited from entering associated critical sections that access the same resource.

With a task, mutual exclusion can easily be constructed:

```
task type T is
  entry A (...);
  entry B (...);
    .
    .
    .
end T;

task body T is
  -- The resource is represented by the definition
  -- of some appropriate data structure.
begin
  loop
    select
      accept A(...) do
        .
        .
        .
      end A;
    or
      accept B (...) do
        .
        .
        .
      end B;
    or
        .
        .
        .
    end select;
  end loop;
end T;
```

Each task of type T will define a new resource. For each of these resources, although entries A B, etc. may give access, the semantics of the task body (with or without a select statement) ensure that only one accept statement at a time can be executing. The accept statement is itself the critical section. As long as the resource is defined within the task body, and is not accessible to 'sub tasks' defined within the same body, then mutual exclusion is provided. Mutual exclusion does not, however, extend to include the evaluation of the actual parameters to an entry call. The evaluation of such parameters in two distinct entry calls may therefore interfere with each other if shared variables are used directly or are influenced by side effects.

Deadlocks are another matter! Consider the following code:

```
task T1 is                          task T2 is
   entry A;                            entry B;
end T1;                             end T2;
task body T1 is                     task body T2 is
begin                               begin
   T2.B;                               T1.A;
   accept A;                           accept B;
end T1;                             end T2;
```

Clearly both tasks will be placed on an entry queue for the other task. They will therefore not be in a position to accept the outstanding call. A task can even call its own entries and deadlock! Guidelines can reduce the possibility of deadlocks (German, 1982) but inherent deadlocks should (must!) be recognised early in the design of systems and evasive action taken.

The following points are pertinent: tasks should be constructed to be either process tasks or synchronisation agents. Process (or active) tasks make entry calls but do not have entries. Synchronisation agents (or passive tasks) accept entry calls but make no calls themselves. Entry calls from within rendezvous should only be used when absolutely necessary. Where a collection of non-concurrent resources is accessed by a number of tasks then:

(i)   Tasks should use resources one at a time if possible.
(ii)   If (i) is not possible then all tasks should access the resources in the same predefined order.
(iii)   If (i) and (ii) are not possible then the tasks controlling access to the resources must be designed to take appropriate remedial action. For example resources could be pre-emptively removed from tasks using a timeout structure.

With deadlocks there is no substitute for proving that they cannot occur in the first place!

The property of liveness or indefinite postponement is relevant in a number of areas. Entries themselves are queued FIFO and therefore cannot lead to postponements; a select statement is however non-deterministic. If there is more than one open accept alternative then the ARM says that the choice of which is to be selected is arbitrary. Interestingly the GREEN language (an early version of Ada) defined the choice to be 'random':

> *"The rule for choosing one of the open alternatives has been stated to be at random. This should be treated in a statistical sense. It should not be possible for a program to detect the algorithm used."* (Rationale for Design of the Green Programming Language).

Luckily this requirement that the run-time system supports a random number generator has been dropped. An implementation may interpret 'arbitrarily' as it wishes but a good implementation should ensure that the acceptance of a particular entry is not indefinitely postponed. Indeed, rather than use a pseudo-random number a FIFO algorithm could be applied to the heads of each of the entry queues. However, no particular model of fairness can be assumed and the programmer should not rely on this to give a specific synchronisation.

To ensure liveness, select statements can be constructed to force the system to examine each queue in turn:

```
loop
  select
    accept A;
  else
    null;
  end select;
  select
    accept B;
  else
    null;
  end select;
  select
    accept A;
  or
    accept B;
  end select;
end loop;
```

This structure would, of course, get very tedious if a large number of entries was involved! The final select statement is needed to delay the owner task if no outstanding entry calls exist (otherwise the task would loop around and poll the entry queues). With a single processor system it can be assumed that all tasks will in turn be given access to the processor. The run-time system would normally support a 'first in first out' queue of tasks that are in the state 'executing'. (The optimisation of task switching may, in some circumstances, require other scheduling schemes). Only when priorities are used (see chapter 11) could a task be indefinitely postponed from the processor.

This chapter will be concluded by given a solution to the dining philosophers program that was outlined in section 3.5.

```
procedure DINING_PHILOSOPHERS is
  package ACTIVITIES is
    procedure THINK;
    procedure EAT;
  end ACTIVITIES;

  use ACTIVITIES;
  N : constant := 5;  -- number of philosophers.
  type PHILOSOPHERS_RANGE is new INTEGER range 0..N-1;

  task type PHILOSOPHERS is
    entry NUMBERING (P : PHILOSOPHERS_RANGE);
  end PHILOSOPHERS;

  task type CHOPSTICK_CONTROL is
    entry PICK_UP;
    entry PUT_DOWN;
  end CHOPSTICK_CONTROL;

  task DEADLOCK_PREVENTION is
    entry ENTERS;
    entry LEAVES;
  end DEADLOCK_PREVENTION;

  CHOPSTICKS : array (PHILOSOPHERS_RANGE)
                 of CHOPSTICK_CONTROL;
  PHILOSOPHER : array (PHILOSOPHERS_RANGE)
                 of PHILOSOPHERS;
  package body ACTIVITIES is separate;
  task body PHILOSOPHERS is separate;
  task body CHOPSTICK_CONTROL is separate;
  task body DEADLOCK_PREVENTION is separate;
begin
  for P in PHILOSOPHERS_RANGE loop
    PHILOSOPHER(P).NUMBERING(P);
  end loop;
end DINING_PHILOSOPHERS;
```

The procedures THINK and EAT in the package ACTIVITIES will consist of some appropriate delay statement and will be called concurrently by the philosophers who are structured as process tasks. Each of the non-concurrent chopsticks is represented by a synchronisation task.

```
task body CHOPSTICK_CONTROL is
begin
  loop
    accept PICK_UP;
    accept PUT_DOWN;
  end loop;
end CHOPSTICK_CONTROL;
```

Deadlocks are prevented by noting that they can only occur if all of the philosophers wish to eat at the same time. By stopping just one philosopher from entering the eating stage, deadlocks are prevented; moreover, as only one philosopher task is delayed (and therefore freed when a single task stops eating), liveness is preserved.

```
task body DEADLOCK_PREVENTION is
  MAX : constant INTEGER := N - 1;
  PEOPLE_EATING : INTEGER range 0..MAX := 0;
begin
  loop
    select
      when PEOPLE_EATING < MAX =>
        accept ENTERS;
        PEOPLE_EATING := PEOPLE_EATING + 1;
    or
      accept LEAVES;
      PEOPLE_EATING := PEOPLE_EATING - 1;
    or
      terminate;
    end select;
  end loop;
end DEADLOCK_PREVENTION;
```

The philosophers themselves are necessarily programmed as tasks and have a simple life-cycle. In order to know which chopsticks to pick up each philosopher must know its own identity. This is achieved by passing a unique array index from the body of the main procedure to the entry NUMBERING. The process task therefore makes calls upon the other (synchronisation) agents and is not, in the normal execution cycle, called. The use of a single entry to pass identity information at the beginning of the task's execution is one of the few situations in which an entry into an active process task should be used.

```
task body PHILOSOPHERS is
  CHOP_STICK1, CHOP_STICK2 : PHILOSOPHERS_RANGE;
begin
  accept NUMBERING (P : PHILOSOPHER_RANGE) do
    CHOP_STICK1 := P;
  end NUMBERING;
  CHOP_STICK2 := (CHOP_STICK1 + 1) mod N;
```

```
loop
    THINK;
    DEADLOCK_PREVENTION.ENTERS;
    CHOPSTICKS(CHOP_STICK1).PICK_UP;
    CHOPSTICKS(CHOP_STICK2).PICK_UP;
    EAT;
    CHOPSTICKS(CHOP_STICK1).PUT_DOWN;
    CHOPSTICKS(CHOP_STICK2).PUT_DOWN;
    DEADLOCK_PREVENTION.LEAVES;
end loop;
end PHILOSOPHERS;
```

The structure used above assures an indefinite execution of the program. If a limited execution is desired then the PHILOSOPHERS would need to exit from their life-cycle after a number of iterations or after some duration of time. The synchronisation tasks would all have 'or terminate' alternatives on their select statement.

The reliability of this solution is typical of many concurrent Ada programs. Firstly it can be seen that the failure of any of the synchronisation tasks would be disastrous for the program as a whole. A PHILOSOPHER could, however, terminate without affecting the system unless he or she happened to have control of a chopstick at that time. Resources can, in general, be programmed to put themselves back in the resource pool in this eventuality. Assume that there is an upper limit of INTERVAL on the time it takes for a philosopher to eat, such that if a chopstick is not returned within that period the philosopher can be assumed to have died (of overeating!). The body for the task CHOPSTICK_CONTROL would then take the form (including a termination alternative):

```
task body CHOPSTICK_CONTROL is
begin
  loop
    select
      accept PICK_UP;
    or
      terminate;
    end select;
    select
      accept PUT_DOWN;
    or
      delay INTERVAL;
      -- As the philosopher has not called PUT_DOWN he
      -- or she is assumed to be'dead', the chopsticks
      -- can therefore be rescued.
    end select;
  end loop;
end CHOPSTICK_CONTROL;
```

7 TASK TERMINATION, EXCEPTIONS AND ATTRIBUTES

Figure 6.1 illustrates the states that a task can be in after its activation; to be fully incorporated into this diagram are three further states that may be involved in the death of a task:

completion

termination

abnormal

A task is said to be completed when it has finished executing the sequence of statements given in the task's body. Note that, if the task contains an infinite loop, this sequence may not, under normal circumstances, finish executing and the task may never complete.

A task is also said to be completed if an exception is raised during its activation. Consider the following:

```
task body T is
   A : INTEGER range 0..256 := N;
```

If, on elaboration, N has the value 500 then an exception, which is impossible to handle within the task, will be generated and the task will become completed. This will also be the case if any exception is raised and not handled during the execution of the task. Finally, if an exception is raised and handled at the outermost level of the task, then the task becomes completed once the execution of the handler is finished. Note that these exceptions will not be propagated beyond the task; the parent or master task is not directly affected by an exception being raised in a child task, whether it is handled or not.

If the completed task has no dependent tasks then it immediately becomes terminated. However if it is the master of one or more child tasks then it will remain in the completed state until these child tasks have themselves terminated, at which time the master also terminates. A task, once terminated, will remain in that state for the rest of the program (and once the master of the task has terminated, the task can be said to return to the state of 'non-existing'). The condition of being completed, or terminated, can also apply to a block statement or subprogram:

```
procedure FRED is
  task A;
  task B;
    .
    .
    .
begin
  null;              -- Although procedure FRED is
  end FRED;          -- quickly completed it will not
                     -- terminate until task A and
                     -- task B terminate.
```

If tasks A and B do not complete then FRED will never terminate. However if A and B contain open terminate alternatives in select statements then A and B may terminate (although they did not complete) and thus allow FRED to terminate. In general, a task waiting on a select statement with an open terminate alternative may terminate if and only if:

(i)   it depends on some master that is completed, and

(ii) each and every task that depends on that master is either already terminated or is similarly waiting on an open terminate alternative of a select statement.

In these circumstances all tasks dependent on that master will be terminated (collectively) and the master itself will then terminate.

This termination method allows synchronisation tasks to be unconcerned about the duration of their execution as long as they have terminate alternatives on the appropriate select statement. By way of a simple example consider a task type that will provide a safe implementation of a shared variable (i.e. the variable is hidden in a task body):

```
task type SHARED_VARIABLE is
  entry READ  (I : out ITEM);   -- for some type ITEM.
  entry WRITE (I : ITEM);
end SHARED_VARIABLE;

task body SHARED_VARIABLE is
  VAR : ITEM;
begin
  accept WRITE (I : ITEM) do
    VAR := I;
  end WRITE;
  loop
    select
      accept WRITE (I : ITEM) do
        VAR := I;
      end WRITE;
    or
```

```
          accept READ (I : out ITEM) do
             I := VAR;
          end READ;
       or
          terminate;
       end select;
    end loop;
end SHARED_VARIABLE;
```

This example illustrates the use of two accept statements for the same entry. The initial accept ensures that the first operation must be a WRITE; after that, READS and WRITES will be accepted in whatever order is dictated by the dynamics of the program's execution. Provided that at least one WRITE has been accepted then the task will terminate when its master and other relevant tasks are all in a position to do so.

If an attempt is made to rendezvous with a task that is either completed or terminated then the entry call must be refused. This is done by raising an exception at the point of the entry call. The exception raised is TASKING_ERROR which is one of the five predefined exceptions. Even when the entry call has been placed on a task's entry queue it is possible for the called task to complete without accepting that particular call, in which case TASKING_ERROR is again raised. Note that a conditional entry call on a terminated task will still have TASKING_ERROR raised.

As a synchronisation task does not, in general, make entry calls it need not contend with the exception TASKING_ERROR. Reliable process (active) tasks must however take into account the possibility of the exception being raised during their use of synchronisation tasks.

7.1 The Abort Statement

The abort statement is one of the most controversial in Ada. It is defined quite simply:

```
<abort_statement> ::= abort <task_name> {,<task_name>};
```

Any task may abort any other named task by executing this statement:

```
abort BUFFER;
abort PHILOSOPHER(1), PHILOSOPHER(3);
```

If a task is at the receiving end of this statement then it immediately becomes abnormal. Any non-terminated tasks that depend upon an aborted task are also said to be abnormal. This completes the action of the abort statement and the task perpertrating the abort will continue its execution. The effect of becoming abnormal depends upon the state of the aborted task; the following points summarise the consequences:

* No further rendezvous is possible with an abnormal task.
* An abnormal task that is suspended (at an accept, a select or delay statement) becomes completed.
* An abnormal task that has made an entry call but which is not yet in a rendezvous becomes completed; it is removed from the entry queue.
* An abnormal task that has not yet started its activation becomes completed (and, as there are no dependent tasks, terminated).
* An attempt to abort an already abnormal, completed or terminated task is allowed – the effect being null.
* A task making an entry call will have the exception TASKING_ERROR raised if the called task is abnormal or becomes abnormal before, or during, the execution of the rendezvous.
* Finally, if the calling task (of a rendezvous) becomes abnormal during the rendezvous then the rendezvous is completed normally, the called task is unaffected.

If the task was updating a shared variable when it was aborted the value of the shared variable is undefined.

If none of the above situations apply (i.e. the task is merely executing code) then the abnormal task must become completed before it reaches one of the following synchronisation points:

(i)   The end of its activation.
(ii)   The activation of another task.
(iii)   The start or end of an accept statement.
(iv)   A select statement.
(v)   A delay statement.
(vi)   An exception handler.
(vii)   An abort statement.

A consequence of this rule is that an abnormal task which does not reach any of the above points need not be terminated! It could be abnormal but still loop round updating shared variables and using processor cycles. There is no way of ensuring that such a task is forced to complete although on a traditional uniprocessor system it would be normal to terminate the task at once.

The rationale for including an abort statement is that a task may become wayward in its control of some external device. It must therefore be possible to abort this one task without bringing the entire program down. In other situations it may be necessary to abort tasks as part of a deadlock recovery routine. The scope rules dictate that if a master task is aborted then all dependent tasks must also cease their executions.

The inclusion of this statement was made, reluctantly, by the language designers and the ARM gives a clear warning about its use:

> "*An abort statement should be used only in extremely severe situations requiring unconditional termination.*" (*ARM 9.10.10*).

In the rationale for the Green language this view was stated as follows:

> "*The abort statement is provided for emergency use only. Its over use could severely hinder program understanding and validation*".

Nevertheless the fact that a task can abort any other task introduces an interesting circular argument to this rationale. Hoare(1979), who has been particularly critical of this language feature, has made the following remark:

> "*The existence of this statement causes intolerable overheads in the implementation of every other feature of tasking. Its 'successful' use depends on a valid process aborting a wild one before the wild one aborts a valid process - or does any other serious damage. The probability of this is negligible. If processes can go wild, we are much safer without aborts.*"

All the states that an Ada task can be in have now been described; Figure 7.1 illustrates these states.

7.2 Task and Entry Attributes

Both task objects (T) and entries (E) have attributes associated with them. Consider first the attributes concerned with the mapping of the constructs on to the underlying hardware:

T'ADDRESS Returns ADDRESS defined in package SYSTEM; the address of the first storage unit of the task body

T'SIZE Returns INTEGER; the size in bits of the task object.

T'STORAGE_SIZE Returns INTEGER; the number of storage units needed to activate the task object.

E'ADDRESS Returns ADDRESS defined in package SYSTEM; the address of the hardware interrupt vector if an address clause has been given (see section 12.4).

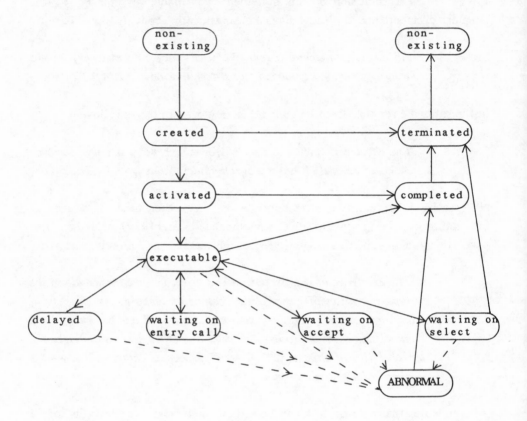

Figure 7.1

These attributes are not employed in the normal course of programming. Other attributes are more useful:

>**T'CALLABLE** Returns BOOLEAN; false if T is completed, terminated or abnormal, otherwise true.
>**T'TERMINATED** Returns BOOLEAN; true if T is terminated, otherwise false.

A task may therefore obtain information about the state of some other task. Care must however be taken if this information is to be used for any type of synchronisation. Thus the following example does not preclude the possibility of TASKING_ERROR being raised:

```
if T'CALLABLE then
  T.CALL;  -- Call some entry in task T.
end if;
```

It is possible that T may have completed (perhaps been aborted) after the attribute was evaluated but before the entry call could be accepted and the rendezvous completed.

Where the attribute CALLABLE is of value, is when a resource wishes to check that the task that presently has access to it is still using the resource and has not terminated without returning it to the resource pool. To do this the resource task must 'know' which tasks are accessing the resource; as the rendezvous is based on a client-server model this is not automatic. A request for resources therefore needs to leave a 'name' that can be used with the attribute CALLABLE. This can take the form of an array index or an access type (see chapter 9).

The specification of the CHOPSTICK resource, illustrated in the previous chapter, could be expanded so that if the call to PUT_DOWN does not take place within time INTERVAL then the resource holder is checked to see if it is still CALLABLE. In this example the clients (philosophers) are represented by an array of tasks and each philosopher has been given a unique number which it will use when requesting chopsticks. The body for CHOPSTICK_CONTROL now becomes:

```
task body CHOPSTICK_CONTROL is
  HOLDER, TEMP : PHILOSOPHER_RANGE;
begin
  loop
    select
      accept PICK_UP (P : PHILOSOPHER_RANGE) do
        HOLDER := P;
      end PICK_UP;
    or
      terminate;
    end select;
    loop
      select
        accept PUT_DOWN (P : PHILOSOPHER_RANGE) do
          TEMP := P;
        end PUT_DOWN;
        exit when TEMP = HOLDER;
        -- Having accepted a call to PUT_DOWN
        -- the identifier P is checked to make sure
        -- it corresponds to the philosopher that
        -- picked up the chopstick.
      or
        delay INTERVAL;
          exit when not PHILOSOPHER(HOLDER)'CALLABLE;
      end select;
    end loop;
```

```
        -- return chopstick to pool
    end loop;
end CHOPSTICK_CONTROL;
```

Unfortunately, this solution involves a busy wait while the task holding the resource is polled to see if it still 'exists'. Hopefully the size of INTERVAL would be such that the inner loop would not be re-executed often. Alternatively the lack of a call to PUT_DOWN in time INTERVAL may indicate a serious malfunction of the philosopher tasks, in which case it may be desirable, rather than to just remove the resources from the task, to abort the philosopher:

```
    -- as before
    or
        delay INTERVAL;
            if PHILOSOPHER(HOLDER)'CALLABLE then
                abort PHILOSOPHER(HOLDER);
            end if;
            exit;
    end select;
```

The 'if' statement is not absolutely necessary but precludes a meaningless abort being generated if the task is already completed or terminated.

Each entry queue has an attribute associated with it that allows the correct length of the queue to be accessible to the owning task:

E'COUNT Returns INTEGER; the number of entry calls presently queued on the entry E. Where E is either a single entry, a family of entries or a single entry of a family.

If E is an entry of task T then E'COUNT can only be used within the body of T but not within a dependent program unit of that body.

The attribute COUNT would appear to be a useful one in enabling a synchronisation task to exercise specific control over outstanding requests. Care must however be taken when using COUNT as its value will not only increase with the arrival of new entry calls but may decrease as a result of a timed entry call. The queue may also shrink if a task is aborted while it is on an entry queue. As the value given by the attribute is therefore, in some senses, a shared variable its use in guards could lead to difficulties. In the protected variable example given earlier in this chapter an arbitrary choice was made between accepting calls to the two entries. This may be inappropriate, for it is usual to give preference to WRITE operations so that READs obtain a more up-to-date value:

```
task type SHARED_VARIABLE is
  entry READ  (I : out ITEM);
  entry WRITE (I :  ITEM);
end SHARED_VARIABLE;

task body SHARED_VARIABLE is
  VAR : ITEM;
begin
  accept WRITE (I : ITEM) do
    VAR :- I;
  end WRITE;
  loop
    select
      accept WRITE (I : ITEM) do
        VAR :- I;
      end WRITE;
    or
      when WRITE'COUNT - 0 =>
        accept READ (I : out ITEM) do
          I :- VAR;
        end READ;
    or
      terminate;
    end select;
  end loop;
end SHARED_VARIABLE;
```

It is possible (although admittedly unlikely) for an interleaving to proceed as follows:

(i)   On execution of the select there is one outstanding WRITE request.

(ii) The guard is evaluated and found to be false; calls to READ are therefore not available to the select.

(iii) The entry to WRITE is removed (externally).

(iv) Select statement is suspended waiting for a call to WRITE.

In this situation no calls to READ will be processed even though there are no WRITE requests.

7.3 Exceptions and Tasks

In addition to the usual rules regarding exceptions a number of further cases are introduced by the tasking model. Firstly, as indicated above, exceptions are not propagated beyond the task in which they were raised. A task will become completed if an exception is raised but not handled within the task. Other tasks are not directly affected by this demise unless they try and rendezvous with the terminated task; in which case the exception TASKING_ERROR will be raised at the point of the entry call. With ANSI standard Ada it is not possible to raise an exception in another task. This was allowed in earlier drafts of the language, but has fortunately been removed; it represented a particularly inappropriate form of unsynchronised communication.

Finally there is the case of what happens if an exception is raised during the execution of a rendezvous. Where there exists an inner block that handles the exception inside the rendezvous then no further consequences arise. If, however, an exception is raised but not handled during a rendezvous then the rendezvous itself is abandoned and the exception is raised both in the calling and called tasks as follows:

(i)   In the calling task the exception is raised at the point of the entry call.

(ii) In the called task the exception is raised at the point immediately after the end of the accept statement.

If the scope of the exception is the body of the called task then in the calling task the exception is anonymous and can only be handled with an 'others' clause. Failure to handle the exception in either the called or calling task will cause that task to become completed.

Consider a task FILE_ACCESS that controls access to a file of records. It has available an entry UPDATE that will write a record to the file at the point indicated by an index:

```
entry UPDATE (I : INDEX; R : SOME_RECORD);
```

Within the body of FILE_ACCESS there is a procedure WRITE that will actually update the file. This procedure will however raise the exceptions FILE_NOT_OPEN and INDEX_OUT_OF_ORDER where necessary. The code associated with the entry UPDATE could take the form :

```
loop
  begin
    select
      accept UPDATE (I : INDEX; R : SOME_RECORD) do
        loop
          begin
            WRITE (I,R);
            exit;
          exception
            when FILE_NOT_OPEN =>
              -- Take whatever action is necessary to
              -- open the file.
          end;
        end loop;
      end UPDATE;
```

```
       or
          -- other alternatives
       end select;
    exception
       when INDEX_OUT_OF_ORDER => null;
    end;
 end loop;
```

With the first error, FILE_NOT_OPEN, it is appropriate for the necessary action to take place within the rendezvous. As a result it does not effect either the calling task or the called task once the rendezvous has been completed. The second error condition, which is associated with the index value being inappropriate, is deemed to be the fault of the calling task and consequently the exception is propagated to this task. The called task is not to be troubled by the error condition, and so the select statement is encased in a block that defines a null exception handler.

This example has been used to illustrate the link between exceptions and rendezvous. It should be noted that, unless the possibility of the index being out of range is very rare, a boolean flag parameter to the entry would be a more appropriate structure for signalling the error condition back to the calling task.

8 TASKS AND PACKAGES

Tasks and packages are syntactically similar and form the major building blocks of Ada programs. They are however quite distinct constructs and it is important that the user should have no misconceptions as to their roles. A package is used to encapsulate logically related items, it is both static and passive. Tasks, on the other hand, are used to facilitate concurrent programming, they can be created dynamically (see chapter 9) and they are active.

Another important distinction lies in what can be contained in their specifications. A task may contain only entry declarations; a package, by comparison, can contain anything other than entry declarations. Where resources are concerned this point is particularly important. Consider two invalid implementations of a buffer:

```
task BUFFERS is
   type BUFFER is limited private;   -- Invalid Ada
   entry PUT (I : ITEM; B : in out BUFFER);
   entry GET (I : out ITEM; B : in out BUFFER);
private
      .
      .
      .
end BUFFERS;

package BUFFERS is
   type BUFFER is limited private;
   entry PUT (I : ITEM; B : in out BUFFER);      -- Invalid
   entry GET (I : out ITEM; B in out BUFFER);    -- Ada
private
      .
      .
      .
end BUFFERS;
```

The task provides the operators for synchronisation but is illegal because types cannot be defined in task specifications. The package does allow for abstract data types but not with entry declarations. (It is interesting to note that the task example would have been legal in GREEN but this leads to other difficulties such as: do the type, or subprogram, declarations still exist once the task has terminated?).

Thus tasks cannot, by themselves, satisfy Bloom's requirement for modularity (see section 3.10). For although resource abstraction can be separated from its use, by using a package, the synchronisation scheme requires a task definition and therefore cannot be hidden (Wellings, 1984b, 1985a). It is necessary to use a combination of a package and a task to provide a powerful resource abstraction mechanism:

```
package BUFFERS is
   type BUFFER is limited private;
   procedure PUT (I : ITEM; B : in out BUFFER);
   procedure GET (I : out ITEM; B : in out BUFFER);
private
        .
        .
        .
end BUFFERS;
```

The package specification defines, in a single unit, a data type to represent the resource and two operators for that resource. These operators are necessarily declared as subprograms. Within the body of the package, or within the private part of the specification, tasks are declared to control synchronisation. In this buffer example it is more appropriate to construct the BUFFER itself as a task:

```
private
   task type BUFFER_TEMPLATE is
      entry PUT (I : ITEM);
      entry GET (I : out ITEM);
   end BUFFER_TEMPLATE;
   type BUFFER is new BUFFER_TEMPLATE;
end BUFFERS;
```

Within the body of the package, calls to the subprograms are converted into entry calls:

```
package body BUFFERS is
   task body BUFFER_TEMPLATE is separate;
   procedure PUT (I : ITEM; B : in out BUFFER) is
   begin
      B.PUT(I);
   end PUT;
   procedure GET (I : out ITEM; B : in out BUFFER) is
   begin
      B.GET(I);
   end GET;
end BUFFERS;
```

The necessary synchronisations are provided, but are hidden within the package body. It is recommended that this 'procedural interface' should be used for all tasks, especially as the package is a far more useful design structure. The overhead introduced by the use of subprograms can be reduced by employing the INLINE pragma. Another advantage of this procedural interface concerns information hidding; for if only certain entries of a task are intended to be called from external program units than the 'private' set is hidden. This would not be the case if the task was declared in the specification part of the package.

An exception to this recommendation is where a conditional or timed entry call is to be used on the resource operators. In this situation the task must be visible (see chapter 15 for an alternative structure); however, a package interface is still recommended, for example with a single buffer:

```
package BUFFER is
   task B is
      entry PUT (I : ITEM);
      entry GET (I : out ITEM);
   end B;
end BUFFER;

package body BUFFER is
   task body B is separate;
end BUFFER;
```

The body of the task must be contained within the body of the package. A conditional entry call would then take the form:

```
select
   BUFFER.B.PUT(X);
else
   raise SOME_EXCEPTION;
end select;
```

8.1 The Readers and Writers Problem

In chapter 3 it was stated that one of the motivations for the rendezvous concept is that a single mechanism provides both synchronisation and data communication. Indeed it can be argued that to use two different concepts (i.e. synchronisation and communication) is misleading as one cannot take place without the other! The Ada rendezvous, like the monitor, is structured around the most common form of synchronisation namely mutual exclusion. And, as has been illustrated, mutual exclusion is assured by defining the resource to be acted upon inside the body of a single task.

Unfortunately, many synchronisation protocols are much more sophisticated and this has led, in other languages, to the use of formal expressions to attempt to state the kinds of synchronisations allowed. A commonly used example of this kind of protocol is the readers and writers problem. Consider a (non-shareable) resource such as a file. Because of multiple update difficulties the necessary synchronisations are such that if one process is writing to the file then no other process should be either writing or reading. If, however, there is no writer process then any number of processes should have read access. Because of this latter property the READ cannot be constructed as an accept statement as only one would be allowed at a time. Rather, a task must be used to synchronise the start and finish of reads and writes, with the data communication taking place via shared objects. Because of this use of shared variables it is imperative that the task specification and the shared variables, are hidden within a package body. Here is a first solution to the readers and writers problem:

```
package READERS_WRITERS is
  procedure READ (I : out ITEM);   -- for some type ITEM.
  procedure WRITE (I : ITEM);
end READERS_WRITERS;

package body READERS_WRITERS is
  procedure PUT (I : ITEM) is separate;
  procedure GET (I : out ITEM) is separate;
  task CONTROL is
    entry START_WRITE;
    entry START_READ;
    entry STOP_WRITE;
    entry STOP_READ;
    entry REQUEST_WRITE;
  end CONTROL;

  procedure READ (I : out ITEM) is
  begin
    CONTROL.START_READ;
    GET(I);
    CONTROL.STOP_READ;
  end READ;

  procedure WRITE (I : ITEM) is
  begin
    CONTROL.REQUEST_WRITE;
    CONTROL.START_WRITE;
    PUT(I);
    CONTROL.STOP_WRITE;
  end WRITE;
```

```
task body CONTROL is
  READERS : NATURAL := 0;
  WRITERS : BOOLEAN := FALSE;
begin
  loop
    select
      when READERS = 0 =>
        accept START_WRITE;
    or
      when not WRITERS =>
        accept START_READ;
        READERS := READERS + 1;
    or
      accept STOP_WRITE;
        WRITERS := FALSE;
    or
      accept STOP_READ;
        READERS := READERS - 1;
    or
      when not WRITERS =>
        accept REQUEST_WRITE;
        WRITERS := TRUE;
    or
      terminate;
    end select;
  end loop;
end CONTROL;
end READERS_WRITERS;
```

The READ procedure enforces the necessary condition synchronisation by first
calling START_READ; this entry will be accepted only when there are no
writer processes active (i.e. when WRITERS = FALSE). By comparison the
pre-conditions for a WRITE are more complex and involves two stages.
Firstly, the need to perform a write must be signalled so that no more reads
are allowed. This is achieved by calling REQUEST_WRITE. Secondly, in
order for the conditions associated with a write to be satisfied, the
START_WRITE call must not be accepted until all readers presently active
have completed their accesses. This is again achieved by an appropriate guard.
In this example the task is used to give synchronisation only. A more efficient
solution to this particular problem can be obtained by using the task to give
the mutual exclusion on the WRITE operation whilst leaving the READ to
perform pre and post synchronisation:

```
task CONTROL is
  entry START_READ;
  entry STOP_READ;
  entry WRITE (I : ITEM);
end CONTROL;
```

```
task body CONTROL is
begin
  loop
    select
      accept START_READ;
      READERS := READERS + 1;
    or
      when READERS = 0 =>
      accept WRITE (I : ITEM) do
        PUT(I);
      end WRITE;
    or
      accept STOP_READ;
      READERS := READERS - 1;
    or
      terminate;
    end select;
  end loop;
end CONTROL;
```

The READ procedure is as before, the WRITE however is much simpler

```
procedure WRITE (I : ITEM) is
begin
  CONTROL.WRITE(I);
end WRITE;
```

This structure has the advantage that the WRITE operation now requires only one rendezvous whereas before it necessitated three.

Finally, with this READERS and WRITERS problem it is usual to give WRITE operations preference. This could be achieved by adding a guard to the START_READ accept statement:

```
when WRITE'COUNT = 0 =>
```

However as was indicated earlier (section 7.2) this is not a completely reliable structure. The first solution given has the benefit that once a WRITE operation is requested (WRITERS = TRUE) then no further START_READS are processed. A solution that requires two rendezvous for a READ and two for a WRITE is therefore necessary to give a reliable solution with WRITE having higher priority:

```
package READERS_WRITERS is
  procedure READ (I : out ITEM);  -- for some type ITEM.
  procedure WRITE (I : ITEM);
end READERS_WRITERS;

package body READERS_WRITERS is
  procedure PUT (I : ITEM) is separate;
  procedure GET (I : out ITEM) is separate;
  task CONTROL is
    entry START_READ;
    entry STOP_READ;
```

```
      entry REQUEST_WRITE;
      entry WRITE(I : ITEM);
  end CONTROL;

  procedure READ (I : out ITEM) is
  begin
    CONTROL.START_READ;
    GET(I);
    CONTROL.STOP_READ;
  end READ;

  procedure WRITE (I : ITEM) is
  begin
    CONTROL.REQUEST_WRITE;
    CONTROL.WRITE(I);
  end WRITE;
  task body CONTROL is
  READERS : NATURAL := 0;
  WRITERS : BOOLEAN := FALSE;
  begin
    loop
      select
        when not WRITERS =>
          accept START_READ;
          READERS := READERS + 1;
      or
        accept STOP_READ;
          READERS := READERS - 1;
      or
        when not WRITERS =>
          accept REQUEST_WRITE;
          WRITERS := TRUE;
      or
        when READERS = 0 =>
        accept WRITE(I : ITEM) do
          PUT(I);
        end WRITE;
        WRITERS := FALSE;
      or
        terminate;
      end select;
    end loop;
  end CONTROL;
end READERS_WRITERS;
```

8.2 The Specification of Synchronisation Packages

The readers and writers problem illustrates the use of a package, with procedure specifications, to encapsulate the necessary synchronisations for some resource usage. The package specification does not however give any indication as to the protocols that the package body will implement. Indeed it is usually not clear that a task can be delayed by calling one of these apparently straightforward procedures. The use of formal comments can help in the readability and understanding of such packages. Moreover, they form a valuable aid in the verification of programs. The simplest property that a synchronisation package can have is that it will give mutual exclusion over the specified subprograms:

```
package SHARED_VARIABLE is
   procedure READ   (I : out ITEM);
   procedure WRITE  (I : ITEM);
   --| mutual_exclusion(READ,WRITE).
end SHARED_VARIABLE;
```

In many more situations the package will act like a monitor in that it not only gives mutual exclusion over the specified subprograms but there is also the possibility that the calling task will be blocked due to some internal state of the resource. A simple example of this structure is the buffer where, for example, a call to GET from an empty buffer will cause the requesting task to be suspended:

```
package BUFFERS is
   type BUFFER is limited private;
   procedure PUT (I : ITEM; B: in out BUFFER);
   procedure GET (I : out ITEM; B : in out BUFFER);
   --| monitor (PUT, GET).
private
   .
   .
   .
end BUFFERS;
```

If the package included a function to test whether the buffer is empty or not (i.e. function EMPTY(B:BUFFER) return BOOLEAN) then this subprogram could be executed in parallel with the other procedures and its name would therefore not appear in the formal comment.

For more sophisticated synchronisations path expressions, (Campbell & Habermann, 1974) can be used to state quite explicitly the protocol that is, or should be, supported by the package body. The following comment implies mutual exclusion:

```
--| path 1 : (READ, WRITE) end
```

Here one procedure is permitted at a time and it is either a READ or a WRITE. In general, the readers/writers algorithm allows a number of simultaneous reads, the associated path expression becomes:

```
--| path 1 : ([READ], WRITE) end
```

the square brackets imply 'derestriction'. If a specific sequence of calls is required then a semicolon can replace the comma:

--| path 1 : (WRITE; READ) end

This now implies that there must be a strict sequence to the calls of the procedures; first WRITE, then READ, then WRITE etc. The appropriate comment for the bounded buffer example can now be developed, firstly there must be a PUT before a GET, so:

--| path 1 : (PUT; GET) end

But this is too restrictive for there can be up to n PUTS before a GET (for buffer size n) i.e. PUT can get ahead of GET by up to n calls:

--| path n : (PUT; GET) end

Unfortunately, this has now removed the mutual exclusion property. For a buffer, a call to PUT can be concurrent with a call to GET but not with another call to PUT; therefore the PUTs and GETs must be protected from themselves:

--| push n : (1 : (PUT); 1 : (GET)) end

If the construct were a stack then mutual exclusion would have to extend to both subprograms. This is indicated by giving a second path restriction - the implication being that both must be obeyed:

--| path n : (PUT; GET), 1 : (PUT, GET)

the first path allows calls to PUT to get ahead of calls to GET by n, the second part states that mutual exclusion on both procedures is necessary.

Path expressions were first defined by Campbell and Habermann (1974), since when a number of extensions and variations have been proposed; for example: Habermann (1975), Lauer and Campbell (1975), Campbell (1976), Flon and Habermann (1976), Lauer and Shields (1978), Lauer *et al* (1979) and Andler (1979). A Pascal-based systems programming language that implements a particular variant is described in Campbell and Kolstad (1979a,b). Although not all forms of condition synchronisation are amenable to being described by such expressions they have proved useful in specifying the semantics of concurrent computations; Shields (1979), Shaw (1980) and Best (1982). It is recommended that if a package is hiding a synchronisation task then some form of formal comment should be used to describe the embedded synchronisations. This comment will be useful both for the design of the system, where the package body may later be coded to the specification described in the comment, and in the general readability and maintainability of the program.

Another possible use of path expressions is in the automatic production of the necessary package body. Goldsack and Moreton (1982) describe a system by which an ordinary package which specifies and implements subprograms can be converted into a synchronisation package by means of a software tool acting upon a path expression comment. The tool expands the package body to include synchronisation tasks and then transforms the subprograms so that they make pre- and post- calls on these synchronisation tasks. Although the code produced is not as efficient as a hand coded version might be, considerable confidence can be placed in the software. Whether an automatic tool is used or not, the systematic coding of such packages from their specifications is clearly appropriate.

8.3 Library Packages and Tasks

Tasks themselves cannot form library units; they may however be contained in a library package or procedure. The task can either be completely hidden within the library package body or it can be specified in the visible part of the package:

```
package QUEUE is
   task BUFFER is
      entry PUT (I : ITEM);
      entry GET (I : out ITEM);
   end BUFFER;
end QUEUE;
```

The body of BUFFER would be contained within the body of QUEUE.

Tasks in a library package are special in that they have a package as master although in general one should consider the package as a passive construct. Library units and the corresponding library unit bodies are elaborated prior to the execution of the main program. If such a unit is a package that contains a task then the task will be activated after the elaboration of the declarative part of the package body. This activation phase will be completed before any statements within the package body are executed. (A null statement is assumed for package bodies without a sequence of statements). The overall effect of this is that a task within a library unit will be executable before the main program is executed.

The ARM unfortunately does not define whether, or when, such tasks are required to terminate. It is advised that 'terminate' alternatives are included on all select statements; this may mean, however, that the 'library' tasks will not be allowed to finish their work before disappearing. If the main procedure terminates (which it can because it is not the master of these tasks) then the run-time system may immediately shut down all tasks. This is particularly irritating if the task is performing an output function for the main program, but after completion of the main program (Burns & Robinson, 1984a). An alternative in these circumstances is to hold up this main program until all the tasks in the library packages have completed their work.

Although tasks cannot form library units a task body can be a subunit. The rules governing the use of this construct are identical to those associated with package bodies as subunits. In particular the subunit can be given an increased context (i.e. it can be declared with access to other library units). For example the package FILE_CABINET is defined as follows:

```
package FILE_CABINET is
   procedure EXTRACT (I : INDEX; R : out REC);
   procedure PLACE (I : INDEX; R : REC);
   -- REC is an externally defined record type
   INDEX_ERROR  : exception;
                      -- raised in EXTRACT and PLACE.
   CLASH_ERROR  : exception;  -- raised in PLACE.
   NULL_ERROR   : exception;  -- raised in EXTRACT.
   --| mutual_exclusion (EXTRACT, PLACE).
end FILE_CABINET;
```

The synchronisation is given as mutual exclusion although the example is of the readers/writers type. Exception are used to indicate an inappropriate index, an attempt to extract from an empty address, or an attempt to place a record on top of another one:

```
package body FILE_CABINET is
   task CONTROL is
      entry PUT (I : INDEX; R : REC);
      entry GET (I : INDEX; R : out REC);
   end CONTROL;

   procedure EXTRACT (I : INDEX; R : out REC) is
   begin
      CONTROL.GET(I,R);
         -- INDEX_ERROR or NULL_ERROR could be raised.
   end EXTRACT;
   procedure PLACE (I : INDEX; R : REC) is
   begin
      CONTROL.PUT(I,R);
         -- INDEX_ERROR or CLASS_ERROR could be raised.
   end PLACE;
   task body CONTROL is separate;
end FILE_CABINET;
```

Only the body of CONTROL requires access to the physical file that is used to store the records, therefore:

```
with DIRECT_IO;
separate (FILE_CABINET)
task body CONTROL is
  package REC_IO is new DIRECT_IO (REC);
  use REC_IO;
  FILE : FILE_TYPE;
  PC : POSITIVE_COUNT;
  TEMP_REC : REC;
  function CONVERT (I : INDEX) return POSITIVE_COUNT
                    is separate;
  NULL_REC : constant REC :=  (...);
begin
  OPEN (FILE, INOUT_FILE, "RECORD FILE");
  loop
    begin
      select
        accept PUT (I : INDEX; R : REC) do
          PC := CONVERT(I);
          READ(FILE, TEMP_REC, PC);
          if TEMP_REC /= NULL_REC then
            raise CLASH_ERROR;
          end if;
          WRITE(FILE, R, PC);
        end PUT;
      or
        accept GET (I : INDEX; R : out REC) do
          PC := CONVERT(I);
          READ(FILE, R, PC);
          if R = NULL_REC then
            raise NULL_ERROR;
          end if;
        end GET;
      or
        terminate;
      end select;
    exception
      when others => null;
    end;
  end loop;
end CONTROL;
```

The function CONVERT transforms a value of type INDEX to one of the subtype POSITIVE_COUNT that is needed to access the file. It is this function that may raise INDEX_ERROR:

```
separate (FILE_CABINET.CONTROL)
function CONVERT (I : INDEX) return POSITIVE_COUNT is
    .
    .
    .
end CONVERT;
```

8.4 Generic Packages with Tasks

Just as tasks cannot form library units they also cannot be used in the specification of a generic. These restrictions are sensible for, as was considered earlier, tasks do not themselves form a general module structure. The logical place to put a task is in a package; be it an ordinary one, a library unit or a generic. Tasks can, of course, be used in the body of a generic. Synchronisation packages can therefore be generalised to form generic library units. The existence of such units can then significantly reduce the effort needed to produce concurrent programs.

One of the most common synchronisation agents required is the buffer. Indeed, the language CHILL provides a general buffer structure. In Ada a generic package of the form given below should be available in all system libraries. The two generic parameters are the size of the buffer and the data type of the objects to be placed and removed from the buffer. For each buffer declared in the user program a task is activated, which encapsulates the data objects used to represent the buffer; mutual exclusion is therefore assured. The synchronisation task is an adaptation of that given earlier; rather than having an extra integer to count the number of items on the buffer it is noted that if TOP = BASE then the buffer is empty and if $(TOP + 1)mod(SIZE + 1) = BASE$ then the buffer is full (i.e. it has SIZE elements in it):

```
generic
  SIZE : POSITIVE;
  type ITEM is private;
package BUFFERS is
  type BUFFER is limited private;
  procedure PUT (I : ITEM; B : in out BUFFER);
  procedure GET (I : out ITEM; B : in out BUFFER);
  --| path SIZE : (1 : PUT); 1 (GET)) end
private
  task type BUFFER_TEMPLATE is
    entry PUT (I : ITEM);
    entry GET (I : out ITEM);
  end BUFFER_TEMPLATE;
  type BUFFER is new BUFFER_TEMPLATE;
end BUFFERS;

package body BUFFERS is
  procedure PUT (I : ITEM; B : in out BUFFER) is
  begin
    B.PUT(I);
  end PUT;

  procedure GET (I : out ITEM; B : in out BUFFER) is
  begin
    B.GET(I);
  end GET;
```

```
task body BUFFER_TEMPLATE is
  subtype BUFF_RANGE is INTEGER range 0..SIZE;
  BUFF : array (BUFF_RANGE) of ITEM;
  TOP, BASE : BUFF_RANGE := 0;
  SP1 : constant POSITIVE := SIZE + 1;
begin
  loop
    select
      when TOP /= BASE =>
      accept GET (I : out ITEM) do
        I := BUFF(BASE);
      end GET;
      BASE := (BASE + 1) mod SP1;
    or
      when (TOP + 1) mod SP1 /= BASE =>
      accept PUT (I : ITEM) do
        BUFF(TOP) := I;
      end PUT;
      TOP := (TOP + 1) mod SP1;
    or
      terminate;
    end select;
  end loop;
end BUFFER_TEMPLATE;
end BUFFERS;
```

9 ACCESS TYPES FOR TASKS

As a task object has a defined type it is possible to provide an access type for that task type:

```
task type T is
    .
    .
    .
end T;

type P is access T;
```

Task types with associated access variables are used where the dynamic generation of tasks is required during program execution. The task object itself is created by the evaluation of an allocator:

```
task type BUFFER is
    entry PUT (I : ITEM);
    entry GET (I : out ITEM);
end BUFFER;

type BUFFER_POINTER is access BUFFER;

PTR : BUFFER_POINTER := new BUFFER;
```

A buffer task object has been created and activated at the point of creation; its 'name' is PTR.all and the entry points are designated PTR.PUT and PTR.GET.

Although static tasks should be used, wherever possible, access variables are an important tool in circumstances where the underlying model requires dynamic creation or where it is necessary to exchange the name of some task object. The rules governing the behaviour of tasks created by an allocator are, however, somewhat different from those already described; in particular:

(a) a task object created by an allocator is activated by the evaluation of that allocator.

(b) unlike a static task object (whose master is that block, subprogram or task that created the object) a task that is created by the evaluation of an allocator is dependent on the unit which contains the access type definition.

The following stylised code illustrates the above points:

```
declare
  task type T;
  type A is access T;
  X : T;
  Y : A := new T;        -- activation of Y.all
  task body T is ...
begin
                         -- activation of X
  declare
    type L is access T;
    P : L := new T;      -- activation of P.all
    Q : T;
    R : A := new T;      -- activation of R.all
    S : A;
  begin
                         -- activation of Q
    S := new T;          -- activation of S
  end;                   -- awaits completion of Q and P.all
end;                     -- awaits completion of Y.all,
                         -- X, R.all and S.all
```

In this example Y.all, P.all and R.all become activated during the elaboration of the declarative parts of the blocks; by comparison the static tasks X and Q are only activated after the elaboration phase. The task designated by S.all illustrates how a task can be created, at any time, by the action of the allocator. Differences in the termination of tasks is best illustrated by comparing the three tasks P.all, Q and R.all. All of these tasks are 'declared' in the inner block; Q is a static task and therefore has this inner block as its master, P is an object of type L which is declared within this inner block, thus the task designated by P.all has the same master as Q. However R.all is obtained from the access type A which is declared in the outer block. As a consequence of this the inner block may terminate before R.all.

One of the main uses of access variables is in providing another means of naming tasks. The example given in section 5.3 showed how a task may be made aware of its own name by passing an array index as a parameter to an initialisation entry call (each task is a unique element in this array). Another method makes use of an access variable:

```
type T;              -- This is an incomplete declaration.

type T_NAME is access T;

FRED, JILL : T_NAME;

task type T is
  entry INITIALISE (NAME : T_NAME);
    .
    .
    .
end T;

task body T is
  ME : T_NAME;
    .
    .
    .
begin
  accept INITIALISE (NAME : T_NAME) do
    ME := NAME;
  end INITIALISE;
    .
    .
    .
end T;

FRED := new T;  -- The new tasks are
JILL := new T;  -- suspended on entry INITIALISE.

FRED.INITIALISE(FRED);
JILL.INITIALISE(JILL);
```

Within the body of the task use can be made of ME; for example, it could be passed as a parameter and used to construct a return call.

One of the inevitable consequences of the use of access variables is the possibility of producing aliases and anonymous tasks. If FRED and JILL are two variable of the same access type (the access type being obtained from a task type) then the following is illegal:

```
FRED.all := JILL.all;     -- not legal Ada
```

a task type is always limited private and therefore comparisons and assignments are not allowed. However

```
FRED := JILL;
```

is quite legal and means that FRED now designates the same task as JILL. As a consequence, the task that was designated by FRED is now anonymous and can never be accessed again; in particular, as it cannot be named so it cannot be aborted if it turns out to be a rogue task. It is desirable therefore that only terminated tasks are made anonymous (Nissen & Wallis, 1984). Duplicated names can also cause difficulties and lead to programs that are difficult to understand. Moreover the use of the abort statement can again lead to erroneous program behaviour; if it is necessary to abort the task designated by FRED above:

```
abort FRED.all;
```

then JILL.all is left 'dangling'. A more reliable solution would be to set all aliases to null before aborting the task:

```
JILL := null;
abort FRED.all;
```

9.1 Agents, Messengers and Mailboxes

The approach adopted in this book for the construction of concurrent programs in Ada has assumed an early recognition, in the design phase of any project, of processes (active) and agents (passive). Processes communicate with each other by the use of buffers; resources are encapsulated within packages and are protected by synchronisation tasks. Processes make entry calls; agents, in general, only accept entry calls (unless they themselves make use of other resources). This architecture is nevertheless limited in that a process must wait until an agent has dealt with its request. In many circumstances a 'no-wait send' is more appropriate. This type of decoupling of the system can be accomplished by using messenger or mailbox tasks as intermediaries between processes and resources.

A messenger task forwards a call (entry or subprogram) for a process; the call must have the form of a message (i.e. no out parameters) so that the process has no need to wait for a reply. Let P be a process task and let a resource package have the following definition:

```
package RESOURCE is
  type MESSAGE is ...
  procedure REQUEST (M : MESSAGE);
end RESOURCE;
```

Within the body of this task there may be a synchronisation task that will delay the processing of calls to REQUEST. If task P wishes to call REQUEST then, for some variable MESS of type MESSAGE, the statement

RESOURCE.REQUEST(MESS);

may unnecessarily delay P.

A messenger task is constructed to pass on the request:

```
task type MESSENGER is
  entry FORWARD (M : MESSAGE);
end MESSENGER;

task body MESSENGER is
  TEMP : MESSAGE;
begin
  accept FORWARD (M : MESSAGE) do
    TEMP := M;
  end FORWARD;
  RESOURCE.REQUEST(TEMP);
end MESSENGER;
```

If this task type is visible to P then the direct call on REQUEST can be replaced by:

```
declare
  PHIDIPPIDES : MESSENGER;
begin
  PHIDIPPIDES.FORWARD(MESS);
end;
```

Unfortunately this block will not terminate until the task PHIDIPPIDES terminates; this defeats the object of having this intermediate task! It is necessary to declare with the messenger task an access type:

```
type MESSENGERS is access MESSENGER;
```

Within P the correct use of the messenger is therefore:

```
declare
  PHIDIPPIDES : MESSENGERS := new MESSENGER;
begin
  PHIDIPPIDES.FORWARD(MESS);
end;
```

the block can now terminate freely and P is not delayed.

Messengers are useful agents if no data is to be returned to the process; unfortunately, this is not usually the case and it is necessary to use a different construct in these circumstances. The agent employed here is a mailbox. Consider first the structure without this intermediary:

```
package RESOURCE is
  type MESSAGE is ...
  type REPLY is ...
  procedure REQUEST (M : MESSAGE; R : out REPLY);
    .
    .
    .
end RESOURCE;
```

Within process P a call of REQUEST would have the form

```
RESOURCE.REQUEST(MESS, REP);
```

A mailbox is a task type that acts as a temporary buffer between the resource and the process. The resource will place the reply in the mailbox; the process will extract the reply from the mailbox when it is ready to do so.

```
task type MAILBOX is
  entry PUT (R : REPLY);
  entry GET (R : out REPLY);
end MAILBOX;

type ADDRESS is access MAILBOX;

task body MAILBOX is
  TEMP : REPLY;
begin
  accept PUT (R : REPLY) do
    TEMP := R;
  end PUT;
  accept GET (R : out REPLY) do
    R := TEMP;
  end GET;
end MAILBOX;
```

The REQUEST procedure then has the following specification:

```
procedure REQUEST (M : MESSAGE; A : ADDRESS);
```

and the calling program might include:

```
declare
  ADD : ADDRESS := new MAILBOX;
begin
  RESOURCE.REQUEST(MESS, ADD);
end;
```

As the parameters of REQUEST are now all of mode in the call to REQUEST could have been done within a messenger agent. Having made the request, process P can now proceed until it requires the reply – this it obtains by making an entry call on ADD.all:

```
ADD.GET(REP);
```

Within the body of RESOURCE the call to REQUEST is converted into an entry call on some synchronisation task SYN:

```
procedure REQUEST (M : MESSAGE; A : ADDRESS) is
begin
  SYN.REQ(M,A);
end REQUEST;
```

The task SYN will have an accept statement of the form:

```
accept REQ (M : MESSAGE; A : ADDRESS) do
  LOCAL_M := M;
  LOCAL_A := A;
end REQ;
-- processing to construct LOCAL_REPLY from LOCAL_M
LOCAL_A.PUT(LOCAL_REPLY);
```

Without the mailbox the processing must take place within the rendezvous:

```
accept REQ (M : MESSAGE; R : out REPLY) do
  -- processing to construct R from M.
end REQ;
```

Notice that an access type is necessary here for a note is made of the name of the buffer task. This can only be constructed as a copy of a pointer to the task rather than the task itself.

The use of messenger and mailbox agents helps to enforce the concurrent nature of the domain and reduces the tendency to tie task executions too closely together. Although a resource control agent will now need to make an entry call on another task, there is the benefit that the resource is receiving requests from a standard messenger and replying to a standard mailbox. Even if processes are aborted, the resource control task will be unaffected, as the agents will in general not themselves be aborted. Generic packages that define messengers and mailboxes for private parameter types can easily be constructed and, together with the generic buffer, form three important building blocks for concurrent programs.

As an example of how agents can improve the reliability of systems consider the readers and writers problem described in the previous chapter. The procedures READ and WRITE that are specified in the resource control package had the following form:

```
procedure READ (I : out ITEM) is
begin
  CONTROL.START_READ;
  GET(I);
  CONTROL.STOP_READ;
end READ;

procedure WRITE (I : ITEM) is
begin
  CONTROL.REQUEST_WRITE;
  CONTROL.START_WRITE;
  PUT(I);
  CONTROL.STOP_WRITE;
end WRITE;
```

If a task that is executing one of these procedures is aborted then the resource itself may be affected. For example, if the task was executing the WRITE procedure and had made a request to write but had not yet called

'STOP_WRITE' then all other calls to use the resource would be delayed, indefinitely. The synchronisations employed by the resource are not resilient to a failure in the calling task. This situation can be improved by providing an agent to perform the synchronisation calls for the user tasks; the write agent would therefore be:

```
task type WRITE_AGENT is
  entry WRITE (I : ITEM);
end WRITE_AGENT;

type WA_PTR is access WRITE_AGENT;

task body WRITE_AGENT is
begin
  select
    accept WRITE (I : ITEM) do
      CONTROL.REQUEST_WRITE;
      CONTROL.START_WRITE;
      PUT(I);
      CONTROL.STOP_WRITE;
    end WRITE;
  or
    terminate;
  end select;
end WRITE_AGENT;
```

The procedure WRITE now consists of creating a new agent followed by a rendezvous with this agent:

```
procedure WRITE (I : ITEM) is
  AGENT : WA_PTR := new WRITE_AGENT;
begin
  AGENT.WRITE(I);
end WRITE;
```

Apart from the overhead of an extra rendezvous, the operation of the READERS_WRITERS package will be unaffected by the use of agents. However, if a calling task is aborted, then the rendezvous with the agent may or may not have commenced. In the first case no calls to CONTROL have yet been made and hence the resource is unaffected (the terminate alternative on the agent allows it to terminate when the unit upon which it depends is left; Barnes, 1984) The second possibility (the rendezvous has started) is also reliable due to the rules governing the aborting of tasks in rendezvous; namely, if the calling task is aborted then the called task is unaffected and the rendezvous will terminate normally (i.e. all the calls to CONTROL will have been made).

9.2 Deallocation and Garbage Collection

For static objects, which have a single name, the scope rules of the language determine when data objects disappear and, therefore, when the memory they occupied can be reused. With dynamic objects the situation is more complex and a number of different strategies for deallocation exist. The two main approaches are:

(i)   the language provides an explicit disposal procedure,

(ii) the run-time system keeps a record of all accesses on a dynamic object and removes it when it is no longer referred to.

Ada provides a generic deallocation procedure that removes storage from designated objects. The procedure does not check to see if there are other references to the object. More significantly here, the ARM (13.10.1.8) prohibits the use of deallocation on access types if the object designated is a task. (To be accurate, the ARM states that the execution of such a procedure will have no effect.)

The use of the run-time system to periodically remove anonymous objects is usually called 'garbage collection'. There is however no requirement on an Ada implementation to provide this facility. The ARM merely rules that if such a facility exists then a task that is anonymous must also have terminated before it can be removed.

The lack of a requirement for a garbage collection facility in Ada is not surprising. Indeed it may be impractical for a real-time language to allow such a facility due to the resulting heavy and unpredictable overheads in execution time (Young, 1982). As the master of a task created by an allocator is that unit which contains the definition of the access type (not the declaration of the access object) then the only way of guaranteeing that a task's stack is completely removed is to have the access type itself go out of scope.

This unfortunate situation is particularly significant when it involves the use of messengers and mailboxes. The resources concerned will usually be defined within library packages as will the agents that are provided to access these resources. With the absence of a garbage collector the run-time system must associate, permanently, some storage with every task that is created by the operation of an allocator, (Wellings, 1984a,b 1985a). Even after the task has terminated it is still possible for a reference to the task to have been retained. The effects of this are quite subtle; an efficient implementation may only reserve a single word for the reference. Nevertheless the continuous execution of the program with the periodic creation and termination of agent tasks will eventually lead to storage exhaustion and program termination. Normal program testing may not be carried out over a sufficient timescale to bring about this condition.

This situation is serious and indicates that many of the example programs produced in text books are unreliable. Nevertheless, agents are useful and powerful program tools. In the next chapter an approach is outlined that makes use of a pool of reusable agents; this has been employed to counter the above difficulties.

10 RESOURCE MANAGEMENT

In many of the applications, for which the Ada programming language will be used, particular attention will have to be focused on the isolation and management of resources, especially those that are, in some sense, limited. Already in this book resource control examples have been given with packages being used to encapsulate the resource, and hidden tasks being structured to give the required synchronisations. In this chapter typical designs for resource management packages will be given and Ada will be examined to see how easy it is to produce the program structures required. This assessment is taken, largely, from Wellings (1984a,b 1985a).

Consider, as an example, a package that controls access to page frames of memory:

```
package PAGE_ALLOCATOR is
  type PAGE_ADDRESS is limited private;
  procedure REQUEST (SIZE : NATURAL;
                     P : out PAGE_ADDRESS);
  procedure FREE (P : PAGE_ADDRESS);
private
    ...
end PAGE_ALLOCATOR;
```

The type PAGE_ADDRESS is appropriate for the structure of the allocation algorithm; it could either be the start address of a set of frames (of length SIZE) or it could be a linked list of frame addresses. A task calling FREE need not state how many frames it is releasing - the allocation procedure will keep track of the number of frames associated with the PAGE_ADDRESS P. This has the benefit of increasing the reliability of the algorithm as a task cannot, in error, release more frames than it has allocated. Security could be further increased, if this is desirable, by having the requesting task leave an identifier that will then be checked against that of the releasing task to ensure that tasks are not attempting to free frames they have no access to.

The above structure is typical of a resource control package in that resources are requested and released with data passing between the package and the clients in order to perform the required transfer of resource. Because the resources are themselves not concurrent (i.e. they cannot be used by an unlimited number of clients concurrently) synchronisation rules must be imposed on the request procedure. The required conditions for resource management are as follows:

(i)   A requester must never be made to wait if sufficient resources are available and the manager is not otherwise occupied.

(ii)   The manager must be resilient in the face of the failure or aborting of requesting tasks. Only if the manager itself fails, should the system deadlock.

(iii)   If resources are lost at any time, due to failure of other tasks, then the manager must continue with a depleted pool.

(iv)   Neither the requester nor the manager must busy wait. If the resources required are not immediately available the requester task must be suspended.

The page frame example involves the control of a number of identical resources. If the requester is restricted to acquiring only one frame at a time then the structure of the management task is straightforward:

```
package body PAGE_ALLOCATOR is
  task MANAGER is
    entry GET (P : out PAGE_ADDRESS);
    entry PUT (P : PAGE_ADDRESS);
  end MANAGER;

  procedure REQUEST (P : out PAGE_ADDRESS) is
    -- SIZE is now 1.
  begin
    MANAGER.GET(P);
  end REQUEST;

  procedure FREE(P : PAGE_ADDRESS) is
  begin
    MANAGER.PUT(P);
  end FREE;

  procedure NEXT(P : out PAGE_ADDRESS) is
  begin
    -- returns address of next free frame.
  end NEXT;

  procedure ADD_FREE (P : PAGE_ADDRESS) is
  begin
    -- add P to free list.
  end ADD_FREE;
```

```
NUMBER_OF_FRAMES : constant := ...;
-- could be a generic parameter

task body MANAGER is
   FREED : NATURAL := NUMBER_OF_FRAMES;
begin
   loop
     select
       when FREED > 0 =>
       accept GET(P : out PAGE_ADDRESS) do
          FREED := FREED - 1;
          NEXT(P);
       end GET;
     or
       accept PUT(P : PAGE_ADDRESS) do
          FREED := FREED + 1;
          ADD_FREE(P);
       end PUT;
     or
       terminate;
     end select;
   end loop;
end MANAGER;
end PAGE_ALLOCATOR;
```

If resources are requested in a fixed quota then the above approach is adequate. The guard ensures that a rendezvous with the calling task will only take place if the request can be fully accommodated. Unfortunately this is not a general property. If the parameter SIZE is included in the request then there is a dilemma - although there are some free frames are there enough to meet a request of SIZE? This problem can be stated as follows:

(i)   The rendezvous with the requester should only take place if there are sufficient resources available.

(ii) The rendezvous must take place in order to read the 'in' parameter that is giving the size of the request.

The Ada guard cannot accommodate these requirements; a single request must be programmed as two distinct rendezvous.

10.1 Algorithms That Require Two Rendezvous

The above situation is of one of a number that have been discussed in this book where it is necessary for a task to make two rendezvous in order to complete what is really a single transaction. This situation leads to real difficulties, as little can be assumed about the behaviour of the two tasks between the rendezvous. The single transaction can in no way be constructed as atomic.

In order to illustrate the difficulties with this structure, two possible solutions will be introduced and criticised:

```
package PAGE_ALLOCATOR_1 is
  procedure REQUEST (S : SIZE; P : out PAGE_ADDRESS);
  procedure FREE (P : PAGE_ADDRESS);
end PAGE_ALLOCATOR_1;

package body PAGE_ALLOCATOR_1 is
  task MANAGER is
    entry GET (S : SIZE; P : out PAGE_ADDRESS;
               DONE : out BOOLEAN);
    entry PUT (S : SIZE; P : PAGE_ADDRESS);
    entry RETRY (S : SIZE; P : out PAGE_ADDRESS;
                 DONE : out BOOLEAN);
  end MANAGER;

  procedure REQUEST (S : SIZE; P : out PAGE_ADDRESS) is
    SUCCESSFUL : BOOLEAN;
  begin
    MANAGER.GET(S,P,SUCCESSFUL);
    while not SUCCESSFUL loop
      MANAGER.RETRY(S,P,SUCCESSFUL);
    end loop;
  end REQUEST;

  procedure FREE (P:PAGE_ADDRESS) is
  begin
    MANAGER.PUT(P);
  end FREE;

  procedure NEXT(P : out PAGE_ADDRESS) is ...
  procedure ADD_FREE(P : PAGE_ADDRESS; S: out SIZE) is ;
          -- ADD_FREE returns the number of pages
          -- released; it calculates this from P.
  NUMBER_OF_FRAMES : constant := ... ;

  task body MANAGER is
    FREED : NATURAL := NUMBER_OF_FRAMES;
    SZ : SIZE;
    procedure TRY(S : SIZE; PA : out PAGE_ADDRESS;
            FREED : in out NATURAL; OK : out BOOLEAN) is
    begin
      if S >= FREED then
        FREED := FREED - S;
        OK := TRUE;
        NEXT(PA);
      else
        OK := FALSE;
        PA:= null;
      end if;
    end TRY;
```

```
begin
  loop
    select
      accept GET(S : SIZE; P : out PAGE_ADDRESS;
                 DONE : out BOOLEAN) do
        TRY(S,P,FREED,DONE);
      end GET;
    or
      accept PUT(P : PAGE_ADDRESS) do
        ADD_FREE(P,SZ);
        FREED := FREED + SZ;
      end PUT;
      for I in 1..RETRY'COUNT loop
        select
          accept RETRY (S : SIZE;P : out PAGE_ADDRESS;
                        DONE : out BOOLEAN) do
            TRY(S,P,FREED,DONE);
          end RETRY;
        else
          exit;
        end select;
      end loop;
    or
      terminate;
    end select;
  end loop;
end MANAGER;
end PAGE_ALLOCATOR_1;
```

With this algorithm a requesting task will first attempt to get S frames by calling GET. If there are not enough free frames then the task will be suspended on RETRY. The only way more free frames can become available is for FREE to be called. When this happens the entry PUT is accepted and the value of FREED is updated. It is now possible for one or more of the sleeping request tasks to be satisfied. Each, in turn, has RETRY accepted and either the resources allocated or the refusal flag set. If the flag is set the calling task will loop around and again be suspended on RETRY. By using the attribute COUNT, and the fact that the entry queues are FIFO, each waiting task is checked to see if it can continue every time resources are released.

This algorithm meets condition 2-4 of those introduced at the beginning of this chapter. In particular, if the calling task fails during a call to request then in all possible situations the resource manager is unaffected:

(i)   Failed while on entry queue for GET - removed from queue.
(ii) Failed during execution of the GET (or RETRY) rendezvous - rendezvous will complete normally, resources may be lost but otherwise manager will continue.
(iii) Failed while on entry queue for RETRY - removed from queue, value of COUNT decremented.

The only other possibility is for the third situation to be such that a value of COUNT has been taken by the MANAGER task before the client task failed. All that will happen here is for the inner 'for loop' to execute one more time than is absolutely necessary with the consequence that either the 'else' clause will be taken or one waiting task will cycle through the RETRY twice.

Where this solution is deficient is in terms of condition 1; it is possible for a task to be suspended within REQUEST although there are ample resources available. Consider the following interleaving:

(a) requesting task calls GET but is not allocated resources as there are insufficient to meet the request.

(b) MANAGER task completes this rendezvous, re-executes the select statement and is suspended.

(c) some other task calls PUT (via procedure FREE), this entry is accepted and completed. Number of resource available is increased.

(d) the MANAGER tests all tasks suspended on RETRY, leaves the inner and outer select statements, loops round, re-executes the outer select and is suspended waiting on either a call to PUT or GET.

(e) the original requesting task now calls RETRY.

In this situation there may be sufficient resources available for the task that has just been suspended in RETRY but the MANAGER will not process RETRYs again until after another call to PUT. This clearly violates the first condition.

The difficulty is a race condition, between the two rendezvous (in this example GET and RETRY) it is not possible to assume that the client task will get to the second rendezvous before the server. No direct variant of this example avoids this problem.

The second example attempts to overcome the shortcomings of the first 'solution' by making the MANAGER task wait until the client task has made the second entry call (only the task body is different in this example):

```
task body MANAGER is
    TOTAL : NATURAL := 0;
            -- Number of tasks waiting on RETRY or
            -- in the process of calling RETRY.
    S_TOTAL : NATURAL;
        -- used as a temporary copy of TOTAL.
    FREED : NATURAL := NUMBER_OF_FRAMES;
    SZ : SIZE;
```

```
begin
  loop
    select
      accept GET(S:SIZE; P:out PAGE_ADDRESS;
                         DONE: out BOOLEAN) do
          if S>= FREED then
            FREED := FREED - S;
            DONE := TRUE;
            NEXT(P);
          else
            DONE := FALSE;
            P := null;
            TOTAL := TOTAL + 1;
          end if;
        end GET;
    or
      accept PUT(P : PAGE_ADDRESS) do
        ADD_FREE(P,SZ);
        FREED := FREED + SZ;
      end PUT;
      S_TOTAL := TOTAL;
      for I in 1.. S_TOTAL loop
        accept RETRY(S:SIZE; P:out PAGE_ADDRESS;
                           DONE:out BOOLEAN) do
          if S>FREED then
            FREED := FREED - S;
            DONE := TRUE;
            TOTAL := TOTAL - 1;
            NEXT(P);
          else
            DONE := FALSE;
            P := null;
          end if;
        end RETRY;
      end loop;
    or
      terminate;
    end select;
  end loop;
end MANAGER;
```

The MANAGER is now totally committed to processing all possible calls to RETRY including those that have not yet been made. This avoids a race condition but commits the MANAGER too strongly; for if the requesting task is aborted then the MANAGER will be deadlocked. Even if a family entry was used so that retries were made on a unique family member there is still the fundamental problem; if the manager waits for the client the algorithm is not resilient to client failure; if the MANAGER does not wait then the client may be unnecessarily delayed due to a race condition.

One means of eliminating the problem of unpredictable aborts, of client tasks, is to use an agent to do the synchronising on behalf of the clients (see chapter 9). The agent will need to make the calls on the MANAGER and return the PAGE_ADDRESS to the client:

```
task type AGENTS is
  entry FORWARD (S : SIZE);
  entry REPLY (P : out PAGE_ADDRESS);
end AGENTS;

type AGENT is access AGENTS;

task body AGENTS is
  LOCAL_S : SIZE;
  LOCAL_P : PAGE_ADDRESS;
  SUCCESSFUL : BOOLEAN;
begin
  accept FORWARD(S:SIZE) do
    LOCAL_S := S;
  end FORWARD;
  MANAGER.GET(LOCAL_S,LOCAL_P,SUCCESSFUL);
  while not SUCCESSFUL loop
    MANAGER.RETRY(LOCAL_S,LOCAL_P,SUCCESSFUL);
  end loop;
  accept REPLY(P:out PAGE_ADDRESS) do
    P := LOCAL_P;
  end REPLY;
end AGENTS;
```

The procedure REQUEST then becomes:

```
procedure REQUEST (S : SIZE;P : out PAGE_ADDRESS) is
  AGE:AGENT := new AGENTS;
begin
  AGE.FORWARD(S);
  AGE.REPLY(P);
end REQUEST;
```

This agent does enable the MANAGER to be unconcerned about the client being aborted, for it only communicates with the agent. Client failure will mean that that particular agent is deadlocked but this will not affect the overall system. The shortcomings of this method are twofold; firstly it is inefficient in terms of context switching (a minimum of 8 task switches being needed). Secondly, as was indicated in chapter 9, without a garbage collector the use of agents is not acceptable for the program will take up an increasing amount of storage as it runs. The only solution that remains, therefore, is to have a finite pool of reusable agents that can be dynamically built if the maximum number of concurrent calls to REQUEST is not known. A complete solution that uses this method is given in the next section.

The lack of a satisfactory solution to this kind of resource allocation problem may lead to changes in the language definition at some time in the future. These difficulties arise as a direct result of the interaction of four language features:

(a) A task must accept an entry call before it knows whether or not it can satisfy any request contained within it.

(b) Once a rendezvous has commenced it is not possible to requeue the calling task directly, it must requeue itself by way of a further entry call.

(c) A task can be aborted unconditionally by any other task.

(d) In general, an accepting task is unaware of the identity of a client task.

Language changes may focus on any of the first three features. An attempt to remove (d) would have too profound a consequence on the nature and structure of the Ada rendezvous. One possible change would be to allow a guard to have access to 'in' parameters and thereby ensure that the associated request could be fully met before accepting the rendezvous. The language SR (Andrews 1982) does have such a mechanism although the implementation may be significantly more time consuming than that used in the present version of Ada. For example, it will not be possible to limit the evaluation of each guard to once per execution of the select statement; each entry call will necessitate re-evaluation of the guard.

Another possibility, discussed by Silberschatz(1984), is to allow a calling task to be requeued during the execution of the rendezvous if a satisfactory termination of the rendezvous is not possible. This can be achieved by introducing an **await** statement which can only be placed within an accept statement, which is itself part of a select statement:

```
await(< boolean_expression >);
```

If the boolean expression evaluates FALSE then the calling task is suspended (an activation record is used to save information about the partial state of the computation) and the select statement is terminated. When the select statement is next executed the boolean expression is again evaluated (at the same time as any guards) and if a TRUE value is obtained the suspended rendezvous can be selected and the execution continued. Clearly more than one rendezvous may be suspended on an await statement; whether the queue discipline is FIFO like the accept statement or priority ordered as Silberschatz suggests is a matter of debate.

In this chapter a single example has been used to illustrate the required structure for a package implementing a resource management algorithm. As indicated in chapter 8 a formal comment should be used within the package specification in order to express the necessary synchronisations.

For many algorithms, these synchronisations can only be expressed in terms of the history of the resource. In the example given earlier, the distribution of free page frames may determine whether or not a request could be met. This distribution is itself a result of previous allocations. Unfortunately there is no succinct form for expressing the history of an object (Hill 1984). With simple algorithms, however, it is possible to provide the necessary information:

```
generic
  MAX : NATURAL;
package RESOURCE is
  procedure PUT(S : NATURAL);
  procedure GET(S : NATURAL);
  -- GET(S) iff MAX - N(GET) + N(PUT) > S
end RESOURCE;
```

A generic is used to introduce the parameter MAX (the maximum number of free resources); the comment should be read as follows - "a call to GET with the parameter value S will be successful if and only if the present number of free resources is greater than S. The present number is obtained by subtracting, from the maximum, the number allocated by successful calls to GET, and adding the number returned by successful calls to PUT".

Where it is natural for a task to require the concurrent usage of more than one type of resource then a single package should be used to encapsulate all of these resources. The package body can then deal with the possibility of deadlocks that could arrive if separate packages are used. A reliable deadlock prevention algorithm will need to know the identity of all requesting tasks in order to impose a 'discipline' on these clients. One possible approach is to list all resources in a predefined order and then make requesters access the resources in that order. Other approaches are possible; however care must always be taken to ensure that the possibility of deadlocks is not inherent in the system design.

10.2 A General Purpose Management Package

An example resource control package which uses agents was given earlier. For each client request a new agent is created; once the request has been met this agent terminates. However, although this simple structure would appear to be adequate it was noted earlier that deallocation difficulties on a system without an appropriate garbage collection facility will lead to storage exhaustion. It is therefore necessary to employ reusable agents.

This section provides code for a generic resource control package. In addition to the conditions described earlier the following criteria is also accommodated:

(a) A task obtaining a resource will leave an identification that may be checked when the resource is returned.

(b) Only sufficient reusable agents will be created to meet the heaviest load yet encountered.

(c) An agent may check to see if the client is still active. If it is not, the agent will return itself to the pool of free agents and return the acquired resources to the resource manager.

(d) All tasks associated with resource management must terminate when the program unit that is using the resource wishes to terminate.

The specification of the generic package is as follows:

```
generic
    MAX : INTEGER;
    DELAY_DURATION : DURATION := 60.0;
    type ADDRESS is private;
    type IDENTITY is private;
    type RESOURCE is private;
    with procedure ALLOCATE(A : ADDRESS; R : out RESOURCE;
                            I : IDENTITY; SUC : out BOOLEAN);
    with procedure DEALLOCATE(R : RESOURCE; I : IDENTITY;
                            AL : out BOOLEAN);
    with function HAS_TERMINATED(I : IDENTITY)
                                            return BOOLEAN;
package RESOURCE_MANAGER is
    procedure REQUEST(A : ADDRESS; R : out RESOURCE;
                            I : IDENTITY);
    procedure RELEASE(R : RESOURCE; I : IDENTITY);
    RELEASE_ERROR : exception;  --raised by RELEASE
    CREATION_ERROR : exception;  --raised by REQUEST
    -- monitor (REQUEST,RELEASE)
end RESOURCE_MANAGER;
```

The parameter MAX stands for the maximum number of agent tasks that can be created. This value can be arbitrarily large, but is included to enable the maximum storage requirement to be evaluated if this is desirable. If a request for resources would cause this maximum number to be invalidated than the exception CREATION_ERROR is raised.

In order to meet criteria (c) above, each agent must poll its client to see if the task is still active. Busy wait loops are, in general, too inefficient unless the frequency of the loop is low. The parameter DELAY_DURATION allows the delay between tests to be specified; the default value is sixty seconds.

The three type parameters allow data structures to be defined to represent the resource, client identification and the address of the resource. Client identification could be an access type for the task, an array index, a request key or some other representation. The address is similarly arbitrary and enables a type to be constructed that will encompass all information necessary to request a particular resource. As no structure is assumed for these three types, within the generic package, RESOURCE, ADDRESS and IDENTITY are all defined as 'private'. This gives the user of this generic package considerable flexibility.

The procedures that actually manipulate the resource must be provided when an instantiation of the generic is undertaken. ALLOCATE will provide a RESOURCE R when given an ADDRESS A; alternatively, the resource may already be allocated in which case the out parameter SUC must be set to FALSE. This procedure also requires an IDENTITY I. To return the resource, DEALLOCATION is provided; this procedure may check to see that the identity of the client returning the resource is equal to that which obtained it. If this is not the case the out parameter AL is set to FALSE. The effect of which will be to raise the exception RELEASE_ERROR. In situations where checking is inappropriate AL must always return TRUE.

The final subprogram parameter is HAS_TERMINATED which, when given an IDENTITY I, should test to see if the task associated with I has terminated. For example, if IDENTITY is an access type for the task type representing the client, then the procedure:

```
function TERM(I  :  IDENTITY) return BOOLEAN is
begin
   return I.all'TERMINATED;
end TERM;
```

would be an appropriate one to 'pass' to HAS_TERMINATED. If this termination check is not required then a simple function which always returns FALSE will suffice.

Having provided two constants, three types and three subprograms it is possible to instantiate a resource control package. (The control package given below is resilient to exceptions being raised in the user defined subprograms). This package provides procedures for requesting and releasing resources. The use of these procedures gives controlled access to the unprotected ALLOCATE and DEALLOCATE subprograms. Care must be taken when instantiating this generic package to ensure that the procedures associated with ALLOCATE and DEALLOCATE cannot be called directly by any other part of the program. Also specified in the generic package are the two exceptions RELEASE_ERROR and CREATION_ERROR; these have already been described.

Before giving the code that constitutes the package body an example of the use of RESOURCE_MANAGER will be given.

```
package PAGE_ALLOCATOR is
   MAX_SIZE : constant := 16;
   type PAGE_ADD is ...
   type SIZE is new INTEGER range 1..MAX_SIZE;
   type KEY is private;
   procedure REQ(K : KEY; PA :   out PAGE_ADD; S : SIZE);
   procedure FREE(K : KEY; PA : PAGE_ADD);
   procedure GET_KEY(K : out KEY);
   KEY_ERROR : exception;  -- raised in REQ
private
   type KEY is
   record
      VAL : INTEGER := INTEGER'FIRST;
   end record;
end PAGE_ALLOCATOR;
```

The resource concerned (PAGE_ADD) is the start address for a block of pages. Requests for pages must state the size of the requirement; SIZE is therefore synonymous with ADDRESS. Identification is undertaken, in this example, by a key mechanism. To obtain a block of pages a client must first acquire a key and then call REQ, for example:

```
GET_KEY(K);
REQ(K,PAGE,8);  -- request for 8 pages
```

To release these pages FREE is called with the same key. The implementation of GET_KEY is very simple; an integer counter cycles around all the integer values. It is therefore possible, although unlikely, for the same key to be given to two active clients. Note, for security the type KEY must be private to stop keys being assigned new values externally; also a record type is used to enable an initial value to be given to objects of type KEY. This initial value is used to ensure that GET_KEY is called by each client; failure to do so will result in the exception KEY_ERROR being raised in REQ. To stop the key value being copied KEY should be defined as limited private; unfortunately the generic RESOURCE_MANAGER presented here must itself copy the key value and hence only a private type is allowed.

```
with RESOURCE_MANAGER;
package body PAGE_ALLOCATOR is
  MAX_REQUESTS : constant := 64;
  CODE : KEY;

  procedure NEXT(S : SIZE; PA : out PAGE_ADD;
                  K : KEY; DONE : out BOOLEAN) is separate;
      -- NEXT allocates pages by keeping a linked list of
          -- free page areas.

  procedure ADD_FREE(PA : PAGE_ADD; K : KEY;
                        ALLOWED : out BOOLEAN) is separate;
    -- ADD_FREE will check K against recorded user of PA.
  function DUMMY(K : KEY) return BOOLEAN is
  begin
    return FALSE;
    --no check on client termination
  end DUMMY;

  package PAGE_MANAGER is new RESOURCE_MANAGER(
          MAX => MAX_REQUESTS,
          ADDRESS => SIZE,
          IDENTITY => KEY,
          RESOURCE => PAGE_ADD,
          ALLOCATE => NEXT,
          DEALLOCATE => ADD_FREE,
          HAS_TERMINATED => DUMMY);
  use PAGE_MANAGER;

  procedure GET_KEY(K : out KEY) is
  begin
    CODE.VAL := CODE.VAL + 1;
    K := CODE;
  exception
    when CONSTRAINT_ERROR =>
      CODE.VAL := INTEGER'FIRST + 1;
      K := CODE;
  end GET_KEY;

  procedure REQ(K : KEY; PA : out PAGE_ADD; S : SIZE) is
    PADD : PAGE_ADD;
  begin
    if K.VAL = INTEGER'FIRST then
      raise KEY_ERROR;
    end if;
    REQUEST(S,PADD,K);
    PA := PADD;
  end REQ;

  procedure FREE(K : KEY; PA : PAGE_ADD) is
  begin
    RELEASE(PA,K);
  end FREE;
end PAGE_ALLOCATOR;
```

10.3 Code for the Generic Package

The package body for RESOURCE_MANAGER has the following
implementation (and for completeness the specification is repeated):

```
generic
  MAX : INTEGER;
  DELAY_DURATION : DURATION := 60.0;
  type ADDRESS is private;
  type IDENTITY is private;
  type RESOURCE is private;
  with procedure ALLOCATE(A : ADDRESS; R : out RESOURCE;
                   I : IDENTITY; SUC : out BOOLEAN);
  with procedure DEALLOCATE(R : RESOURCE; I : IDENTITY;
                             AL : out BOOLEAN);
  with function HAS_TERMINATED(I : IDENTITY)
                                          return BOOLEAN;
package RESOURCE_MANAGER is
  procedure REQUEST(A : ADDRESS; R : out RESOURCE;
                                  I : IDENTITY);
  procedure RELEASE(R : RESOURCE; I : IDENTITY);
  RELEASE_ERROR : exception;  --raised by RELEASE
  CREATION_ERROR : exception; --raised by REQUEST
  -- monitor (REQUEST,RELEASE)
end RESOURCE_MANAGER;

package body RESOURCE_MANAGER is
  type AGENT_OBJECT;
  type AGENT is access AGENT_OBJECT;
  task type AGENT_TASK is
    entry INITIALISE(A : AGENT);
    entry INPUT(ADD : ADDRESS; ID : IDENTITY);
    entry OUTPUT(R : out RESOURCE);
  end AGENT_TASK;
  type AGENT_OBJECT is
  record
    TK : AGENT_TASK;
    PTR : AGENT;
  end record;

  task AGENT_MANAGER is
    -- This task controls access to the pool
    -- of reusable agents.
    entry REQUEST(A : out AGENT);
    entry REPLACE(A : AGENT);
  end AGENT_MANAGER;
  task CONTROL is
    -- This task controls access to
    -- the resource by making
    -- safe calls on ALLOCATE and DEALLOCATE.
    entry REQUEST(A : ADDRESS; R : out RESOURCE;
               I : IDENTITY; SUCCESSFUL : out BOOLEAN);
    entry RETRY(A : ADDRESS; R : out RESOURCE;
               I : IDENTITY; SUCCESSFUL : out BOOLEAN);
    entry RELEASE(R : RESOURCE; I : IDENTITY);
  end CONTROL;
```

```
      procedure REQUEST(A : ADDRESS; R : out RESOURCE;
                                     I : IDENTITY) is
        AGT : AGENT;
      begin
        AGENT_MANAGER.REQUEST(AGT);
        AGT.TK.INPUT(A,I);
        AGT.TK.OUTPUT(R);
      end REQUEST;
      procedure RELEASE(R : RESOURCE; I :IDENTITY) is
      begin
        CONTROL.RELEASE(R,I);
      end RELEASE;
      task body AGENT_TASK is separate;
      task body AGENT_MANAGER is separate;
      task body CONTROL is separate;
    end RESOURCE_MANAGER;
```

The CONTROL task gives mutual exclusion over calls to ALLOCATE and
DEALLOCATE by providing an entry to REQUEST a resource, RELEASE a
resource or RETRY (following an unsuccessful call to REQUEST). All
outstanding calls on RETRY are processed following each call to RELEASE.
The body for CONTROL is:

```
      separate(RESOURCE_MANAGER)
      task body CONTROL is
        SUC : BOOLEAN;
        ALLOWED : BOOLEAN;
        TOTAL : NATURAL := 0;
              -- Number of calls to be accepted on RETRY
        TOTAL_COPY : NATURAL;
      begin
        loop
          begin
            select
              accept REQUEST(A : ADDRESS; R : out RESOURCE;
                  I : IDENTITY; SUCCESSFUL : out BOOLEAN) do
                begin
                  ALLOCATE(A,R,I,SUC);
                exception
                  when others =>
                    SUC := FALSE;
                end;
                SUCCESSFUL := SUC;
              end REQUEST;
              if not SUC then TOTAL := TOTAL + 1; end if;
            or
              accept RELEASE(R : RESOURCE; I : IDENTITY) do
                DEALLOCATE(R,I,ALLOWED);
                if not ALLOWED then
                  raise RELEASE_ERROR;
                end if;
              end RELEASE;
              TOTAL_COPY := TOTAL;
```

```
          for T in 1 .. TOTAL_COPY loop
            accept RETRY(A : ADDRESS; R : out RESOURCE;
                I : IDENTITY; SUCCESSFUL : out BOOLEAN) do
              begin
                ALLOCATE(A,R,I,SUC);
                exception
                  when others =>
                      SUC := FALSE;
                end;
                SUCCESSFUL := SUC;
              end RETRY;
              if SUC then TOTAL := TOTAL - 1; end if;
            end loop;
        or
            terminate;
        end select;
      exception
        when OTHERS => null;
            -- This catches RELEASE_ERROR and exceptions
            -- raised in DEALLOCATE.
      end;
    end loop;
end CONTROL;
```

Requests to CONTROL are made on behalf on a client by an AGENT_TASK. Access to the pool of free agent tasks is controlled by the single task AGENT_MANAGER. The procedure REQUEST in the body of RESOURCE_MANAGER therefore consists of three statements: (1) obtain an agent task - in reality a pointer, AGENT, to such a task; (2) pass address and identification to this agent; and (3) obtain resource, or resources, from the agent, as follows:

```
procedure REQUEST(A : ADDRESS; R : out RESOURCE;
                              I : IDENTITY) is
  AGT : AGENT;
begin
  AGENT_MANAGER.REQUEST(AGT);
  AGT.TK.INPUT(A,I);
  AGT.TK.OUTPUT(R);
end REQUEST;
```

The code for AGENT_TASK is as follows:

```
separate(RESOURCE_MANAGER)
task body AGENT_TASK is
  AGT : AGENT;
  AD : ADDRESS;
  ID : IDENTITY;
  RE : RESOURCE;
  SUCCESSFUL : BOOLEAN;
begin
  accept INITIALISE(A : AGENT) do
    AGT := A;
  end INITIALISE;
```

```
        loop
          select
            accept INPUT(ADD : ADDRESS; ID :IDENTITY) do
              AD := ADD;
              AGENT_TASK.ID := ID;
            end INPUT;
          or
            terminate;
          end select;
          CONTROL.REQUEST(AD,RE,ID,SUCCESSFUL);
          while not SUCCESSFUL loop
            CONTROL.RETRY(AD,RE,ID,SUCCESSFUL);
          end loop;
          loop
            begin
              select
                accept OUTPUT(R : out RESOURCE) do
                  R := RE;
                end OUTPUT;
                exit;
              or
                delay DELAY_DURATION;
                  if HAS_TERMINATED(ID) then
                    CONTROL.RELEASE(RE,ID);
                    -- The resources are returned to CONTROL
                    exit;
                  end if;
              or
                terminate;
              end select;
            exception
              when others => null;
                -- Catches exceptions raised in HAS_TERMINATED
            end;
          end loop;
          AGENT_MANAGER.REPLACE(AGT);
                -- Return to free pool
        end loop;
      end AGENT_TASK;
```

The agent task takes responsibility for replacing itself in the pool of free
agents by calling REPLACE in AGENT_MANAGER. It must therefore be
initialised with a pointer to itself. The code for AGENT_MANAGER is:

```
separate(RESOURCE_MANAGER)
task body AGENT_MANAGER is
  TOP : AGENT := null; -- points to next free agent
  TEMP_AGENT : AGENT;
  NUMBER_CREATED : NATURAL := 0;
begin
  loop
    begin
      select
        accept REQUEST(A : out AGENT) do
          if TOP = null then   -- no free agent
            if NUMBER_CREATED < MAX then
              -- create new agent task
              TEMP_AGENT := new AGENT_OBJECT;
              TEMP_AGENT.TK.INITIALISE(TEMP_AGENT);
              A := TEMP_AGENT;
              TEMP_AGENT := null;
              NUMBER_CREATED := NUMBER_CREATED + 1;
            else
              raise CREATION_ERROR;
            end if;
          else   -- there is a free agent
            TEMP_AGENT := TOP;
            TOP := TOP.PTR;
            TEMP_AGENT.PTR := null;
            A := TEMP_AGENT;
            TEMP_AGENT := null;
          end if;
        end REQUEST;
      or
        accept REPLACE(A : AGENT) do
          TEMP_AGENT := A;
        end REPLACE;
        TEMP_AGENT.PTR := TOP;
        TOP := TEMP_AGENT;
        TEMP_AGENT := null;
      or
        terminate;
      end select;
    exception
      when CREATION_ERROR => null;
    end;
  end loop;
end AGENT_MANAGER;
```

Finally, it should be remembered that although this generic package is structured to meet all the design criteria outlined earlier, its use may be expensive in computer time. A single call to request a resource will involved, at least, seven context-switches!

11 TASK SCHEDULING

The use of the concept of concurrency leads to a model of tasking in which each task is executing on its own logical processor. Unfortunately, few implementations will have the luxury of one processor per task and, as a result, there will be situations in which more tasks wish to execute than there are processors on which to run them. In this situation, it is necessary for the run-time system to choose which tasks to execute and, by implication, which are delayed.

On a single or limited processor system the ARM gives no guidance on how tasks should be interleaved; however, in order to minimise wasteful task switching many implementations will choose the following algorithm. A task, once it is executing on a processor, will continue to execute until it is no longer in the state of 'executable'. Its removal from this state will only occur if it:

(a) completes its execution,

(b) executes a delay statement,

(c) executes an entry call,

(d) elaborates a sub-task,

(e) executes an accept statement upon which no entry call has been made,

(f) executes a select statement in which there is no else part and no outstanding entry calls on any open accept alternatives.

The only exception to this rule occurs if there is an interrupt entry into some other task, see chapter 12. A consequence of this scheduling algorithm is that if a task does none of the above actions then it will continue, indefinitely, on the processor and delay all other tasks. For example, a task continually testing the value of a shared variable may, if no delay statement is built into the loop, have complete control of the processor. The task that wants to execute, so that it can update the shared variable, will never be swapped in to do so.

From portability considerations, any Ada program must execute reliably on a single processor or distributed system. Programmers must, therefore, exercise an element of cognitive dissonance so that they can simultaneously use fully parallel and restricted sequential models of their programs. The restrictive model prohibits the use of busy waits (which may be acceptable in parallel systems); the parallel model debars the use of shared variables because of multiple update difficulties (although on a single processor implementation, only one task will be updating the variable at a time).

In situations where there are more processes wishing to run than can be accommodated it is often useful, particularly in operating systems, to prescribe priorities to each process so that the run-time system can make a more sensible decision as to which process to run. Priorities can be used in Ada by means of a pragma.

11.1 The Priority Pragma

When a task becomes suspended, the next task to run will be chosen arbitrarily from the set of tasks able to run, unless priorities have been assigned to tasks. In the absence of priorities it can be assumed that the run-time system will be fair, in that a task that is executable will not have to wait indefinitely before it is actually executing (unless a set of tasks has monopolised the available processors so that no tasks are being suspended).

A task can be assigned a priority by placing the appropriate pragma in the task specification or task type specification:

```
task BUFFER is
   pragma PRIORITY(X);
   entry PUT(I : ITEM);
   entry GET(I : out ITEM);
end BUFFER;
```

where X is a static expression of subtype PRIORITY (of type integer). A task's priority cannot, therefore, be changed during execution of the program. The range of PRIORITY is implementation dependent (it could be only 1..1!) and is defined in the predefined library package SYSTEM. A low value of X implies a low priority. Not all tasks within a program need to be given priorities but, once given, a task cannot change its priority. (In addition to tasks, the main program may also be assigned a priority.) The significance of assigning a priority to a task is given by the following rule from the ARM:

"If two tasks with different priorities are both eligible for execution and could sensibly be executed using the same physical processors and same physical resources, then it cannot be the case that the task with the lower priority is executing while the task with the higher priority is not."(ARM 9.8.4).

This rule is somewhat imprecise. No mention is made of tasks without priorities or tasks with identical priorities, and hence nothing should be implied. In addition, the phrase 'could sensibly be executed' is hardly a formal definition of allowable semantics but it is necessary to prevent inappropriate task switching in a highly distributed implementation.

Where two tasks are in rendezvous, then the priority of the rendezvous itself is the higher value of the priorities of the two tasks concerned. This rule is necessary to ensure that a high priority task is not unnecessarily held up merely by being in a rendezvous with a low priority one. If only one of the tasks has a priority then the rendezvous will have a priority of at least that value.

Caution must be taken when using priorities; the ARM itself warns that:

"Priorities should be used only to indicate relative degrees of urgency; they should not be used for task synchronisations", (ARM 9.8.6).

In particular it should not be assumed that just because task X has been given a higher priority than task Y, then the execution of X precludes that of Y. A move to a distributed architecture may allow both tasks to execute. Moreover any implementation is allowed to map all priority levels onto a single value and thereby remove the usefulness of the priority system.

The main role of priorities is to deal with critical responce requirements when the system is heavily loaded. The most critical responces should be dealt with by tasks of highest priority. Priorities have, however, a role in the fine tuning of a developed system. An analysis of a working system may indicate that certain queues are relatively long and by giving a higher priority to the tasks that are extracting objects from these queues an improvement in performance may be observed. In all situations only a small range of priorities should be used and these should be isolated into a library package (Nissen & Wallis, 1984):

```
package PRIORITIES is
  HIGH_PRIORITY : constant PRIORITY := ... ;
  MID_PRIORITY  : constant PRIORITY := ... ;
  LOW_PRIORITY  : constant PRIORITY := ... ;
end PRIORITIES;
```

Within the program, reference should only be made to these constants. The recoding of this package for different implementations is trivial.

It is important to emphasise that the priority pragma only applies to tasks that are executable. It has no effect, for example, on the queue of tasks waiting on an entry call. This queue is FIFO (First in First Out) even though a high priority task may be behind a low priority one. Moreover, if a task executes a select statement of the form:

```
select
  accept HIGH;
or
  accept LOW;
end select;
```

then, if there are outstanding calls on both entries the choice made by the select is still arbitrary even if the calling tasks have different priorities. Once the choice has been made, then the priority of the rendezvous will reflect the priority of the calling task. The relative priorities of the tasks at the head of the entry queues are not, however, used to make the choice. To overcome these difficulties the program must be structured to enforce its own scheduling requirements. This can often be achieved effectively by using a family of entries. It is advisable for a program not to rely on the FIFO structure of the queue associated with an entry. Not only does it prevent priority ordering but it reflects the order in which calls arrive at the task not the order in which they were made. On a distributed system this could be significant.

11.2 Use of Entry Families for Scheduling

In chapter 5 a family of entries was used to split a single entry queue into three separate queues. Any call upon the entry would then be placed onto the particular queue indicated in the call:

```
type A_PRIORITY is (HIGH, MEDIUM, LOW);
task SERVER is
  entry REQUEST (A_PRIORITY) (...);
end SERVER;
```

a typical call would be

```
SERVER.REQUEST(LOW)(...);
```

Within the body of the task, a select statement is constructed so that priority
is given to calls coming in on the HIGH family entry:

```
task body SERVER is
EMPTY : BOOLEAN;
begin
  loop
    select
      accept REQUEST (HIGH) (...) do
         .
         .
      end REQUEST;
    or
      when REQUEST(HIGH)'COUNT = 0 =>
        accept REQUEST (MEDIUM) (...) do
           .
           .
        end REQUEST;
    or
      when REQUEST(HIGH)'COUNT   = 0  and
           REQUEST(MEDIUM)'COUNT = 0   =>
        accept REQUEST (LOW) (...) do
           .
           .
        end REQUEST;
    end select;
  end loop;
end SERVER;
```

In chapter 6 it was noted that in the situation where timed entry calls were
being made (or calling tasks were aborted) then it is possible for a structure
of the above kind to behave incorrectly. A call to the HIGH entry could be
withdrawn after the guards for the other entries have been evaluated (to
FALSE) but before the entry was accepted. The effect of this is that calls to
the other family entries will be blocked until a call to 'HIGH' terminates the
select statement.

Another criticism of the above code is that for a large family the
necessary guards become somewhat excessive (for a 1000 member family the
guard on the lowest value would need to contain 999 boolean evaluations!).
An alternative structure involves looping through all the possible values of
the family:

```
task body SERVER is
  ...
begin
  loop
    for P in A_PRIORITY loop
      select
        accept REQUEST (P) (...) do
          ...
        end REQUEST;
        exit;
      else
        null;
      end select;
    end loop;
  end loop;
end SERVER;
```

The task loops through the values of A_PRIORITY in the order required until it finds an outstanding entry call. Having accepted this call it exits from the inner loop and tries to find a high priority entry again. If no entries are outstanding then it returns via the outer loop to try again.

This last point immediately raises a question about this 'solution', for it uses a busy wait loop which is polling for requests. A reliable and efficient algorithm must separate the acceptance of outstanding entry calls from waiting for the first new entry call to arrive. If there are no outstanding calls then the server task must be suspended on a select statement that will accept the first incoming call, whatever its priority:

```
task body SERVER is
  EMPTY : BOOLEAN ;      -- no outstanding calls.
begin
  loop
    loop
      EMPTY := TRUE;
      for P in A_PRIORITY loop
        select
          accept REQUEST (P) (...) do
            ...
          end REQUEST;
          EMPTY := FALSE;
          exit;
        else
          null;
        end select;
      end loop;
      exit when EMPTY;
          -- will only exit when no requests
          -- have been found.
    end loop;
```

```
         select
           accept REQUEST (HIGH) (...) do
                  .
                  .
           end REQUEST;
         or
           accept REQUEST (MEDIUM) (...) do
                  .
                  .
           end REQUEST;
         or
           accept REQUEST (LOW) (...) do
                  .
                  .
           end REQUEST;
         or
           terminate;
         end select;
       end loop;
     end SERVER;
```

The second half of this task body which will accept any incoming call (or terminate) must, of necessity, explicitly name each family entry and will be lengthy for large families as a consequence. If the family size is such that this length is a problem then one must again use a two-rendezvous solution. One entry (not a family) is used to announce that a request call is about to be made; the other entry is the usual REQUEST family. All calls to REQUEST must be preceded by a call to ANNOUNCE. This can be assured by hiding the required synchronisations in a package:

```
         package RESOURCE is
           type SOME_PRIORITY is new INTEGER range 0..999;
           procedure REQUEST(P : SOME_PRIORITY; ... );
         end RESOURCE;

         package body RESOURCE is
           task SERVER is
             entry ANNOUNCE;
             entry REQUEST (SOME_PRIORITY) (...);
           end SERVER;

           procedure REQUEST(P : SOME_PRIORITY;...) is
           begin
             SERVER.ANNOUNCE;
             SERVER.REQUEST(P)(...);
           end REQUEST;

           task body SERVER is separate;
         end RESOURCE;
```

When there are no outstanding calls the SERVER task will be suspended on 'select ANNOUNCE' or 'terminate'. When there are entry calls SERVER will loop through the priorities accepting calls to REQUEST or further calls to

ANNOUNCE (which must be given preference):

```
begin
  loop
    select
      accept ANNOUNCE;
    or
      terminate;
    end select;
    loop
      EMPTY := TRUE;
      for P in SOME_PRIORITY loop
        select
          accept ANNOUNCE;
          EMPTY := FALSE;
          exit;
        or
          when ANNOUNCE'COUNT = 0 =>
            accept REQUEST(P)(...) do
              .
              .
              .
            end REQUEST;
            EMPTY := FALSE;
            exit;
        else
          null;
        end select;
      end loop;
      exit when EMPTY;
    end loop;
  end loop;
end;
```

To remove the possibility of a client task being aborted while executing
ANNOUNCE an agent task could be employed to make the two calls on
SERVER. (Such algorithms were discussed in the previous chapter).

11.3 Alternative Language Designs

Family entries can be used to schedule the use of a resource but
are clearly not as powerful as the concept of scheduling within operating
systems. A package that provides a procedure REQUEST will most probably
also specify another called RELEASE. The task controlling the resource will
only work properly if client tasks release resources appropriately. Even if a
higher priority task requires the resource there is nothing (short of abort!)
that the server can do until the task that holds the resource releases them,
nevertheless scheduling is important in resource dominated applications.

Finally in this chapter, it is interesting to compare the above
program examples with those that would emanate from a different language
design. The language occam provides syntactical forms that make the

programming of priorities much simpler. Occam, like Ada and many other languages, enables a priority to be attached directly to a process; however, where occam differs is in its form of the select statement (called ALT in occam). There are two constructs of interest. First, a select can be forced to be 'non-arbitrary'; in Ada-style syntax this would take the form:

```
priority select              -- not legal Ada
  accept REQUEST(HIGH)(...) do
  .
  .
  .
  end REQUEST;
or
  accept REQUEST(MEDIUM)(...) do
  .
  .
  end REQUEST;
or
  accept REQUEST(LOW)(...) do
  .
  .
  end REQUEST;
end select;
```

The priority select takes the textual order of the alternatives as the criterion for arbitrating between two or more outstanding calls. For example, if there were calls to REQUEST(MEDIUM)(...) and REQUEST(LOW)(...) then the MEDIUM one would be taken because it is textually first. The second useful construct removes the need to list all the members of a family as distinct accept statements. For example:

```
for J in SOME_PRIORITY select     -- not legal Ada
  accept REQUEST(J)(...) do
  .
  .
  end REQUEST;
end select;
```

would be equivalent to:

```
select
  accept REQUEST(1)(...) do
    .
    .
    .
  end REQUEST;
or
  accept REQUEST(2)(...) do
    .
    .
    .
  end REQUEST;
or
    .
    .
    .
or
  accept REQUEST(999)(...) do
    .
    .
    .
  end REQUEST;
end select;
```

The inclusion of delay, terminate or else clauses could easily be incorporated into this syntax. For instance, a select statement could be defined to have a 'family select' as one of its possible alternatives:

```
select
  accept ANNOUNCE;
    .
    .
    .
or
  for J in A_PRIORITY select      -- not legal Ada
    accept REQUEST(J)(...)
      .
      .
      .
    end REQUEST;
  end select;
end select;
```

Guards could also be used. The semantics of the above forms are identical to those that would appertain had the select been written out in full.

By combining the two contructs discussed above, the code for handling a large family of entries, using a priority algorithm, would be:

```
loop
  select
    for J in SOME_PRIORITY priority select
                                      -- not legal Ada
      accept REQUEST(J)(...) do
        .
        .
        .
      end accept;
    end select;
  or
    terminate;
  end select;
end loop;
```

This is clearly more concise, and thus liable to be more error free, than the code given earlier in this chapter for 'true' Ada.

12 LOW-LEVEL PROGRAMMING

One of the intended application areas for Ada is the production of embedded systems. The major difficulty in developing such systems is the design and implementation of device drivers. A device driver is a task that has sole responsibility for controlling access to some external device. Although this is clearly a key area in the production of embedded systems, the Ada model is untested here, and it is far from obvious that the facilities that Ada provides are adequate for the job.

A hardware device is an object which is operating in parallel with other elements of the system. It is logical therefore to consider the device as being a hardware 'task'. However Ada does not provide a normal rendezvous or even a shared variable interface to these tasks although it does enable the programmer to specify the exact form of the interface (down to the bit level) using representation clauses. Alternatively it allows code inserts for invoking special machine instructions to be used if necessary. Corresponding to each device there is generally a software task, called a device driver, which can encapsulate these low-level features.

Assembler or machine code inserts are obviously at variance with the abstract constructs of the rest of the language and should only be used when absolutely necessary.

12.1 Machine Code Inserts

The machine code insertion mechanism enables programmers to write Ada code which contains visible non-Ada objects. This is achieved in a controlled way by only allowing machine code instructions to operate within the context of a subprogram body. Moreover, if a subprogram contains code statements then it can contain only code statements and 'use' clauses (comments and pragmas being allowed as usual).

As one would expect the details and characteristics of using code inserts are largely implementation dependent; implementation-specific pragmas and attributes may be used to impose particular restrictions and calling conventions on the use of objects defining code instructions. A code statement has the following structure:

```
code_statement ::= type_mark'record_aggregate;
```

The base type of the type_mark must be declared within a predefined library package called MACHINE_CODE. It is this package that provides record declarations (in standard Ada) to represent the instructions of the target machine. The following example is from the ARM (13.8.7):

```
M : MASK;
procedure SET_MASK; pragma INLINE(SET_MASK);

procedure SET_MASK is
  use MACHINE_CODE;
begin
  SI_FORMAT'(CODE => SSM.B => M'BASE_REG.D => M'DISP);
  -- M'BASE_REG and M'DISP are implementation-specific
  -- predefined attributes
end;
```

The pragma INLINE instructs the compiler to include in-line code, rather than a procedure call, whenever the subprogram is used.

Even though this code insertion method is defined in Ada the ARM makes it quite clear (13.8.4) that an implementation need not provide a MACHINE_CODE package. If it does not, the use of machine code inserts is prohibited.

12.2 Pragma INTERFACE

This facility allows a procedure or function specification to be used as an interface between Ada and subprograms written in other languages. The pragma names the language (and thereby the calling convention) and the subprogram (see ARM 13.9). For example:

```
package FORT_LIB is
  function SQRT(X : FLOAT) return FLOAT;
  function EXP(X : FLOAT) return FLOAT;
private
  pragma INTERFACE(FORTRAN.SQRT);
  pragma INTERFACE(FORTRAN.EXP);
end FORT_LIB;
```

Ada bodies for the subprograms are not given in the Ada program which is in contrast to the use of machine code inserts.

Again, there is no requirement on any implementation to support any particular language INTERFACE. However, if an interface to the assembler of the target machine is provided then it is clearly possible to write input–output routines in assembler and use them as ordinary subprograms within an Ada program.

12.3 Representation Clauses

Representation clauses are a compromise between abstract and concrete structures. They are described in most Ada text books and are outlined below. Four distinct specifications are available.

    (a) Length clauses: maximum bit length of objects, maximum storage space for tasks.

    (b) The literals of an enumeration type may be given specific internal values.

    (c) Record components can be assigned offsets and lengths.

    (d) An object may be positioned at a specific address.

If an implementation cannot obey a specification request then the compiler must reject the program. As an example of the use of representation clauses, consider the control status register of a disc drive, this register is illustrated in Figure 12.1:

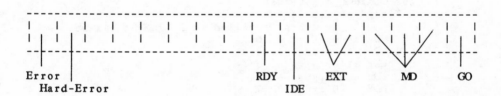

Figure 12.1

Error, Hard-Error, RDY (Ready) IDE (interrupt enable) and GO are all two-state variables that are best thought of as flags:

```
type FLAG is (OFF,ON);
```

with 0 representing OFF and 1 giving ON (this being the default representation). The 'Mode of Operation' covers three bits but provides only four operations:

```
type MODE is (RESET, WRITE, READ, SEEK);
```

The required internal codes for these four states are 0,1,2 and 4; this is specified as follows:

```
for MODE use (0,1,2,4);
```

As long as the sequence is still strictly increasing, any representation is allowed. The Memory Extension Bits can be mapped onto a type which is restricted to three bits by a length clause:

```
type MEB is new INTEGER range 0..3;
for MEB'SIZE use 3;
```

Having constructed each individual component, the register itself can be represented as a record; firstly, in standard Ada:

```
type CONTROL_STATUS is
  record
    GO   : FLAG;
    MD   : MODE;
    EXT  : MEB;
    IDE  : FLAG;
    RDY  : FLAG;
    HARD_ERROR : FLAG;
    ERROR : FLAG;
  end record;
```

The record type can then be structured using offset and length clauses.

```
for CONTROL_STATUS use
  record at mod 2;
          -- This is called an alignment clause.
    GO  at 0 range 0..0;
    MD  at 0 range 1..3;
    EXT at 0 range 4..5;
    IDE at 0 range 6..6;
    RDY at 0 range 7..7;
    HARD_ERROR at 1 range 6..6;
    ERROR at 1 range 7..7;
  end record;
```

For example, MD is to be placed at the storage unit 0 using bits 1,2 and 3; ERROR is to be found in the storage unit 1 at bit 7. The 'storage unit' is implementation dependent and for this example is deemed to have the value 8. (The value of this unit is contained within the predefined library package SYSTEM). The alignment clause ensures that the record is placed at an even byte boundary. To constrain the system to use only 16 bits in total for an object of type CONTROL_STATUS another length clause is used.

```
for CONTROL_STATUS'SIZE use 16;
```

Finally a data object to represent the control register must be defined and placed at the correct memory location; this is the physical address of the register:

```
CONTROL_REGISTER : CONTROL_STATUS;
for CONTROL_REGISTER use at 8#777404#;
```

Having now constructed the abstract data representation of the register, and placed an appropriately defined variable at the correct address, the hardware register can be manipulated by assignments to this variable:

```
CONTROL_REGISTER := (GO    => ON,
                     MD    => READ,
                     EXT   => 0,
                     IDE   => ON,
                     RDY   => OFF,
                     HARD_ERROR => OFF,
                     ERROR => OFF);
```

The use of this record aggregate assumes that the entire register will be assigned values at the same time. To ensure that 'GO' is not set before the other fields of the record it may be necessary to use a temporary control register:

```
TEMP_CR : CONTROL_STATUS;
```

This temporary register is then assigned control values and copied into the real register variable:

```
CONTROL_REGISTER := TEMP_CR;
```

The code for this assignment will ensure that the entire control register is updated in a single action.

After the completion of the I/O operation the device itself may alter the values on the register; this is recognised in the program as changes in the values of the record components:

```
if CONTROL_REGISTER.ERROR=ON then
  raise DISK_ERROR;
end if;
```

The object CONTROL_REGISTER is therefore a collection of shared variables, which are shared between the device control task and the device itself. Appropriate synchronisations between these two concurrent (and parallel) processes are necessary to give reliability and performance. Condition synchronisations must ensure that the correct sequence of events takes place between the hardware and its driver. This is usually achieved by implementing a model which is essentially that of two coroutines. Permission to access registers shared between them is passed from software to hardware and back again.

This structure will provide mutual exclusion, as only one process will be updating shared variables at a time. There remains the question of what form the condition synchronisation should take. The two most common are:

(i)   polling,

(ii) interrupt driven

Whichever is used on any particular device is a property of the hardware as well as the system software. Polling cannot, therefore, be eliminated if it is the only method available for examining the condition of the device. If polling is used, then the busy wait loop must incorporate a delay statement so that the device task does not monopolise the processor. Alternatively the whole task can be periodic.

12.4 Interrupt Handling

Interrupt driven hardware incorporates, at a fundamental level, a synchronisation primitive into the structure of the processor. When the device wishes to communicate with its driver (for example to indicate that some required data is now available) it sets a flag in the processor (on a single processor system). The operating system suspends the process that is executing on the processor and designates the code it wishes to have executed as a result of the occurrence of the interrupt. This code is usually called the interrupt handler.

With an embedded system the Ada run-time system is, essentially, the operating system. The interrupt handler takes the form of some Ada source code. An interrupt can be considered as a rendezvous call from a device (the hardware task) to an 'interrupt entry' in the device controller (the software task).

An entry point that is to be used for handling interrupts is designated by associating with the entry specification an address clauses, for example:

```
task INTERRUPT_HANDLER is
  entry CONTACT;
  for CONTACT use 16#180#;
end INTERRUPT_HANDLER;
```

The address '16#180#' is given in the form required by the implementation;
the meaning of this address clause is given below. A body for this task could
have the simple structure:

```
task body INTERRUPT_HANDLER is
begin
  -- interrupt enabled using a
  -- representation-clause
  loop
    accept CONTACT do
      -- some appropriate action
    end CONTACT;
  end loop;
end INTERRUPT_HANDLER;
```

This straightforward structure defines a task that will loop around and deal
with a single source of interrupts. With other devices it may be appropriate to
enable interrupts only for the time during which an interrupt could occur.
Consider a task that is acting as a device driver for a printer:

```
task PRINTER_DRIVER is
  entry PRINT_REQUEST(L : LINE);
  entry INTERRUPT;
  for INTERRUPT use 8#440#;
end PRINTER_DRIVER;
```

The use of the name 'INTERRUPT' is not significant; readability
considerations dictate that this is usually the most appropriate name to use.
A body for the task PRINTER_DRIVER would then have the form:

```
loop
  accept PRINT_REQUEST (L : LINE) do
    COPYL := L;
  end PRINT_REQUEST;
  -- set up data registers using COPYL
  -- set up control register,
  -- including interrupt enable.
  accept INTERRUPT;
    -- disable interrupts.
    -- check error conditions.
end loop;
```

This driver task will accept a request to do a print operation from another
task in the system. By using appropriate data structures and representation
clauses the hardware registers will be set up so as to instruct the device to
undertake the required action.

The driver task will then be delayed waiting for a call to the entry INTERRUPT. When the device has completed its operation, (i.e. the line has been printed), it will raise an interrupt; the run-time system will then translate this into an entry call on INTERRUPT. The driver will accept the rendezvous and proceed to undertake whatever error checking is necessary. Finally, the driver task will loop round to be ready to process another request.

In situations where the hardware device must be timed-out then a select statement with a delay alternative will cater efficiently for normal requirements:

```
select
  accept INTERRUPT;
or
  delay TIME_OUT;
    raise TIME_OUT_ERROR;
end select;
```

One of the benefits of using the same interfacing mechanism for communicating with hardware is that in the development stage of the software the hardware task can be replaced with a real task that is simulating the action of the device. This task can 'share' the data structures representing the registers and make calls to the INTERRUPT entry. From the point of view of the driver there is no distinction between a hardware and a software entry call.

12.5 Properties of Interrupt Entries

As was indicated above, an entry call can be associated with an actual interrupt by including an address clause with the entry specification. There is, however, no predefined meaning or interpretation for this 'address'. It may correspond to the hardware interrupt vector or may be used to specify the priority of the interrupt.

The type of the interrupt may be such that it is lost if not immediately processed, in this case the interrupt has the form of a conditional entry call. Alternatively the hardware call may behave as a timed entry call if it has not been handled in some required time interval or if a second interrupt appears and effectively overwrites the first call, (interrupts are not usually queued).

Where information is passed with the interrupt, the associated entry call can have parameters onto which this data can be mapped. Only 'in' parameters are allowed. The type of this data would usually be integer. As the meaning of these parameters is particularly implementation–dependent they are not recommended for use (Hibbard *et al*, 1981). Rather, it is preferable to use only parameterless entry calls and employ representation clauses to read any related data from specific locations.

In order to ensure that interrupts are handled quickly, all hardware tasks are deemed to have priorities greater than those available to software tasks. As the interrupt handler takes the form of a rendezvous between a hardware and a software task, the priority of the rendezvous is that of the hardware task. Therefore this rendezvous must take precedence over all other tasks that are executing. It is this circumstance that could cause another task to be suspended, even though it has not changed its state from being executable. After the driver task has executed the interrupt rendezvous, the suspended task may continue executing or, because of fairness consideration, another waiting task may proceed.

When considering interrupt entries and priorities it is important to remember those factors that were discussed in the previous chapter. If an entry is being used for software and hardware entry calls then the FIFO definition of the entry queue will mean that it is possible for a hardware call to be behind a software call even though it has a higher priority. Moreover one cannot assume that a select statement will choose the interrupt entry in preference to other accept statements.

Although all hardware tasks have higher priorities than all software tasks there is no predefined method of assigning different priorities to these hardware processes. If the implementation allows, the address specification may be used to give a priority to the interrupt (and by association the hardware device that causes that interrupt), the implication being that a high priority interrupt will have preference over a lower one. Unfortunately there is little (perhaps nothing!) that programmers can do to construct their own interrupt model and much of the required system software will need to be provided by the run–time system. It is asking a lot of the compiler implementors to build a run–time system suitable for all applications. Ada has yet to prove itself as a widely usable implementation language for device drivers as there is no provision for tailoring this run–time system.

Another potentially dangerous consequence of the rules concerning priorities is that on a limited processor system a software task doing critical work cannot stop itself from being suspended while a low priority task deals with a low priority interrupt, Consider the following:

```
task ALARM_WARNING is
  pragma PRIORITY(HIGH_PRIORITY);
  entry ALARM;
  for ALARM use at 16#100#;
end ALARM_WARNING;

task body ALARM_WARNING is
begin
  loop
    accept ALARM do
      -- Actions here cannot be interrupted by
      -- any software task or by any other interrupt
      -- entry if priority interrupts are supported
      -- and ALARM has the highest such priority.
    end ALARM;
      -- Action here cannot be interrupted by any
      -- software task but may be suspended if any
      -- interrupt entry call is made on any task
      -- in a position to accept such a call.
  end loop;
end ALARM_WARNING;
```

What the above indicates is that all necessary actions must be taken inside the rendezvous with the hardware task.

Because of the need to task switch before the interrupt handler can be executed, valuable time will be lost, which in some applications is significant. To cater for this difficulty the ARM states:

> "*Interrupt entry calls need only have the semantics described above; they may be implemented by having the hardware directly execute the appropriate accept statement.*" (*ARM 13.5.1.5*).

Finally, if an accept statement that is associated with an interrupt entry is contained in a select statement with an 'or terminate' alternative an implementation may impose further restrictions on the conditions required for this terminate alternative to be taken.

12.6 Low-Level Input-Output

In order to standardise on the control of physical devices the ARM (14.6) explicitly provides a package called LOW_LEVEL_IO. Within this package, data types are defined that represent devices and exchangeable data. Also defined are two procedures, SEND_CONTROL and RECEIVE_CONTROL, that can be used to communicate control information between system devices and the Ada program. By overloading these procedures, subprograms are defined for all devices:

```
package LOW_LEVEL_IO is
   -- declarations of DATA_TYPE and DEVICE_TYPE
   procedure SEND_CONTROL(DEVICE : DEVICE_TYPE;
                          DATA : in out DATA_TYPE);
   procedure RECEIVE_CONTROL(DEVICE : DEVICE_TYPE;
                             DATA : in out DATA_TYPE);
   -- declarations of overloaded procedures
end LOW_LEVEL_IO;
```

As the physical declarations of each machine and device vary, the meaning of the control data exchanged is implementation dependent. For example, a device driver task may wait on a parameterless interrupt entry and then call LOW_LEVEL_IO.RECEIVE_CONTROL to obtain further information about the reason for the interrupt.

The bodies of the overloaded control procedures will be given in the body of LOW_LEVEL_IO. These procedures may contain code statements. Unfortunately, when a task calls one of these subprograms there is no indication as to whether or not the task will be delayed or, more significantly, whether the entire program will be delayed as a result.

The simultaneous use of high and low level input-output facilities could clearly result in unreliable software. It is, therefore, necessary to limit the visibility of the low-level routines to the body of that object that implements the high level facilities. Each device should have its own device driver that is encapsulated within a package that exports procedures for accessing the device (i.e. the package provides a virtual device). Within the body of the device driver, external objects are accessed via either:

(a) LOW_LEVEL_IO

(b) a package encapsulating representation clauses.

In addition, interrupts (and other asynchronous external events) will need to be trapped as entry calls mapped onto the appropriate place in memory. Within the context of a software development project it is important to ensure that only "authorised and qualified" programmers have access to the more sophisticated input-output routines (Pyle, 1979).

12.7 Appendix F

There are, within Ada, a controlled and limited number of places where implementation-dependent characteristics can become visible. A number of these have been discussed in this chapter. The ARM recommends that each and every Ada implementation should include an appendix, called Appendix F, that describes all these non-standard characteristics. Items listed in each Appendix F include:

(a) The form, allowable use and effect of every implementation-dependent pragma.

(b) The name, type and effect of every implementation-dependent attribute.

(c) The specification of the package SYSTEM (see below).

(d) The list of all restrictions on representation clauses.

(e) The interpretation of expressions that appear in address clauses, including those for interrupt.

(f) Any implementation-dependent characteristics of the input-output packages (including the interpretation of types and subprograms that appear in LOW_LEVEL_IO).

The predefined library package called SYSTEM includes the definitions of certain configuration-dependent characteristics. In the visible part of the package the following must be provided (ARM 13.7.2):

```
package SYSTEM is
    type ADDRESS is implementation_defined;
    type NAME is implementation_defined_enumeration_type;

    SYSTEM_NAME : constant NAME := implementation_defined;

    STORAGE_UNIT   : constant := implementation_defined;
    MEMORY_SIZE    : constant := implementation_defined;

    -- System-Dependent Named Numbers:

    MIN_INT        : constant := implementation_defined;
    MAX_INT        : constant := implementation_defined;
    MAX_DIGITS     : constant := implementation_defined;
    MAX_MANTISSA   : constant := implementation_defined;
    FINE_DELTA     : constant := implementation_defined;
    TICK           : constant := implementation_defined;

    -- Other System-Dependent Declarations

    subtype PRIORITY is INTEGER
                    range implementation_defined;

    ...
end SYSTEM;
```

An allowable alternative form to that given above uses pragmas for SYSTEM_NAME, STORAGE_UNIT and MEMORY_SIZE.

12.8 A Simple Driver Example

A common class of equipment to be attached to an embedded
computer system is that of the analogue to digital converter (ADC). The
converter samples some environmental factors such as temperature or
pressure; it translates the measurements it receives, which are usually in
millivolts, and provides scaled integer values on a register. Consider a single
converter that has a 16 bit result register at hardware address 8#150000#
and a control register at 8#150002#. The computer is a 16 bit machine and
the control register is structured as follows:

Bit	Name	Meaning
0	A/D Start	Set to 1 to start a conversion.
6	Interrupt Enable/Disable	
7	Done	Set to 1 when conversion is complete.
8-13	Channel	The Converter has 64 analogue inputs, the particular one required is indicated by the value of the channel.
15	Error	Set to 1 by the converter if device malfunctions.

The driver for this ADC will be structured as a task so that the interrupt it
generates can be processed as an entry call. This task will, however, be
defined within a library package:

```
package ADC is
   MAX_MEASURE : constant := (2**16)-1 ;
   type CHANNEL is new INTEGER range 0..63;
   subtype MEASUREMENT is INTEGER range 0..MAX_MEASURE;
   procedure READ (CH: CHANNEL ; M : out MEASUREMENT);
   CONVERSION_ERROR : exception;
end ADC;
```

For any request, the driver will make three attempts before raising the
exception. The package body contains only the driver task:

```
package body ADC is
   task DRIVER is
      entry READ (CH : CHANNEL; M : out MEASUREMENT);
      entry INTERRUPT;
      for INTERRUPT use at 8#100#;
   end DRIVER;

   procedure READ(CH : CHANNEL; M : out MEASUREMENT) is
   begin
      DRIVER.READ(CH,M);
   end READ;

   task body DRIVER is separate;
end ADC;
```

The data structures necessary to represent the registers are specified within a package:

```
package ADC_DATA_DEFS is
   REG_ADDRESS : constant := 8#150002#;
   BUF_ADDRESS : constant := 8#150000#;
   BITS : constant := 16;
   type BUFFER is new INTEGER range 0..MAX_MEASURE;
   for BUFFER'SIZE use BITS;
   type FLAG is (DOWN, SET);
   type CHAN is new CHANNEL;
   for CHAN'SIZE use 6;
   type CONTROL_REGISTER is
   record
      AD_START : FLAG;
      IE    : FLAG;
      DONE  : FLAG;
      CH    : CHAN;
      ERROR : FLAG;
   end record;
   for CONTROL_REGISTER use
   record at mod 2;
      AD_START at 0 range 0..0;
      IE at 0 range 6..6;
      DONE at 0 range 7..7;
      CH at 1 range 0..5;
      ERROR at 1 range 7..7;
   end record;
   CR : CONTROL_REGISTER;
   BUFF : BUFFER;
   for CR use at REG_ADDRESS;
   for BUFF use at BUF_ADDRESS;
end ADC_DATA_DEFS;
```

The body of DRIVER is:

```
with ADC_DATA_DEFS;   use ADC_DATA_DEFS;
task body DRIVER is
begin
  loop
    begin
      accept READ(CH : CHANNEL; M : out MEASUREMENT) do
        for I in 1..3 loop
          CR := (AD_START => SET,
                 IE      => SET,
                 DONE => DOWN,
                 CH   => CHAN(READ.CH),
                 ERROR => DOWN);
          accept INTERRUPT;
          if CR.DONE=SET and ERROR=DOWN then
            M := INTEGER(BUFF);
            return;
          end if;
        end loop;
        raise CONVERSION_ERROR;
      end READ;
    exception
      when CONVERSION_ERROR => null;
    end;
  end loop;
end DRIVER;
```

In the control loop, the task waits on a call to READ; the parameters of this entry call give a channel number from which to read, and an output variable for the actual value read. Inside the accept an inner loop attempts three conversions; the control register, CR, is set up with the start and interrupt-enable flags up and the error and finished flags down. In order to set up the representation of the data type for channel, its type, CHAN, must be declared within the body of ADC_DATA_DEFS. However, an external type, CHANNEL, must be made available in the visible part of the package. Therefore CHAN is derived from CHANNEL and the parameter READ.CH is converted from type CHANNEL to type CHAN (CH => CHAN(READ.CH)).

Once the interrupt has arrived (as a parameterless entry call) the driver task tests to make sure that CR.DONE has been set and that the error flag has not been raised. If this is the case, the out parameter M is constructed, again using a type conversion, from the value on the buffer register. (Note that this value cannot be out of range for the subtype MEASUREMENT). Three conversions are attempted. If none are acceptable, the exception CONVERSION_ERROR is raised, and not handled, inside the rendezvous. This exception is therefore propagated back to the calling task and is raised again after the accept statement in the driver task. A simple null handler will prevent further consequences for the driver.

The above example illustrates that it is often necessary when writing device drivers to convert objects from one type to another. In these circumstances the strong typing features of Ada can be an irritant. It is, however, possible to circumvent this difficulty by using a generic function that is provided as a predefined library unit:

```
generic
    type SOURCE is limited private;
    type TARGET is limited private;
function UNCHECKED_CONVERSION(S : SOURCE) return TARGET;
```

For example rather than have:

```
M := INTEGER(BUFF);
```

It is possible to first instantiate a conversion function:

```
function CONVERT is new
    UNCHECKED_CONVERSION(BUFFER,MEASUREMENT);
```

The conversion then takes the form:

```
M := CONVERT(BUFF);
```

If this construct were used MEASUREMENT could be defined as a type rather than a subtype (the subtype being needed in the original code as the conversion was undertaken using 'INTEGER').

The effect of unchecked conversion is to copy the bit pattern of the source over to the target. The programmer must make sure that the conversion is sensible and that all possible patterns are acceptable to the target.

13 IMPLEMENTATION OF ADA TASKING

In keeping with the usual role for a language reference manual, little further information, other than the semantics of the language, is given on how the tasking model should be implemented. Compiler writers must nevertheless construct a system that will efficiently map Ada programs onto the underlying hardware. Two key aspects of this mapping concern processor allocation and memory management.

13.1 Processor Allocation

A number of concurrent programming languages, such as Modula, are designed solely for single processor systems. Their implementations require a run-time system that will schedule the concurrent objects of the program so that they share the processor. Other languages (for example occam) are intended for use, primarily, in multiprocessor environments. Here concurrency will imply parallelism and a mechanism must be used to allocate processes to processors.

Ada is intended to function in both of these situations:

"Parallel tasks may be implemented on multicomputers, multiprocessors, or with interleaved execution on a single physical processor" (ARM 9.0.5).

Indeed it is also permitted for different parts of a single task to be executed on different processors as long as the effect of the execution is the same as it would have been on a single processor. All present implementations of Ada use a single processor and run all tasks upon it. Using Ada for distributed systems presents some difficulties which will be discussed later in this chapter.

Although many operating systems, e.g. UNIX, (trademark AT&T) provide logical processes, a number of early compilers for Ada have chosen to map entire programs onto one logical process. This has the unfortunate disadvantage that if one task makes an I/O request then the host operating system will suspend the process and thereby block all other tasks even though they are executable (Fantechi, 1984). An experimental system which does map tasks onto logical processes is PULSE (Wellings, 1984c, 1985a).

13.2 Memory Management

Most modern high-level languages are implemented using a stack-based memory management system. The available run-time storage is organised as a single stack with code and static data at the bottom and free storage at the top. A stack pointer is positioned at the bottom of the free area. As memory is allocated the stack pointer moves up the stack and as memory is released it moves down. Storage must therefore be freed in the reverse order to that of allocation. Most operations take place on the top of the stack. For example, to add two objects together involves copying each object onto the top of the stack (stack pointer increases by 2), performing a plus operation (this replaces the two objects with the result; stack pointer decreases by 1) and returning the top of the stack value into the appropriate position in the stack (stack pointer again decreases by 1). The whole operation therefore involves the stack growing by two elements and then returning to its original size.

The only mechanism that does not employ a 'last in first out' structure is the storage use of the allocator. Languages that have this type of pointer facility require a heap that is managed separately. Often the heap is placed at the very top of the free area and grows down towards the rest of the stack. The free area is therefore effectively being attached from both ends.

When a subprogram is called, a new activation record is placed on the top of the stack which includes local variables and a return address. Chains of subprogram calls, therefore, cause no difficulty; nor does recursive calling or reentrant usage. As Ada has recursive subprogram calls and data structures whose size is only calculated at run-time it encourages the use of a stack-based memory management structure. What loss of efficiency there might be by not utilising fully the available hardware registers is compensated for by portability considerations. A project involved in defining a portable virtual machine for Ada (called the A-machine) has adopted a stack machine architecture (Ibsen, 1984).

With a multi-tasking program each task can, to some extent, be seen as as separate program and so each task will have its own stack. These stacks are however not entirely unrelated. The point of creation of a task is

dependent on some state of the parent (master). A child task may also require
access to shared variables held on its parent's stack. From these consideration
a structure known as a **cactus stack** is used. A cactus stack consists of a
variable number of stacks; one for each task in the program. Consider the
following code:

```
procedure MAIN is
  A, B : INTEGER;
  task T1;
  task body T1 is
    G, H : INTEGER;
    task T3;
    task body T3 is
      I, J : INTEGER;
    begin
      null;            -- null actions given for simplicity
    end T3;
  begin
    null;
  end T1;
  C, D : INTEGER;      -- These declarations should be
                       -- placed inside an inner block
                       -- as they follow the declaration
                       -- of a task body.
                       -- These inner blocks have however
                       -- been omitted for clarity.
  task T2;
  task body T2 is
    K, L : INTEGER;
  begin
    null;
  end T2;
  E, F : INTEGER;
begin
  null;
end MAIN;
```

The outer level variables A and B are shared by all three tasks and the main
program; at the other extreme, I and J are only accessible in task T3. As each
task is created a corresponding branch on the cactus stack is constructed.
When all three tasks are present the stack will take the following form:

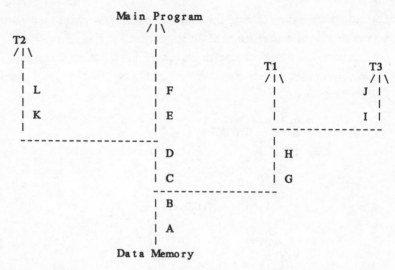

The stack for T3 is grafted onto the stack for T1 which is itself attached to the main stack. Therefore T3 has access to I and J, also H and G, and subsequently A and B. A branch on the cactus stack disappears when the associated task terminates. It is a consequence of the termination rules of Ada that a task can only terminate if its children also terminate. A branch cannot thus become detached. Within a single task the cactus branch behaves like a normal linear stack.

13.3 Task Switching

If more than one task is to execute on a processor then task (or context) switching must be performed. This action is analogous to an operating system switching from one process to another. The dynamic information necessary to execute a task is usually called the task execution context and is contained in a data structure known as the task activation record. For example with the portable A-machine design (Ibsen, 1984) the activation record includes:

> **Program Counter**- the address of the next instruction that the task will execute.
>
> **Stack Pointer**- the address of the top of the task's branch on the cactus stack.
>
> **Block Level**- the static level of the current executing block.
>
> **Exception Address**- the address of the exception handler for the executing block, if there is one.

Dynamic Procedure Link- the return address to the calling subprogram.

Dynamic Block Link- the return address to the preceding block.

In order to switch tasks the old task's activation record (or part of it) must be stored (on the stack) and the new task's record mounted. This action can be expensive in machine cycles and has led to criticism of the tasking model. If the switching is inefficient then time-critical applications may not be programmable in Ada. Two methods of reducing the overhead are possible: hardware constructed as an 'Ada Machine' must context switch in a small number of instructions, preferable only one! The other approach is to optimise the code so that fewer task switches are needed. This transformation, and example timings, is considered in the next section.

13.4 Habermann and Nassi Optimisations

Where processors are in short supply it will be necessary for the tasks to be 'sequentialised' so that they can share the available processors. This will usually, though perhaps not inherently, lead to the introduction of significant inefficiences. The main costs arise from the need to manage the organisation of a cactus stack and, more significantly, in the performance of context switching. To move from executing task A to executing task B involves saving the state of the current running task, A, and restoring the context of task B. Consider the following three simple programs:

```
procedure MAIN_PROC is
   JOB : constant := 200_000;
   J : INTEGER := 0;
   procedure ADD(I : in out INTEGER) is
   begin
      I := I + 1;
   end ADD;
begin
   loop
      ADD(J);
      exit when J = JOB;
   end loop;
end MAIN_PROC;

procedure MAIN_TASK1 is
   JOB : constant := 200_000;
   J : INTEGER := 0;
   task T is
      entry ADD(I : in out INTEGER);
   end T;
```

```
      task body T is
      begin
        loop
          accept ADD(I : in out INTEGER) do
            I := I + 1;
          end ADD;
        end loop;
      end T;
   begin
     loop
       T.ADD(J);
       exit when J = JOB;
     end loop;
   end MAIN_TASK1;

   procedure MAIN_TASK2 is
     JOB : constant := 200_000;
     J : INTEGER;
     task T is
       entry ADD(I : in out INTEGER);
     end T;
     task body T is
     begin
       loop
         select
           accept ADD(I : in out INTEGER) do
             I := I + 1;
           end ADD;
         or
           terminate;
         end select;
       end loop;
     end T;
   begin
     loop
       T.ADD(J);
       exit when J = JOB;
     end loop;
   end MAIN_TASK2;
```

The first program, MAIN_PROC, makes 200,000 identical procedure calls; the second, MAIN_TASK1, contains two concurrent objects with one making 200,000 entry calls upon the other. In this second example, after the main program has exited from its loop the task will still be active but suspended on the accept. The program is therefore deadlocked. To remove this deadlock the third program, MAIN_TASK2, places the accept statement in a select statement with a terminate alternative. The value of the constant JOB is sufficiently high to minimise the effects of different termination behaviours between the three programs. Start-up times can be calculated by running the program with JOB equal to 1.

It is illuminating to compare the relative execution times of these programs. If the time taken to execute the first program is taken to be 1 then the best value the author has observed for the second program is 17 and for the third 22. These programs have been run on a number of Ada systems, including six validated compilers, in order to get these values. A number of the compilers tested produced code that resulted in a ratio worse than 200 to 1! The best results were obtained on the University of York (UK) Ada system. With this compiler (running on a VAX 750) a single simple rendezvous takes, approximately, one millisecond.

This cost of a context switch is exacerbated in Ada due to the increased number of processes that the language forces users to create. In order for a client task to extract some data from a buffer task three separate switches may occur:

(i)   Buffer task reaches select statement, there are no outstanding requests; it is suspended.

(ii)   Client task issues an entry call. It is suspended.

(iii) Buffer task executes accept statement, loops and is suspended.

(iv)   Client task has been made executable and continues.

The buffer must be constructed as a task in order to protect its subprograms from concurrent usage. By comparison, a language which supports monitors can give the same protection but will implement this buffer example with no context switches.

A solution to this dilemma is to allow the thread of control of the client task to act as a proxy for the buffer and execute the accept statement itself. The buffer task is thereby implemented more as a monitor than an individual, full Ada task. This type of approach was first discussed by Habermann and Nassi in 1980 and their paper represents one of the most important published on Ada. Indeed their work has been used to justify the inefficient nature of the tasking model! (It can, of course, be argued that the model is not intrinsically inefficient but that machine design is at present inappropriate.) In order to indicate the nature of the optimisation consider a simple server task:

```
task A is
  entry E(...);
end A;
task body A is
begin
  loop
    accept E (...) do
      ...
    end E;
  end loop;
end A;
```

The task has no data of its own and has no executable statements (in effect) outside the accept. The reason E is structured as an accept is, presumably, to give mutual exclusion over request calls. Other tasks in the program will make calls on A.E.

A naive implementation of this task will give it a unique data context and the use of E will involve two or three context switches. An optimised structure replaces the accept statement with an ordinary procedure, the necessary synchronisations (i.e. mutual exclusion) being performed by a semaphore. All calls to E are implemented using pre- and post-synchronisation protocols:

```
Wait(mutex)
  E(...)
Signal(mutex) - for a semaphore mutex
```

The effect of this transformation, which could be performed by the compiler, is to remove the context switches (E is now a common procedure) at the cost of performing primitive operations on a semaphore. Semaphores being low-level constructs (see chapter 3) are easier to implement in an efficient manner.

Clearly, not all tasks can be optimised in this way. Hilfinger (1982) attempts to define classes of tasks which are amenable to such restructuring and labels them monitor tasks and agents. A monitor task is a collection of protected routines - the entries of the task - which are executed in mutual exclusion; usually any code outside the accept statements is small and serves a purely administrative function. Examples of agent tasks are given in chapter 9. Like monitors, agent tasks involve a trivial amount of computation outside the rendezvous.

In the general algorithm described by Habermann and Nassi not all of the required processing is performed on the calling task's stack; however, their algorithm will deal with exceptions being raised during rendezvous, nested accept statements, aborts and the existence of more than one accept body for an entry. The result is to reduce the number of context switches by one in most circumstances. In more restricted situations it may be possible to remove the process altogether (Schauer, 1982) and thereby not only limit the number of context switches required but also reduce the costs of managing the cactus stack. This is achieved by

(a) moving all statements that are outside a rendezvous into the preceding rendezvous, for example, rather than:

```
accept GET(I : out ITEM) do
  I := BUFF(BASE);
end GET;
BASE := (BASE + 1) mod SP1;
```

the code becomes:

```
accept GET(I : out ITEM) do
  I := BUFF(BASE);
  BASE := (BASE + 1) mod SP1;
end GET;
```

(b) structuring each accept statement as a procedure.

(c) encapsulating all statements that precede the first accept statement into a 'start procedure'.

(d) replacing each guard by a test, with the result that a closed guard will cause the task to be suspended on a semaphore (or similar primitive).

(e) replacing each entry call by the corresponding procedure call.

(f) replacing the task initialisation by a call to the start procedure.

Given these possible modifications it is reasonable to ask, though perhaps not to expect, that a compiler should recognise the possibility of optimisation and produce code accordingly. A more realistic requirement, in the short term, is for a compiler to support a pragma that will enable the programmer to request that the associated task be 'optimised out of existence'. This is analogous to the use of the pragma INLINE for removing actual procedure calls.

The availability of this optimise pragma would necessarily have an effect on the style of the programmer, though only in one aspect would this style be at variance to that discussed in this book. Passive tasks that encapsulate resources and receive requests without generating entry calls themselves, unless they are to lower order resource management tasks, will tend to have the simple structure that will support optimisation. Only in the organisation of what should be included in an accept statement is there any contradiction. To minimise the coupling between tasks only the statements absolutely necessary should be included in the rendezvous; however, to simplify the optimisation it is better to have all statements included explicitly within an accept statement. Note that the termination of an optimised task is commensurate with the requirements of the ARM.

Other optimisations are possible with the Ada tasking model; Stevenson (1980) proposes a strategy by which a calling task that can immediately execute a rendezvous does so. This 'order of arrival' scheme again reduces the average number of context switches required. The use of specified priorities can also be employed to reduce the number of times the run-time support system need be invoked (Wellings, 1985a,b). For more subtle optimisations it is necessary that formal methods be used to ensure the validity of proposed transformations.

13.5 Programming Multiprocessor Systems

Although Ada is designed for programming multiprocessor and distributed systems, where more efficient execution would be expected, no real implementation of an Ada program on this type of architecture has yet taken place. Nevertheless, considerable attention has been given to the need to use Ada on this type of system; for example, a feasibility study has been carried out for the European Community by SPL (Stammers et al, 1983; also available as Tedd et al, 1984). It is also true that, for program portability, attention to distribution must be given now, as many of the single processor Ada software systems of today will, at some point in the future, be transferred to multiprocessor systems.

With tightly coupled distributed systems, where all processors have access to the same memory space, the difficulties are primarily for the compiler writers rather than application developers. If the programmer has not relied upon only one task running at a time to give some required synchronisation (in which case the program is erroneous anyway) then the transfer of code to a multi-processor system should not present problems. The allocation of dynamically created tasks to actual processors by the run-time system is, however, more complex; particularly if there are still not enough processors and some tasks have to be time-sliced.

One of the advantages of using a language like Ada in tightly coupled distributed systems is that a decomposition of a program into those parts that can be executed in parallel is explicitly represented in the code. This should assist in achieving the performance improvements that should be manifest from the use of more processors but often does not occur (Enslow & Saponas, 1981). However, although the task would appear to be the most natural means of decomposing a system into concurrent elements it is also possible to map purely sequential code onto a multiprocessor architecture. For example, let T1 and T2 be two tasks sharing a processor, and assume that T1 calls a procedure P1. It is possible to place P1 on another processor so that T1 makes a remote procedure call every time it calls P1. With this structure T1 could be suspended while P1 is being executed, thus allowing T2 to execute in parallel with P1. In this model tasks are only used to represent concurrent objects running on the same processor.

Although Ada has a model of concurrency that is amenable to parallel execution (i.e. the tasking model) it was noted earlier that if it is necessary to pass to each task some initialisation data this cannot be done during task creation other than by using global variables. This can lead to an unexpected bottleneck if there is a large number of tasks that must be initialised, in sequence, by a rendezvous from some parent task. A bottleneck can also arise if a single message is to be broadcast to a large number of other tasks. Again the semantics of the Ada rendezvous leads to a sequential, and therefore inefficient solution.

A possible way of improving on the algorithms that lead to the above bottlenecks is to have each task responsible for receiving and passing on the message (Burns, 1985). If each task passed on the message to two other tasks (i.e. the tasks are structured as a tree) then, if it can be assumed that the distributed system will allow a rendezvous between tasks A and B to proceed in parallel with a rendezvous involving tasks C and D, considerable improvements in speed can be achieved. For example, if 1,500 tasks require initialising, then rather than 1,500 sequential rendezvous only parallel rendezvous activities are required at the cost of a minimal amount of extra processing.

Although the above approach makes a significant reduction in the time taken to initialise a collection of tasks, even better performance can be achieved if each of the tasks involved is prepared to call more than two of its peers. The effect now is to delay all tasks until the complete collection is initialised. This will usually be the preferred approach for with many applications the overall effectiveness of the distributed system will be measured in terms of the slowest component task, i.e. the one that is last to be initialised. The following code implements such an algorithm:

```
procedure MAIN is
  MAX : constant := 1023;
  subtype TASK_RANGE is INTEGER range 0 .. MAX;
  task type TK is
    entry INITIALISE(B,T : TASK_RANGE);
  end TK;
  SET : array(TASK_RANGE) of TK;
  BASE,NEW_BASE : TASK_RANGE;
  TOP : INTEGER range
          TASK_RANGE'FIRST-1 .. TASK_RANGE'LAST;
  task body TK is
    MY_NUMBER : TASK_RANGE;
    -- other declarations
  begin
    declare
      BASE,NEW_BASE : TASK_RANGE;
      TOP : INTEGER range TASK_RANGE'FIRST-1
            .. TASK_RANGE'LAST;
    begin
      accept INITIALISE(B,T : TASK_RANGE) do
        MY_NUMBER := T;
        BASE := B;
        TOP := T - 1;
      end INITIALISE;
      while TOP >= BASE loop
        NEW_BASE   := (TOP + BASE)/2;
        SET(TOP).INITIALISE(NEW_BASE,TOP);
                --top half of remaining group
        TOP   := NEW_BASE - 1;
      end loop;
    end;
        .
        .
        .
  end TK;
begin
  TOP := TASK_RANGE'LAST;
  BASE := TASK_RANGE'FIRST;
  while TOP >= BASE loop
    NEW_BASE := (TOP + BASE)/2;
    SET(TOP).INITIALISE(NEW_BASE,TOP);
            --top half of remaining group
    TOP := NEW_BASE - 1;
  end loop;
end MAIN;
```

Each task is presented, during initialisation, with a range of uninitialised tasks (B..T). For simplicity the task's own name (number) is the top element of the range (T). Following the rendezvous, the task splits its given range in two and passes the top half over to another task. It then takes the bottom half and repeats the process; i.e. it splits it in two, passes top half on, and so on. Eventually the bottom half will consist of a single task (TOP = BASE) and, having passed this task on, it will have completed its initialisation role. With this algorithm an easy formula is available for evaluating the time it takes to initialise tasks. In N time intervals (measured in units of rendezvous) $2^{**}N-1$ tasks can be initialised. For example if N=14 over sixteen thousand tasks can be catered for. Table 13.1 gives some values for N.

	Number of Rendezvous						
	4	6	8	10	12	14	16
Maximum Number of Initialised Tasks	15	63	255	1023	4095	16383	65535

TABLE 13.1

Loosely Coupled Distributed Systems. It is in the programming of systems in which the processors do not share memory that Ada is most problematic. If tasks are in separate machines then they cannot run efficiently if they share data. Downes and Goldsack (1980), when considering preliminary Ada, introduced the concept of a 'zone' task in order to remove this source of inefficiency. A zone task runs on its own processor and may communicate with other zone tasks by using the rendezvous mechanism (only). This rendezvous is also restricted by not allowing parameters to be access types. The use of a zone task is similar in concept to the virtual node structure found in a number of languages designed for the programming of distributed systems; for example the "guardian" of extended CLU (Liskov, 1982) and Argus (Liskov & Scheifler, 1983), and the "network module" of Starmod (Cook, 1979).

In preliminary Ada the task was static, but this is no longer the case and it is therefore more appropriate to define the virtual node as a "network package" (Wellings 1984b). A network package may only have tasks and type declarations in its specification. Again, access types are not allowed as parameters to entries. In order to have non-shared access to library packages it must be possible for each network package to instantiate its own copy. All library packages would therefore need to be generic.

A more detailed discussion of the virtual node concept as it applies to Ada is given in the SPL report (Stammers *et al*, 1983; Tedd *et al*, 1984).

In a loosely coupled system, rendezvous across the system will be implemented by an exchange of messages by the underlying distribution network. The existence of such a network introduces some significant factors. It has already been noted (chapter 6) that a timed entry with time zero, or negative, will be deemed equivalent to a conditional entry call. Thus the time necessary to query the called task (across the network) to see if a rendezvous is immediately possible will not be taken into account for a timed entry call with zero time. By comparison a timed entry call with a small delay may never be successful, even if the called task is prepared to rendezvous, as all the time specified may be used by the network's distribution system.

With network systems it is usually necessary to consider the behaviour of the running software if the network partitions or if a subset of the available processors fail. With a network partition, the distribution system is unable, either temporarily or permanently, to pass the messages necessary for task A to rendezvous with task B (A and B being on different machines). The analysis here is somewhat complex as there may be up to six messages needed to perform a single rendezvous and the network partition could occur at any point in this sequence leaving the run-time systems of the two machines in an unsynchronised relationship. In some circumstances a timed or conditional entry call will enable the calling task to remove itself from the rendezvous request if the network partitions. However in other situations, it will be the reply messages that are lost (or postponed) and even a conditional entry call will block the calling task indefinitely.

One of the requirements of Ada is for it to deal with error conditions, and yet no predefined exceptions exist that relate to network problems such as partitioning. Moreover, the reliability of a network is not of such a high level that these error conditions can be left to the lower communication level of the distributed system (Reynolds *et al*, 1983).

Of similar importance is the consequence of a processor or node crash. With tightly coupled systems it may be possible for the run-time system to move all tasks associated with the fated processor onto other identical processors. Even if this were possible it may be inappropriate for loosely coupled systems. A discussion of fault-tolerant distributed systems programmed in Ada is given by Knight and Urquhart(1984). Again, Ada does not directly address this error condition. The only way of satisfactorily modelling a processor crash is to consider that all tasks running on that processor have been aborted (the abort statement being executed, logically, by the dying processor as a form of last rites). If this is the case then the possibility of tasks being aborted is real and hence the analysis given earlier concerning the abort statement should be considered for programs that are destined for distributed execution. A difficulty with extending the semantics of the abort to include processor failure is that some tasks running on non-failed machines may also be aborted if their master is on a failed processor. For example, if the processor running the main program unit crashed then all tasks would need to be aborted, which is clearly not desirable. To prohibit this, either the main program could be dealt with differently or the effect of the abort could be limited to a network package. The reason all children must be made abnormal with their parent is because they may access objects in their parent's domain. If parent and child were in different network packages, there would be no such objects; a child need not therefore perish with its parent.

An alternative approach to multicomputer execution is to consider the complete software system as a set of distributed Ada programs that communicate outside the language. This is the structure adopted in PULSE (Wellings *et al*, 1985a); agent tasks, called mediums, are in effect supported by the operating system. Program tasks can make entry calls on these mediums in order to interact with other programs.

One further, and more minor, topic to consider with distributed systems is the use of the real-time clock as provided by the standard package CALENDAR. It should not be assumed that all tasks are given access to the same clock and hence time should not be used as a synchronisation tool. This would be bad practice anyway even on a non-distributed architecture.

The partitioning of Ada programs for implementation on distributed hardware is a complex, though important, problem. Nevertheless it is beyond the scope of this book to consider this area further. A more detailed discussion can be found in the work of Cornhill (1983a,b 1984).

14 PORTABILITY

Portability was one of the key criteria governing the design of Ada. It is clear that, in the foreseeable future, the lifespan of the software elements of a system will be far longer than that of its hardware components. A system may be re-hosted three of four times during its existence and with each of these transformations the reliability of the enhanced system will depend, to a large extent, on the portability of the software. Even during the development of a 'one-off' system, portability can have a number of economic and technical advantages. If the design and development of some system is timetabled to take, say, five years then with non-portable languages the hardware would need to be bought in year one and used for developing the software. Using a portable language the software can be 'implemented' first, on a different machine, with the hardware being bought in year five. And four years can make an appreciable difference to the cost and performance of computer equipment.

A number of features of the Ada project have been designed to improve the portability of software written in this language. The avoidance of subsetting and supersetting, an agreed single language standard and the compiler validation exercises all make their contribution to reducing the adverse effects that compilers can have on portability. However compiler writers still have many options (both real and because of the ambiguity of certain aspects of the language specification) and it has proved useful for Ada-Europe to produce a portability guide (Nissen & Wallis, 1984). The issues explicitly linked to tasking are considered below.

A strict interpretation of the term 'portable' would require the behaviours of the executing software to be identical on the two hardware configurations involved. This is clearly an unhelpful definition as one of the reasons for re-hosting the software may have been to get better performance. The behaviour would not therefore be identical; one would be faster. With sequential programs, this non-portable feature is easy to isolate; with real-time multitasking programs it is more difficult. As well as the absolute execution times of tasks changing, their relative executions may vary. The program is unlikely to have identical real-time behaviour; this will be particularly significant if the architecture has changed from a single to a multiple processor one.

With multitasking software, portability must be considered not by the criterion of identical behaviour but in terms of continually satisfying its functional specification. This will include operational aspects as well as time-dependent properties. Notwithstanding these points, it would be somewhat alarming if the behaviour of a retargeted system were grossly different from that previously experienced.

A number of portability issues relate to the comparative performances of distributed and non-distributed processing and these were considered in the last chapter. It must be emphasised at this point, however, that shared variables can have a detrimental effect upon performance; if the processors do not share memory. The unsynchronised or erroneous use of shared variables is also a point at which bugs can be introduced into the software. On one implementation, due to fortuitous timings, the software may behave reliably with this unprotected use of shared objects; on another errors may become manifest.

The following are a number of specific points aimed at removing, or isolating, non-portable features of the language. These points are taken, primarily, from the portability guide referenced above:

(a) Task Activation

No assumptions should be made about the order in which tasks, which are declared together, are activated. The declarations of tasks should not cause side effects.

(b) Task Termination

No assumption should be made about the termination of tasks defined within library packages (see 15.2.3).

(c) Entry Parameters

The evaluation of parameters to entry calls should not have side effects, as no assumptions can be made about the order of evaluation. In particular, a parameter must not have a side effect which affects other parameters of the same entry.

(d) Entry Families

An implementation may restrict the range of entry families. This should be checked before re-targeting.

(e) Entry Queues

Although each entry queue is FIFO, this is in terms of requests arriving at the queue. This need not correspond to the order in which the requests were made.

(f) Type DURATION

The type DURATION is machine-dependent and is therefore a source of difficulties and possible unreliability. DURATION is guaranteed to have a range of -86400.0 .. +86400.0; a greater range, even if supported on a particular machine, should not be used. The accuracy of the type (i.e. its delta) will vary from machine to machine. Only the accuracy necessary for the application should be used and this should be checked before re-targeting. The mapping of delays, measured in terms of objects of type DURATION, on to the model numbers of the implementation may cause minor alterations to the behaviour of the re-targeted system.

(g) Guards

No assumption should be made about the order of evaluation of guards. Guards must not, therefore, have side effects that interfere with other guards.

(h) Selective Waits

If more than one accept alternative is in a position to be chosen (i.e. they all have open guards and outstanding entry calls) then an arbitrary choice is made. No reliance should be placed on the actual algorithm used on any particular implementation. For example, it should not be assumed that the textually first alternative is chosen or that the algorithm is fair.

(i) Conditional and Timed Entry Calls

The definition of the term 'immediate' may not be as expected, particularly in distributed systems; see chapter 6.

(j) Priorities

An implementation may restrict the range of priorities. More significantly, an implementation may map all specified priorities onto a single value. In addition, on a multiprocessor architecture a low priority task may run in parallel with a higher priority one. As a consequence of these points, no essential behaviour should depend upon this pragma. It has a use in 'fine tuning' but this is not a portable feature. A re-targeted system will have a number of real-time differences and fine tuning, if necessary, will need to be re-established.

(k) Aborts

No assumption should be made about when, if at all, a task being aborted is actually terminated.

(l) The Pragma SHARED

The pragma SHARED need not be supported on all systems and its effect, in terms of the objects to which it can be applied, is implementation dependent. Its use is not recommended.

(m) Representation-Clauses

Clearly any program that uses representation clauses is unlikely to be portable. A good modular structure to the program, however, will isolate the non-portable packages for re-coding. Where the interrupt model of the hardware has changed, considerable redesign of the driver tasks may be necessary.

15 PROGRAMMING STYLE FOR ADA TASKING

The bulk of this book has been structured as a tutorial introduction to those features of the Ada programming language that are concerned with concurrency. These tasking features are both flexible and powerful and can therefore be abused. It is possible to write Ada programs in which many nested levels of tasks are used, tasks liberally make entry calls and accept rendezvous requests, excessive overloading is employed and access types are used on all occasions. These programs will have many interesting properties worthy of discussion at academic gatherings; they do not, however, have anything to do with programming real applications in Ada.

The orthogonality of the language design implies that the programmer must discipline himself or herself to use a style that is simple but effective. A style and portability guide has already been published for Ada (Nissen & Wallis, 1984) and in this chapter we bring together a number of important points that have been made in this guide, the preceding chapters and elsewhere (for example Abbott, 1982; Abbott & Booch 1982; and Gardner *et al*, 1983).

15.1 Design of Concurrent Programs

It is beyond the scope of this book to present a comprehensive software engineering design methodology aimed at the language Ada. Other books have undertaken this work, for example 'Life Cycle Support in the Ada Environment' (McDermid & Ripken, 1984). Nevertheless, it is possible to isolate important features of a design process that are, in essence, independent of the actual methodology employed.

The only construct that can give concurrency in Ada programs is the task and it has three main roles:

(i)   To model objects that have a concurrent existence in the problem domain. These may be called active tasks.

(ii)   To exploit the parallel hardware of an implementation by defining parallel algorithms.

(iii)   To provide controlled support to active tasks in the form of monitors, buffers, agents, resource managers and synchronisers. These may be called passive tasks.

A task should be used for one, and only one, of the above functions. In particular, they should not act as both passive and active tasks (an active task may have an entry for initialisation). Where the problem domain defines two processes which the implementation hardware can run in parallel then the corresponding tasks should be considered active in the sense of being in class (i).

The use of Ada to implement parallel algorithms is largely untried as code generators for multiprocessor architectures are not yet available. A task is, however, a high-level structure and an Ada program typically contains a few, sizeable, active tasks. It might appear inappropriate to use Ada in highly parallel architectures, for which a language like occam would seem to be better suited - for an example of the use of Ada in coding parallel algorithms see Cohen (1982). Nevertheless, with conventional multiprocessor hardware, faster algorithms are clearly possible if the program is structured to exploit the parallel architecture. These algorithms would, on the other hand, probably be quite inefficient on single processor implementations. It is recommended that such algorithms be programmed as functions or procedures with the necessary tasks being defined within the subprogram. All these tasks should terminate naturally.

By comparison, passive tasks should be hidden within packages that specify procedures for manipulating the controlling tasks. Each procedure will usually contain a simple entry call that has the same parameters as those used in the procedure call. These packages will, in general, provide controlled access to resources that are shared between two or more active tasks. In terms of design, early recognition should be made of these shared objects, be they records, files or devices. Package specifications, together with some form of comment that will indicate the kind of synchronisations necessary, can then be given. This is all that is required to code the active tasks. The packages themselves can be constructed using standard techniques as there is only a limited variety of these passive tasks. All buffers can be instantiated from a simple generic package, and resource control packages can also be constructed in a straightforward manner.

In many situations, the relationship between an active and a passive task will match the familiar client/server model. The passive or server task must, therefore, be concerned with matters of liveness and fairness; it will be called by many clients and must ensure that they are dealt with adequately.

The design of an active task should be no more complex than that of a sequential program that makes use of library packages. Where one active task wishes to communicate with another, the communication should, whenever possible, model a consumer/producer relationship with a buffer task (defined within a package) being used to loosen the coupling between the two active processes.

It would be advantageous if the decomposition defined by the design process could isolate the specifications of the active and passive processes. Unfortunately, in three respects this is not possible.

(a) The need to program different priorities to active tasks.

(b) The need for active tasks to make timed/conditional entry calls on 'resources'.

(c) The need for active tasks to identify themselves to server tasks.

One consequence of "task A" having a higher priority than "task B" is that if they are both requesting a resource then A should be dealt with first. The FIFO definition of an entry queue does not allow this behaviour and therefore a family of entries must be declared and used by the passive task;

```
type CLASS is (HIGH,MEDIUM,LOW);

package RESOURCE is
  procedure REQUEST (C : CLASS; ...);
end RESOURCE;

package body RESOURCE is
  task CONTROLLER is
    entry GET (CLASS) (...);
  end CONTROLLER;
  procedure REQUEST (C : CLASS; ...) is
  begin
    CONTROLLER.GET(C)(...);
  end REQUEST;
  task body CONTROLLER is separate;
end RESOURCE;
```

Any client task would need to pass a parameter of type CLASS to the requesting subprogram. An outline of how to program tasks that have entry families is given in chapter 11.

If the behaviour of an active task is such that a direct timed or conditional entry call is appropriate then it is necessary for the passive task to be visible in the package specification. In many ways this is inappropriate; for example the synchronisations necessary for the controlled resource may be such that more than one entry point is involved (see chapter 10). An alternative solution is to have the timed entry call embedded in the resource control package; i.e. rather than have:

```
package RESOURCE is
  task CONTROLLER is
    entry GET (...);
          .
          .
  end CONTROLLER;
end RESOURCE;
```

with the call:

```
select
  RESOURCE.CONTROLLER.GET(...);
or
  delay D;
  raise INPUT_ERROR;
end select;
```

the package could be constructed:

```
package RESOURCE is
  procedure REQUEST (DU : DURATION; ...);
end RESOURCE;
```

with the call:

```
RESOURCE.REQUEST(D, ...);
```

The timed entry call, perhaps constructed as a double request (see chapter 6) is then made within procedure REQUEST:

```
procedure REQUEST(DU : DURATION; ...) is
  -- example using only a single entry call
begin
  select
    CONTROLLER.GET(...);
  or
    delay DU;
    raise INPUT_ERROR;
  end select;
end REQUEST;
```

In both of these examples the exception INPUT_ERROR is raised at the point of the call if the request is not accepted within the required time period.

Finally, reliability requirements may make it necessary for server tasks to know the identity of their clients. (With the Ada model of the rendezvous this is, in general, not the case.) This situation can arise when:

(a) it is necessary to check that a task releasing resources actually has them to release (but this can also be achieved by checking a private key that is allocated with the resource, see chapter 10),

(b) a deadlock prevention algorithm requires a case history of client-resource dependencies,

(c) a fairness algorithm requires that the volume of resources allocated to each client is limited.

Care must be taken with (b) and (c) for if a client task merely loops round and re-requests, then this in itself could lead to the indefinite postponement of other tasks. A task's identification may be passed to a server package by using either an array index (for an array of tasks) or an access value (of the task itself) as a parameter.

Having isolated those passive tasks that require family entries, timed/conditioned entry calls or client identification it is possible to develop and implement the component tasks of the concurrent program. If the number of active processes in the system is fixed, as it will be in most process control applications, then they should be represented by static tasks. Only in situations where domain objects enter and leave the system should the dynamic generation of tasks be employed. This will be the case in an air traffic control system where each plane in the controlled air space is allocated a task:

```
task type PLANE is
  entry INITIALISE (R:REC);
        -- For some appropriate record type
end PLANE;

type A_PLANE is access PLANE;

procedure NEW_PLANE (R:REC) is
  P: A_PLANE;
begin
  P := new PLANE;
  P.INITIALISE(R);
end NEW_PLANE;
```

Whichever task is responsible for setting up new PLANE tasks will call the procedure NEW_PLANE. Note that all of these PLANE tasks will be anonymous. (See 15.2.10). This solution may also be unacceptably slow if the time it takes to create and initialise the new task is significant.

15.2 Summary

The following is a summary of points from previous chapters that will assist in the production of legible, maintainable and correct concurrent programs. These guidelines appertain only to considerations of tasking, which, although important, is only one aspect of significance in the production of Ada programs.

15.2.1 Shared Variables

Shared variables should not normally be used to communicate data between concurrent tasks. Only when two tasks are clearly acting as coroutines should they have access to shared objects. If, two, or more concurrent tasks wish to update a shared variable then they should do so by calling subprograms that translate requests into entry calls for a controller (passive) task.

15.2.2 Passive Task Termination

All passive tasks should have terminate alternatives on their select statements so that they will terminate if, and only if, that entire section of the program wishes to terminate. In these circumstances it is impossible for a passive task to terminate before its clients (unless, of course, it fails or is aborted). If it is desirable for the task to perform a final 'autopsy' before terminating (perhaps writing to a file) then a CLOSE_DOWN entry should be defined which is called as a 'last rite'. For programs that do terminate naturally this can be easily achieved by defining the active tasks in an inner block:

```
procedure FRED is
  -- declaration of passive task types and objects
begin
  declare
    -- declaration of active task types and objects
  begin
    null;
  end;
  -- CALL CLOSE_DOWN in all passive tasks
end FRED;
```

The inner block will not terminate until all the active tasks have. It is then safe to close down all the support tasks.

15.2.3 Library Task Termination

Tasks cannot of themselves form library units. However, it is quite possible, and useful, for library packages and subprograms to contain tasks. The ARM does not define how a task within a library package terminates in the case where the main program has terminated. In particular, it cannot be assumed that a 'library' task will be allowed to complete its present action. These tasks should be coded to have terminate alternatives on their select statements and to have all of their processing contained within accept statements.

15.2.4 Contents of Accept Statement

In general, an accept statement should contain only those statements that must be executed during the inter-task rendezvous. This will usually mean the minimum amount of processing necessary to construct any 'out' parameters of the entry call and record the value of those 'in' parameters that will be used after the termination of the rendezvous. If this rule is obeyed then maximum parallelism will ensue. Not withstanding this rule it was noted in chapter 13 that code optimisation is easier to undertake if a passive task has no executable statements, other than loop and select constructs, outside accept statements.

15.2.5 No-Wait Send

If it is desirable for a task not to be delayed in sending a message to another task then a single agent task can act as an intermediary for the calling task (see chapter 9). The agent is delayed waiting for the server to receive and process the message; the calling task merely copies the message over to the agent (by means of an entry call) and proceeds. If an agent is used, then the calling task must make no assumptions about the arrival of its message; it cannot even be sure that the server task is still executing. Another possible difficulty with agent tasks is considered in 15.2.7.

15.2.6 No-Wait Receive

Complementary to no-wait send; an intermediary can be used to receive data for an active process. Rather than wait for a rendezvous to terminate, an agent can be used as a 'mailbox' for the ensuing communications. Only when the active task requires the data need it wait on the agent, which will usually be in a position to forward the 'mail' immediately. See below for a possible difficulty with agents.

15.2.7 The Use of Agents

Care must be taken with agent tasks if they are formed by the action of an allocator on a global access type. Unless a garbage collector is present, which is doubtful in a real-time system, each agent will require a permanent memory location even after it has terminated. For non-terminating programs a pool of reusable agents should be employed.

15.2.8 Aborts

The use of the abort statement should be avoided if at all possible. Its existence in the language makes it difficult to produce reliable code for resource management packages (see chapter 10). One must, however, cater for the use of abort, for even if the present version of the program does not use the feature, future 'upgrades' may introduce it. The use of agents can minimise the damage caused by clients being aborted.

15.2.9 Task Types and Objects

Where there is only one task associated with a task type then that task type should be anonymous. This avoids the introduction of unnecessary names. However, where several tasks have identical structure they should be declared from a common task type.

15.2.10 Anonymous Tasks

A task should not be made anonymous (i.e. when it has been created by the action of an access type that is then re-assigned) unless it has terminated. If there is a dynamic number of tasks then they should be structured as a linked list. For example, at the end of the previous section a variable number of PLANE tasks was needed in an air traffic control system. Rather than have each of these tasks become anonymous, after they have been created, a record can be constructed and added to a list:

```
task type PLANE is
  entry INITIALISE (R:REC);
end PLANE;
type A_PLANE is access PLANE;
type LIST_ELEMENT;
type LIST is access LIST_ELEMENT;
type LIST_ELEMENT is
  record
    NAME : SOME_TYPE;
    NODE : A_PLANE;
    NEXT : LIST := null;
  end record;
procedure NEW_PLANE (R : REC; L : out LIST) is
  P : A_PLANE := new PLANE;
begin
  P.INITIALISE(R);
  L := new LIST_ELEMENT;
  L.NAME := R.NAME;
  L.NODE :=P;
end NEW_PLANE;
```

a call of NEW_PLANE would have to form;

```
NEW_PLANE(R,TEMP_L);
END_NODE.NEXT := TEMP_L;--assuming list is not empty
END_NODE := TEMP_L;
```

where END_NODE (of type LIST) is a pointer to the last plane to be initialised. A record could be removed by reallocating pointers.

15.2.11   Task and Entry Attributes

All of the attributes associated with a task or an entry should be used with care. T'TERMINATED = TRUE is reliable, as once a task has terminated it must remain in that state; T'TERMINATED = FALSE can however be misleading as T might terminate before any action, based on the assumption that it hasn't, can be taken. Similarly T'CALLABLE can only be used if the value FALSE is sought. Using the exact value given by the entry attribute COUNT is also dangerous as it can increase (by a new call being made) or decrease (due to a timed entry call or an abort) at any time.

15.2.12   Select Statement Guards

A guard should never use shared variables. Moreover, the collection of all guards for each select statement should be related in such a way that it is impossible for each of the guards to have the value FALSE. (Select alternatives that do not have a guard are considered to have TRUE as a default guard). At the commencement of the execution of a select statement, all guards are evaluated. They are evaluated just once. Guards may call boolean functions, but side effects should not be allowed.

15.2.13 Busy Waits

Busy waits should always be avoided; on limited processor systems they waste processing cycles and on distributed architectures they can also lead to excessive network traffic. In order for a task to delay itself to some time T in the future, the delay statement:

```
delay  T - CALENDAR.CLOCK;
```

will give a delay of at least the required amount. An agent may busy wait (with a relatively long period) on SOME_TASK'TERMINATED (where the agent is waiting on SOME_TASK to call it) in order to return itself to the agent pool.

15.2.14 Passive Tasks

A passive task should, in general, define and receive entry calls but not make any. The only exception to this is when a resource management task must make requests on 'lower order' resources that are themselves protected by tasks.

15.2.15 Deadlock Prevention

To avoid mutual deadlock, two active tasks should not call each other directly and, in general, N tasks should not form a cycle of requests. Data communication can take place in both directions with the Ada rendezvous and hence one of the tasks can take the role of master for the communication. Wherever possible an intermediate passive task should be defined on which both of the active tasks make entry calls. Deadlock can also occur when tasks wish to make use of more than one non-concurrent resource. A single resource management task (embedded within an appropriate package) should be used to gain access to all resources that may be used concurrently.

15.2.16 Priorities

Only a small number of priority levels should be used and all tasks should be given a priority if any are. The priority of a task that does not contain the pragma is undefined, it might be high or low!

If any entry specification has an address clause then it will (should) be used for a rendezvous with the hardware - i.e. handling an interrupt. This rendezvous will have a higher priority than any specified in the program.

Priorities should only be used for 'fine tuning' and not as a means of ensuring particular synchronisations. The explicit programming of priorities using family entries is needed to overcome the FIFO structure of entry queues.

16 FORMAL SPECIFICATIONS

In this chapter attention is focused, albeit only briefly, on the significant topic of formal specification. Formal models of Ada tasking are urgently needed in order to give complete operational semantics for Ada; and, as a consequence of this, the means by which we can confidently express the behaviour of multitasking Ada programs. Only when these models exist will it be possible to assert that programs are free from deadlocks, are safe, and are fair. Unfortunately, although specification and verification techniques are well understood with sequential languages, a host of different techniques have been proposed for expressing the equivalent properties of a language such as Ada. Among the techniques proposed are predicate transition nets (Genrich & Lautenbach, 1979 and de Bondeli, 1983), relational semantics (Jones, 1983), temporal logic (Lamport, 1983; Barringer & Kuiper, 1983 and Barringer *et al*, 1984) and interval logic (Schwartz *et al*, 1983). Considerations vary from the theoretical (Pnueli & DeRoever, 1982 and Li, 1982) to those oriented toward a subset of the language (Clemmensen 1982). A short review of these models will be given below.

One of the benefits of a formal model is to have the ability to prove that two programs are equivalent. It is then possible to define allowable transformations that change a program into a different but equivalent form. The main motivation for this is the production of programs that are more efficient to implement. Beneficial transformations would be those that:

(a) increased the parallelism for multiprocessor implementations
(b) reduced the amount of context switching on single processor implementations.

16.1 Program Verification and Specification

The designers of Ada were not required to provide an operational semantics for the language. They chose not to and, as a result, a number of ambiguities surround particular aspects of the language. The interactions between shared variables and rendezvous parameters is one such topic. As indicated earlier, a formal method of describing the semantics of Ada programs is of value not just in resolving any ambiguities in the languages design but in:

    (a) teaching how the Ada tasking construct works.

    (b) debugging/verifying existing Ada programs.

    (c) specifying/designing new Ada programs.

There is a need to classify the various methods available for formal specification. Barringer (1984) attempts to do this by first introducing a list of assessment criteria;

> *"clearly, the criteria should include the usual motherhood about formal methods (carried over from sequential program development), that is, that they are formal, understandable to the non-mathematician, teachable, free from implementation bias, applicable to programming in the large etc."*

Other important factors are: applicability, modularity, expressiveness, abstractness, adaptability, usability, practicality and exercisability. Of the main methods available path expressions have already been discussed in chapter 8. Three further formalisms will now be described.

16.2 State-Transition Semantics

    Figure 7.1 represents an informal description of the states that a task can be in; also the actions that transpose a task from one state into another have been discussed. A formal definition of these semantics is an attempt to give a rigorous description of these states and transitions. Having obtained these axioms it is then possible to develop proof rules for analysing the behaviour of concurrent programs. Two such schemes have been described by Barringer and Mearns(1982) and Gerth and DeRoever(1984). Neither of these is complete in the sense of considering all aspects of Ada tasking. To give an indication of the analysis necessary to provide a complete operational semantics, a small fragment of the language will be specified using just one of the possible methods. This specification will follow that given by Pnueli and DeRoever(1982).

    The model presented below is based on the assumption that the behaviour of a concurrent program can be defined in terms of the sequential execution of interleaved atomic instructions, taken one at a time, from a single task each time. The language subset does not, therefore, allow for the use of shared variables. Indeed, it contains only a fixed number of tasks, assignment statements, if and loop statements, entry calls, accept statements and selective waits (in which only accept alternatives are allowed). It excludes subprograms and blocks. A program P in this language subset thus consists of a collection of tasks T1...Tm and a set of variables defined within these tasks y1...yn. Each of these variables will have a value from some domain Di; this domain will include the possibility of the variable being as yet undefined. Each of the tasks Ti will have a set of entries Ei declared – this set may of course be empty.

The execution of the program P is represented as a progression of states. Each state, S, being completely specified by the 'location' of each task and the value of each variable:

```
S - < (T1 at location) & (T2 at location) & ...
        & (Tm at location); d1, d2 ... dn >
```

where di is contained in the domain Di.

The location of each task determines the state of that task; therefore, at the initialisation of the program all tasks are 'NOT_CREATED' and all variables are undefined:

```
S0 - < (T1 at NOT_CREATED) & (T2 at NOT_CREATED) & ...
         & (Tm at NOT_CREATED); undefined, undefined, ... >
```

The sequence of states S0,S1,... is an interleaving of the sequence of states for each task Si0,Si1,...; where Sip is the pth state of task i. There is no requirement for any of these sequences to terminate.

An expression is a mapping from some of the set of variables onto a single value (constants are taken to belong to the set of variables). For convenience, an expression is taken to act on all variables and is represented by the function, f. An assignment to the variable yj therefore has the form:

```
yj :- f(y)
```

where y is the set of variables y1, y2, ... yn. The value of the expression in any particular state is given by f(d). Using this notation the assignment statement can be defined as follows:

```
    < ... (Ti at yj := f(y); S) & ...; d >
-> < ... (Ti at S) & ...;
        d1, d2 ... dj-1, f(d), dj+1 ... >
```

The assignment statement belongs to task Ti; the metasymbol 'at' implies that the task is about to execute the following state. In this case the following state is an assignment; the one after that is represented by S. The action of the assignment transition is to move task Ti to be 'at S', in doing so one of the variables has been updated. Although y represented the set of all variables the requirement that tasks do not share variables implies that yj is a variable of Ti as were the members of y upon which the function f had any non-null action.

The transition represented by the if statement is straightforward:

```
    < ... (Ti at if f(y) then
           S1 else S2 end if; S) & ...; d >
 -> < ... (Ti at S1; S) & ...; d >
```

provided f(y) = TRUE, or

```
    < ... (Ti at if f(y) then
           S1 else S2 end if; S) & ...; d >
 -> < ... (Ti at S2; S) & ...; d >
```

when f(y) = FALSE.

Similarly the while loop transition has two possible actions depending upon the value of a boolean expression:

```
    < ... (Ti at while f(y) loop B end loop ; S) & ...; d >
 -> < ... (Ti at B; while f(y) loop
              B end loop ; S) & ...; d >
```

provided f(y) = TRUE, and

```
    < ... (Ti at while f(y) loop B end loop; S) & ...; d >
 -> < ... (Ti at S) & ...; d >
```

provided f(y) = FALSE.

Semantics of the Rendezvous. The rendezvous requires two tasks to be in appropriate states and the transition will involve the simultaneous movement of both tasks. Let e be an entry of task Tj. A simple rendezvous transition is, therefore, represented as

```
    < ... (Ti at e(u; v); Si) & ...
           (Tj at accept e(f: in; g: out); B; end e; Sj)
           & ...; d >

 -> < ... (Ti at rendezvous e; Si) & ...
           (Tj at f := u; B; v := g; end e; Sj) & ...; d >
```

The parameters of the rendezvous, if any, are split into groups of 'in' and 'out'. A variable may be contained in both groups and is thus an 'in out' parameter. The actions to be performed by Tj are clearly laid out. With a select statement the transition is:

```
< (Ti at e(u; v); Si) & ...
  (Tj at select ... or when f(y) ->
  accept e(f: in; g: out); B; end e;
  Sj; ... end select; Sc) & ...; d >

-> < Ti at rendezvous e; Si) & ...
   < Tj at f := u; B; v := g; end e; Sj; Sc) & ...; d >
```

B is again the state representing the body of the accept statement, Sj is the state (or states) following the accept and Sc is the state after the select statement. In order for the above transition to take place, f(y) must equal true; however this is a necessary but not sufficient requirement as Tj may rendezvous with a different task on a different accept alternative. The choice of alternative is 'arbitrary'; no requirement of fairness is enforced by the language definition. Having moved through the states f := u; B and v := g, the task Tj is now ready to terminate the rendezvous:

```
< ... (Ti at rendezvous e; Si) & ...
  (Tj at end e; Sj; Sc) & ...; d >

-> < ... (Ti at Si) & ... & (Tj at Sj; Sc) & ...; d >
```

Clearly, considerable work is needed to extend the above analysis to include all features of the tasking model: for example, exceptions (Li, 1982), dynamic creation of tasks, aborts and shared variables. A movement from an interleaved to a true parallel model of the concurrency is given by Lehmann, Pnueli and Stavi(1981).

Particularly difficult to analyse, by any specification method, are those features of the language that incorporate real-time dependencies. (Some advances have been made in this area recently by Shyamasundar et al, 1984). For example, consider the interaction of two tasks executing on two different processors. Task A executes a select statement with an else clause. At the same time, task B makes a call on one of the entries of task A; this entry has an associated accept statement in the select statement (and is open). On this multiprocessor system the relative speeds of the processors that are executing tasks A and B will determine whether task A accepts the entry call or, if task B is slightly slower, executes the else part. Incorporating relative processor speeds into a model of the formal semantics for the language is far from trivial! However as a first step one would like to be able to detect race conditions, speed dependencies, deadlock possibilities, etc.

16.3 Temporal Logics

Temporal logic is an extension to propositional and predicate calculi, with new operators being introduced in order to express properties relating to real-time. It is a formal method that suits well that type of operational semantic description given earlier. There are four temporal operators usually defined: [], <>, O and U. The operator **always,** [], implies that the following property will hold true in all future states; for example [] $(X > 0)$ states that X will always be greater than zero. The operator **sometime,** <>, means that the following property will hold true at some moment in the future; e.g. <> $(y > N)$ implies that eventually y will take a value greater than N. The operators **next,** O, and **until,** U, are less used in this type of analysis. Combinations of operators are allowed, for example:

$$[] ((y > 0) => <> (y > N))$$

states that whenever y has a greater value than zero there will be a future moment when y is greater than N.

This type of logic is particularly useful in arguing about the liveness or fairness of algorithms represented by an Ada program; the following assertion:

$$(Ti \ at \ e: \ S) => <> (Ti \ at \ S)$$

implies that if task Ti calls entry e (in some other task) then eventually the rendezvous will be completed (with no exceptions being raised) and Ti will be in a position to execute the next state. Program termination can be expressed, in its most general sense, as

$$(Ti \ at \ NOT\_CREATED) =>$$
$$<> (Ti \ after \ TERMINATED) \ for \ all \ i$$

Such applications of temporal logic illustrate its use in verifying existing programs rather than in the hierarchical specification and rigorous development of new ones. It is possible to criticise the logic as being too global and non modular, it being usually necessary to possess the complete program in order to analyse any part thereof. To overcome these difficulties it is possible to extend the formalism so that the transitions themselves effectively become propositions in the logic. This approach has been advocated by Lamport (1983), Barringer and Kuiper (1983) and Barringer *et al,* (1984). Another criticism arrives out of the low level properties of the temporal operators which can lead to complex formulae that are themselves difficult to verify! The higher order operators of interval logic (Schwartz *et al*, 1983) are an attempt to enhance the expressiveness of temporal logics.

16.4 Predicate-Transition Nets

The use of Place-Transition nets (Brauer, 1980) for modelling the behaviour of concurrent systems was proposed by C.A. Petri over twenty years ago. These nets are constructed as marked directed bipartite graphs from two types of nodes; S-elements denoting local atomic states and T-elements denoting transitions. The arcs of the graph provide the relationship between the S and T elements. Markings on the graph represent tokens over the S-elements; the movement of a token represents a change in the state of the program. Rules are used to specify when and how a token may move from one S-element to another via a transition element.

Place-Transition nets have the useful characteristics of being simple, abstract and graphical, and provide a general framework for analysing many kinds of distributed systems. They have the disadvantage that they can produce very large and unwieldy representations. To allow for a more concise modelling of such systems Genrich and Lautenbach (1979 and 1981) introduced Predicate-Transition nets. With these nets an S-element can model several normal S-elements (similarly T-elements) and the tokens, which originally had no internal structure, can be 'coloured' by tuples of data which may be constants or variables.

De Bondeli (1983) has developed a detailed predicate-transition net model for tasking in Ada. The results of this work are, at times, complex and beyond the scope of this book. They clearly have a role in understanding the Ada variant of concurrency and can play a part in the design of concurrent programs particularly in the control flow aspects of systems design.

17 CONCLUSION

17.1 Is The Tasking Model Useful?

The frustrating time period is over; validated Ada compilers have, at last, become widely available. Ada has been tried on a number of projects and has, in general, proved to be successful in meeting its design aims. A closer examination of these applications, however, reveals that little experience has yet been gained in using the tasking features or in programming real-time systems. The package construct, private types, separate compilation and generics have all combined to provide a well designed, sequential programming language. Unfortunately one cannot be as confident about the tasking features. Consider all the ways in which the tasking model can be criticised:

(i)   It is difficult to implement efficiently.

(ii)   It is extremely difficult to give a formal description of the semantics of the real-time features.

(iii)   The existence of the abort statement makes it difficult to argue about other language features or to provide reliable code.

(iv)   The deallocation of storage used by terminated tasks is not always possible without the use of a garbage collector which is not required by the ARM.

(v)   The use of shared variables and the pragma SHARED is contentious.

(vi)   The mapping of tasks onto distributed hardware is far from trivial.

(vii)   The notion of priority is vague and weak.

In the face of these criticisms is the Ada tasking model of use? A defence of Ada would argue that although present implementations appear to be inefficient this is not an inherent property of the language and the next generation of compilers must (and will) perform better. The lack of a formal definition, although unfortunate, will not inhibit the development of reliable code as the existence of such a model would be used by very few programmers anyway. As for the other criticisms, they can be countered by adopting a programming style that results in the issues being of academic interest only.

The resolution of this debate will only be made when sufficient experience of actually using tasking has been amassed. Language changes may then be considered for some features (see below).

What is clearer is that Ada will introduce to many thousands of programmers the facilities of concurrency and will thereby extend the conceptual framework of the professional programmer. Whether Ada allows for a natural and effective expression of this concept of concurrency is again a matter of debate.

This book has attempted to discuss in detail all aspects of the tasking model; and to do so in sufficient detail to allow reliable production of concurrent Ada programs to be undertaken. Example generic buffers, resource controllers, messengers and mailboxes have been given. These should greatly facilitate the production of Ada code.

Although the tasking model is more problematic than other areas of the language, an Ada programmer must not evade a responsibility to understand the model and gain experience in using it. The decision to use tasking (and how to use it) must be made from knowledge not ignorance.

17.2 Language Improvements

At various places within this book suggestions have been made for possible improvements to the tasking model. These comments are now summarised so that a more complete picture can be given.

17.2.1 Storage Deallocation

Simple 'use once' agent tasks are an important programming tool. Often, these tasks are created by the action of an allocator with the associated access type being declared at the outer-most level of the program, or in a library package. Although these agents terminate once they have been used, it is not possible for the run-time system to deallocate all associated storage as there could still be an object (of the same access type) pointing to the terminated task. The result is that for each agent created, there must be some memory permanently reserved. With long running programs, storage exhaustion is an inevitable consequence, if there is no garbage collection.

The only reliable way of using such agent tasks, is to support a pool of reusable agents; this is an unnecessarily complex software structure – see chapter 10. Some means of instructing the run-time system to deallocate all storage used by a terminated task is required. Note, the predefined generic procedure UNCHECKED_DEALLOCATION can not be applied to task objects (ARM 13.10.1.8).

17.2.2 A More Expressive Rendezvous

Many more transactions could be programmed as a single rendezvous if a somewhat more powerful rendezvous mechanism was supported. It is often the case that synchronisation rules prohibit certain transactions taking place (e.g. adding to a full buffer) and yet a rendezvous may need to start before the rule can be checked. (e.g. adding N objects to a buffer with M free slots; is M $>=$ N ?). The result is that many types of (conceptually single) transaction require two rendezvous. There are changes that would eradicate this problem, two of which were discussed:

(a) Allow guards to have access to 'in' parameters of entry calls.
(b) Allow a rendezvous to be requeued (i.e. suspended) during its execution.

With the second approach an accept alternative of a select statement would be allowed to contain an 'await' statement; for example:

```
await (M >= N);
```

If the boolean expression evaluates FALSE, the rendezvous is suspended and that execution of the select statement is terminated. A subsequent execution of that select statement will re-test the expression and may resume the suspended rendezvous (Wellings, 1984b; Silberschatz, 1984).

17.2.3 Pragma INLINE(task_object)

One of the reasons that programs with tasks are presently inefficient in their execution is the proliferation of passive tasks that the tasking model requires and the subsequent large number of context switches that must be performed. Optimisations exist (in theory) that would remove certain kinds of tasks by replacing accept statements by protected procedure calls that can be executed without a context switch. The extension of the pragma INLINE (or the creation of a new differently named pragma) to apply to tasks would enable the programmer to control this kind of optimisation by requesting that the named task is implemented as, in effect, a monitor.

17.2.4 Entry Families and the Select Statement

It is often useful to have a select statement where each alternative is an accept on a different member of an entry family. For large families, the necessary code becomes long-winded. However this could be improved by introducing syntactical forms that combine entry families and the select statement - see chapter 11. This type of change has also been recommended by Gehani and Cargill (1984) to remove the polling bias that exists when using families.

17.2.5 Priority

The concept of priority within Ada is weak; no minimum set of levels need be supported by an implementation, the behaviour of the select statement takes no account of priority, all tasks generated from the same task type must have the same priority, and tasks that have not been allocated a priority can not be assumed to have a low one. (As a result if one task out of a hundred must be given a high priority all the other ninety-nine must be explicitly given a low priority). In addition there is no obvious method of assigning priority levels to 'hardware tasks' (external devices making interrupt entry calls). The model that Modula (Wirth, 1977a,b,c) implements for interacting with external events appears to be much more powerful.

17.2.6 Distribution of Tasks

This book has not gone into great detail about the execution of Ada programs on multiprocessor or distributed hardware. The reasons for this limited coverage being that little experience has yet been obtained in this area. Nevertheless some language changes, motivated by the particular difficulties of distribution, have been discussed:

(a) The introduction of a "network package" (or virtual node) as the object that is mapped onto processors. A network package may only have tasks and type declarations in its specification. Access types are not allowed.

(b) The introduction of a new predefined exception to deal with network partitioning.

(c) The extension of the semantics of abort to take into account processor failure. If a processor fails, all tasks running on it are assumed to have been aborted. However, in order for the aborting of a parent (master) not to affect child tasks running on other processors, the rules governing the abort would have to be changed so that the knock-on effect of the abort is restricted to a network package.

17.2.7 Library Task Termination

The conditions for termination of tasks that are defined in library units should be specified. In particular such a task should not be terminated (when the main program unit terminates) while it is in the executable state.

The above improvements would not add to the complex nature of the tasking model; rather they would lead to a model that is easier to use, has increased expressive power and is easier to implement efficiently.

REFERENCES

Abbott, R.J. (1982a). Ada style guide (draft). The Aerospace Corporation, Los Angeles.

Abbott, R.J. & Booch, G. (1982b). A usage guide for Ada. The Aerospace Corporation, Los Angeles.

Andler, S. (1979). Predicate path expressions. Conf. Rec. 6th ACM Symp. on Prin. of Programming Languages, pp. 226-236.

Andrews, G.R. (1981). Synchronising resources. ACM Trans. Prog. Lang. and Systems vol 3, no.4, pp. 405-430.

Andrews, G.R. (1982). The distributed programming language SR - mechanisms, design and implementation. Software-Practice & Experience vol 12, no.8, pp. 719-754.

Andrews, G.R. & Schneider, F.B. (1983). Concepts and notations for concurrent programming. Computing Surveys vol 15, no.1, pp. 3-43.

A.R.M. (1983). J. Ichbiah et. al., Reference manual for the Ada programming language. ANSI/MIL-STD-1815A.

Balzer, R.M. (1971). PORTS - A method for dynamic interprogram communication and job control. Proc. AFIPS Spring Jt. Computer Conf (Atlantic City, N.J.) vol 38, pp. 485-489, Arlington, Va.: AFIPS press.

Barnes, J.G.P. (1982). Ada and parallelism. Tool and Notions for Programming Construction, ed. Neel, D., pp. 272-306 Cambridge University Press.

Barnes, J.G.P. (second edition 1984). Programming in Ada. Addison-Wesley.

Barringer, H., Kuiper, R. & Pnueli, A. (1984a). Now you may compose temporal logic specifications. Proc. of the 13th ACM Symp. on the theory of computing, Washington.

Barringer, H. (1984b). Formal specification techniques for parallel and distributed systems - a short review. Ada-Europe working group on formal methods for specification and development.

Barringer, H. & Mearns, I. (1982). Axioms and proof rules for Ada tasks. IEE Proc. vol 129, no.2.

Barringer, H. & Kuiper, R. (1983). Towards the hierarchical, temporal logic, specification of concurrent systems. Proc. of the STL/SERC workshop on the analysis of concurrent systems.

Ben-Ari, M. (1982). Principles of concurrent programming. Prentice Hall, Englewood Cliffs, NJ.

Best, E. (1982). Relational semantics of concurrent programs (with some applications). Proc. IFIP WG2.2 Conf.

Bloom, T. (1979). Evaluating synchronisation mechanisms. Proc. 7th Symp. Operating System Primitives, pp. 24-32.

de Bondeli, P. (1983). Models for the control of concurrency in Ada based on predicate transition nets. presented at meeting of Ada-Europe working group on formal methods for specification and development, Brussels.

Brauer, W. (ed) (1980). Net theory and applications. Lecture Notes in Computer Science, Springer Verlag.

Brinch Hansen, P. (1972). Structured multi-programming. Comm. ACM vol 15, no.7, pp. 574-578.

Brinch Hansen, P. (1973a). Concurrent programming concepts. ACM Computer Surveys, vol 5, no.4, pp. 223-245.

Brinch Hansen, P. (1973b). Operating system principles. Prentice Hall, Englewood Cliffs, NJ.

Brinch Hansen, P. (1975). The programming language Concurrent Pascal. IEEE Trans. on Software Eng. vol 2, pp. 199-207.

Brinch Hansen, P. (1978). Distributed processes: A concurrent programming concept. Comm. ACM vol 21, no.11, pp. 934-941.

Brinch Hansen, P. (1981). Edison: a multi-processor language. Software-Practice & Experience vol 11, no.4, pp. 325-361.

Burns, A. & Robinson, J. (1984a). A prototype Ada dialogue development system. Ada UK News.

Burns, A. & Robinson, J. (1984b). Tool requirements for the implementation of user-interfaces in Ada. Ada UK News.

Burns, A. (1984c). Early experiences in providing Ada training. Information Technology Training vol 2, no.1, pp. 29-31.

Burns, A. & Kirkham, J.A. (1985a). The construction information management system prototypes in Ada. accepted for publication in Software, Practice and Experience.

Burns, A. (1985b). Efficient initialisation routines for multi-processor systems programmed in Ada. to be published in Ada Letters.

Campbell, R.H. & Habermann, A.N. (1974). The specification of process synchronisation by path expressions. Lecture Notes in Computer Science. vol 16, pp. 89-102, Springer Verlag.

Campbell, R.H. (1976). Path expressions: A technique for specifying process synchronisation. PhD Thesis, Computing Laboratory, Univ. of Newcastle-upon-Tyne.

Campbell, R.H. & Kolstad, R.B. (1979a). Path expressions in Pascal. Proc. 4th Intl. Conf on Software Eng. (Munich), pp. 212-219.

Campbell, R.H. & Kolstad, R.B. (1979b). Practical applications of path expressions to systems programming. University of Illinois.

Clemmensen, G.B. (1982). A formal model of distributed Ada tasking. Proc. of the AdaTec Conf. on Ada, pp. 224-237.

Cohen, N.H. (1982). Parallel quicksort: An exploration of concurrent programming in Ada. Ada Letters, pp. 61-68.

Cook, R.P. (1979). *MOD - A language for distributed programming. Proc. 1st Int. Conf. on distributed computing systems, pp. 233-241.

Cornhill, D., Beane, J. & Thelen, K. (1983a). Design for the prototype execution environment. Distributed Ada Project, Honeywell, Systems & Research Center, 2600 Ridgeway Parkway, P.O. Box 312, Minneapolis, USA.

Cornhill, D. (1983b). A survivable distributed computing system for embedded application programs written in Ada. Ada Letters.

Cornhill, D. (1984). Four approaches to partitioning Ada programs for execution on distributed targets. IEEE Computer Society 1984 Conference on Ada Applications and Environments, pp. 153-164.

Dahl, O.J., Myhrhang, B. & Nygaard, K. (1968). The Simula 67 command base language. Norwegian Computer Centre.

Dannenberg, R.B. (1984). Arctic: A functional language for real-time control. Carnegie-Mellon.

Dennis, J.B. & Weng, K.K.S. (1979). An abstract implementation for concurrent computation with streams. Proc. of the 1979 Int. Conf. on parallel processing.

Dennis, J.B. (1980). Data flow supercomputers. Computer vol 13, pp. 48-56.

Dijkstra, E.W. (1968a). Cooperating sequential processes. Programming Languages, ed. F., Genuys, Academic Press, New York, NY.

Dijkstra, E.W. (1968b). The structure of 'THE' multi- programming system. Comm. ACM vol 11, no.5, pp. 341-346.

Dijkstra, E.W. (1971). Hierarchial ordering of sequential processes. Acta Inf. vol 1, pp. 115-138.

Dijkstra, E.W. (1975). Guarded commands, nondeterminancy and formal derivation of programs. Comm. ACM vol 18, no.8, pp. 453-457.

Donner, M. (1983). The design of OWL - A language for walking. SIGPLAN Notices Symp. on prog. lang. issues in software systems.

Downes, V.A. & Goldsack, S.J. (1980). The use of the Ada language for programming a distributed system. The Real Time Programming Workshop, Graz.

Downes, V.A. & Goldsack, S.J. (1982). Programming embedded systems with Ada. Prentice Hall, Englewood Cliffs, NJ.

Enslow, P. & Saponas, T. (1981). Distributed and decentralised control in fully distributed processing systems - a survey of applicable models. GIT-ICS-81/02, Georgia Institute of Technology.

Fantechi, A. (1984). Interfacing with real environments from Ada programs. Ada Letters vol 4, no.2.

Flon, L & Habermann, A.N. (1976). Towards the construction of verifiable software systems. Proc. ACM Conf Data SIGPLAN Notices vol 8, no.2, pp. 141-148.

Francez, N. & Pnueli, A. (1978). A proof method for cyclic programs. Acta Inf. vol 9, pp. 133-157.

Gardner, M.R., Brubaher, N., Dahlke, C., Goudhard, B. & Ross, D.L. (1983). Ada programming style. Intellimac Inc, Rockville, M.D.

Gehani, N.H. & Cargill, T.A. (1984). Concurrent programming in the Ada language: the polling bias. Software-Practice & Experience vol 14, no.5, pp. 413-427.

Genrich, H.J. & Lautenbach, K. (1979). The analysis of distributed systems by means of predicate transistion nets. Lecture notes in computer science vol 70, pp. 123-146, Springer Verlag.

Genrich, H.J., Lautenbach, K. & Thiagarajan, P.S. (1980). Elements of general net theory. Lecture notes in computer science vol 84, Springer Verlag.

Genrich, H.J. & Lautenbach, K. (1981). System modelling with high level petri nets. Theoretical computer science vol 13.

German, S.M. (1982). Monitoring for deadlocks in Ada tasking. Proc. of the AdaTec Conf. on Ada, pp. 10-25.

Gerth, R. & DeRoever, W. P. (1984). A proof system for concurrent Ada programs. Science of Computer Programming, vol 4, pp. 159-204.

Goldsack, S.J. & Moreton, T. (1982). Ada package specifications: path expressions and monitors. IEE Proc. vol 129, no.2, pp. 49-54.

Habermann, A.N. (1975). Path expressions. Dept. of Computer Science Carnegie-Mellon Univ., Pittsburgh, Pennsylvania.

Habermann, A.N. & Nassi, I.R. (1980). Efficient implementation of Ada tasks. Tech Rep CMU-CS-80-103, Carnegie-Mellon Univ.

Hibbard, P., Hisgen, A., Rosemberg, J. & Sheiman, M. (1981). Programming in Ada: examples. Studies in Ada Style, Springer Verlag.

Hilfinger, P.N. (1982). Implementation strategies for Ada tasking idioms. Proc. of the AdaTec Conf. on Ada, pp. 26-30.

Hill, A.D. (1983). Towards an Ada-based specification and design language. Ada UK news vol 4, no.4.

Hill, A.D. (1984). ASPHODEL - An Ada compatible specification and design language. Ada UK News vol 5, no.4, pp. 42-48.

Hoare, C.A.R. (1972). Towards a theory of parallel programming. Operating system techniques, ed. C.A.R., Hoare, & R.H., Perrott, Academic Press, New York, NY.

Hoare, C.A.R. (1974). Monitors: An operating system structuring concept. Comm. ACM vol 17, no.10, pp. 549-557.

Hoare, C.A.R. (1978). Communicating sequential processes. Comm. ACM vol 21, no.8, pp. 666-677.

Hoare, C.A.R. (1979). Subsetting of Ada, Draft Document.

Hoare, C.A.R. (1981a). The emperor's old clothes. Comm. ACM vol 24, no.2, pp. 75-83.

Hoare, C.A.R. (1981b). A calculus for total correctness for communicating sequential processes. Science of computer programming vol 1, pp. 49-72.

Hoare, C.A.R. (1984). Occam programming manual. Prentice Hall, London.

Ibsen, L. (1984). A portable virtual machine for Ada. Software-Practice & Experience vol 14, pp. 17-29.

Jones, C.B. (1983). Specification and design of parallel programs. Proc. of IFIP 83, pp. 321-332.

Kirkham, J.A., Burns, A. & Thomas, R.J. (1984). The use of structured system analysis in the rapid creation of information management systems prototypes written in Ada. Ada Letters vol 4, no.1.

Knight, J.C. & Urquhart, J.I.A. (1984). On the implementation and use of Ada on fault-tolerant distributed systems. Ada Letters vol 4, no.3, pp. 53-64.

Krieg-Bruckner, B. & Luckham, D.C. (1980). Anna: Towards a language for annotating Ada programs. SIGPLAN Notices vol 15, pp. 128-138.

Lamport, L. (1983). Specifying concurrent program modules. ACM Trans. Prog. Lang. and Systems vol 5, no.2, pp. 190-222.

Lauer, P.E. & Campbell, R.H. (1975). Formal semantics of a class of high level primitives for coordinating concurrent processes. Acta Inf. vol 5, pp. 297-332.

Lauer, P.E. & Shields, M.W. (1978). Abstract specification of resource accessing disciplines: adequacy, starvation, priority and interrupts. 13, pp. 41-59.

Lauer, P.E., Torrigiani, P.R. & Shields, M.W. (1979). COSY: A system specification language based on paths and processes. Acta Informatica vol 12, pp. 109-158.

Lehmann, D., Pnueli, A. & Stavi, J. (1981). Impartiality, justice and fairness: The ethics of concurrent termination. Automata, Languages and Programming, Lecture Notes in Computer Science vol 115, pp. 264-277, Springer Verlag.

Li, W. (1982). An operational semantics of multitasking and exception handling in Ada. Proc. of the AdaTec Conf. on Ada, pp. 138-151.

Liskov, B.L. (1982). On linguistic support for distributed programs. Proc. IEEE Symp. Reliability in Distributed Systems and Data-base Systems, pp. 53-60.

Liskov, B.L. & Scheifler, R. (1983). Guardians and actions: linguistic support for robust, distributed programs. ACM Trans. Prog. Lang. and Systems vol 5, no.3, pp. 381-404.

Lomet, D.B. (1977). Process structuring, synchronisation and recovery using atomic transactions. SIGPLAN Notices vol 12, no.3, pp. 128-137.

May, D. & Taylor, R. (1984). Occam - an overview. Microprocessors and microsystems vol 8, no.2, pp. 73-79.

McDermid, J & Ripken, K (1984). Life cycle support in the Ada environment. Cambridge University Press.

McGettrick, A. (1982). Program verification and Ada. IEE Proc. vol 129, no.2, pp. 55-62.

McGraw, J.R. (1982). The VAL language: description and analysis. ACM Trans. Prog. Lang. and Systems vol 4, no.1, pp. 44-82.

Mitchell, J.G., Maybury, W. & Sweet, R. (1979). Mesa language manual version 5.0. Rep CSL-79-3, Xerox Palo Alto Research Center.

Nissen, J. & Wallis, P. (1984). Portability and style in Ada. Cambridge University Press.

Nygaard, K. & Dahl, O.S. (1978). The development of the SIMULA languages. SIGPLAN Notices vol 13, no.8, pp. 245-272.

Peterson, J. & Silberschatz, A. (1983). Operating system concepts. Addison Wesley, Reading, MA.

Pnueli, A. & De Roever, W.P. (1982). Rendezvous with Ada - A proof theoretical view. Proc. of the AdaTec Conf. on Ada, pp. 129-137.

Pyle, I.C. (1979). Input/Output in high level programming languages. Software-Practice & Experience vol 9, pp. 907-914.

Pyle, I.C. (1981). The Ada programing language. Prentice Hall, Englewood Cliffs, NJ.

Pyle, I.C. (1983). Using Ada for specification and Design. IUCC Bulletin vol 5.

Reynolds, P.F., Knight, J.C. & Urquhart, J.I.A. (1983). The implementation and use of Ada on distributed systems with high reliability requirements. Final report on NASA grant no NAG-1-260.

Robinson, J. & Burns, A. (1984). The use of multi-level adaptive user interfaces in improving user-computer interaction. Symposium on Empirical Foundations of Information and Software Science, Atlanta, USA.

Robinson, J. & Burns, A. (1985). A dialogue development system for the design and implementation of user interfaces in Ada. The Computer Journal vol 28, no.1, pp. 22-28.

Schauer, J. (1982). Vereinfachung von prozess - Systemen durch seqentialisievung. 30/82, Institut fur Informatik, Bericht.

Schonberg, E. & Schonberg, E. (1985). Highly parrallel Ada - Ada on an ultracomputer. Ada in use, Proc. of the Ada Int. Conf. Paris.

Schwartz, R.L., Melliar-Smith, P.M., Vogt, F.H. & Plaisted, D.A. (1983). An interval logic for higher-level temporal reasoning. NASA Contractor report 172262, SRI International, California.

Shaw, A.C. (1980). Software specification languages based on regular expressions. Software Development Tools, ed. W.E., Riddle, & R.E., Fairley, pp. 148-175 Springer Verlag.

Shields, M.W. (1979). Adequate path expressions. Proc. Int Symp Semantics of Concurrent Computation, Lecture Notes in Computer Science vol 70, pp. 249–265, Springer Verlag.

Shyamasundar, R.K., De Roever, W.P., Gerth, R., Koymans, R. & Arun-Kumar, S. (1984). Compositional semantics for real-time distributed computing. Technical report RRU–CS–84–6, Utrecht University.

Silberschatz, A.L. (1984). On the synchronizations mechanism of the Ada language. Proc. 7th Hawaii Int. Conf. System Science.

Snyder, G. & Gorden, M. (1983). The BYRON program development language in the Ada integrated environment. ISDOC/PRISE Review meeting.

Stammers, R. & et. al. (1983). A feasibility study to determine the applicability of Ada and APSE in a multi-microprocessor distributed environment. SPL International, Research Centre, The Charter, Abingdon.

Stevenson, D.R. (1980). Algorithms for translating Ada multi-tasking. SIGPLAN Notices vol 15, no.11.

Tedd, M., Crespi-Reghizzi, S. & Natali, A. (1984). Ada for multi-processors. Cambridge: Ada Companion Series, Cambridge University Press.

Wellings, A. J., Tomlinson, G. M., Keeffe, D. & Wand, I. C. (1984a). Communication between Ada programs. Proceedings of the IEEE Conference on Ada Applications and Environments, pp. 145–152.

Wellings, A. J. (1984b). Distributed operating systems and the Ada programming language. D. Phil. Thesis, Department of Computer Science, University of York.

Wellings, A. J., Keeffe, D. & Tomlinson, G. M. (1984c). A problem with Ada and resource allocation. Ada Letters vol 3, no.4.

Wellings, A. (1984d). The select statement considered harmful. private communication.

Wellings, A. J., Keeffe, D., Tomlinson, G. M. & Wand, I. C. (1985a). PULSE - An Ada-based Unix-like distributed operating system. Academic Press.

Wellings, A.J. (1985b). The use of Ada tasking in the implementation of a distributed operating system. Ada UK News.

Welsh, J. & Bustard, D.W. (1979). Pascal-Plus - Another language for modular multiprogramming. Software-Practice & Experience vol 9, pp. 947–957.

van Wijngaarden, A. & et. al. (1975). Revised report on the algorithmic language ALGOL68. Acta Inf. vol 5, pp. 1–236.

Wirth, N. (1977a). Modula: A language for modular multiprogramming. Software-Practice & Experience vol 7, pp. 3–35.

Wirth, N. (1977b). The use of Modula. Software-Practice & Experience vol 7, pp. 37–65.

Wirth, N. (1977c). Design and implementation of Modula. Software-Practice & Experience vol 7, pp. 67–84.

Wirth, N. (1977d). Toward a discipline of real-time programming. Comm. ACM vol 20, no.8, pp. 577–583.

Wirth, N. (1982). Programming in Modula-2. Springer Verlag.

Yemini, S. (1982). On the suitability of Ada multi-tasking for expressing parallel algorithms. Proc. of the AdaTec Conf. on Ada, Arlington, pp. 91–97.

Young, S.J. (1982). Real time languages. Ellis Horwood.

Young, S.J. (1983). An introduction to Ada. Ellis Horwood.

INDEX